SCEPTICISM AND BELIEF IN HUME'S DIALOGUES CONCERNING NATURAL RELIGION

ARCHIVES INTERNATIONALES D'HISTOIRE DES IDEES
INTERNATIONAL ARCHIVES OF THE HISTORY OF IDEAS

106

STANLEY TWEYMAN

SCEPTICISM AND BELIEF IN HUME'S DIALOGUES CONCERNING NATURAL RELIGION

STANLEY TWEYMAN

SCEPTICISM AND BELIEF IN HUME'S DIALOGUES CONCERNING NATURAL RELIGION

1986 **MARTINUS NIJHOFF PUBLISHERS**
a member of the KLUWER ACADEMIC PUBLISHERS GROUP
DORDRECHT / BOSTON / LANCASTER

Distributors

for the United States and Canada: Kluwer Academic Publishers, 101 Philip Drive, Assinippi Park, Norwell, MA 02061, USA
for the UK and Ireland: Kluwer Academic Publishers, MTP Press Limited, Falcon House, Queen Square, Lancaster LA1 1RN, UK
for all other countries: Kluwer Academic Publishers Group, Distribution Center, P.O. Box 322, 3300 AH Dordrecht, The Netherlands

Library of Congress Cataloging in Publication Data

Tweyman, Stanley, 1942–
    Scepticism and belief in Hume's Dialogues concerning
natural religion.

    (Archives internationales d'histoire des idées ;
106)
    Bibliography: p.
    Includes index.
    1. Hume, David, 1711–1776. Dialogues concerning
natural religion. 2. Natural theology. 3. Skepticism.
4. Belief and doubt. I. Title. II. Series.
B1493.D523T94 1985   210   84–20619
ISBN 90–247–3090–2
ISBN 90-247-3090-2 (this volume)
ISBN 90-247-2433-3 (series)

Copyright

PRINTED IN THE NETHERLANDS

To my daughter Justine Susan

To my daughter, Joanne Susan.

Table of Contents

VIII

Preface

In the pages that follow, an attempt is made to examine those sections of the *Dialogues Concerning Natural Religion* which deal with the Argument from Design – the argument which purports to prove that certain observed similarities between the design of the world and machines of human contrivance countenance reasoning by analogy to the conclusion that the cause of the design of the world resembles human intelligence. The sections which deal with the Argument from Design, and with which I am therefore concerned, are Parts I through VIII and Part XII.

I argue that a clue to Hume's discussion of the Argument from Design is to be found in Section XII of the first *Enquiry*, in which Hume presents his most thorough analysis of philosophic dogmatism and scepticism. The *Dialogues*, as will be shown, follows precisely Hume's recommendations in this Section for bringing the dogmatist to the position which Hume himself endorses – 'mitigated scepticism.' It is, then, the position of the mitigated sceptic which is elaborated in Part XII of the *Dialogues*. The belief in an intelligent designer of the world is shown to be akin to certain other beliefs discussed by Hume – causality, physical objects, a continuing self – which are usually referred to in the literature as 'natural beliefs.' The mitigated sceptic's defense of the unknowability of the divine nature is seen to be in accordance with Hume's view that whatever is believed naturally cannot be known or understood.

All references to the *Dialogues Concerning Natural Religion* are from The Library of Liberal Arts edition, edited by N.K. Smith (The Bobbs-Merrill Company, Jnc., Indianapolis, New York, 1947). References to the *Natural History of Religion* are from *Hume on Religion*, edited by Richard Wollheim (World Publishing Company, Cleveland, 1964). The Selby-Bigge edition of Hume's *Treatise of Human Nature* has been used (Oxford at the Clarendon Press, 1955), as well as the Selby-Bigge edition of Hume's *Enquiries Concerning the Human Understanding and Concerning the Principles of Morals* (Oxford at the Clarendon Press, second edition, 1963). References to Nelson Pike's work on Hume are taken from Pike's edition with commentary on the *Dialogues Concerning Natural Religion* (The Bobbs-Merrill Company, Inc., Indianapolis, New York 1970).

X

The love and support I receive from my parents, Fay and Dave Tweyman, my wife Barbara, my daughter Justine, and my brother Martin are given without limit and without reservation; my hope is that they understand what their love and support mean to me.

Glendon College, York University
Toronto, Ontario, Canada

Introduction

Of all Hume's philosophical writings, the *Dialogues concerning Natural Religion* is perhaps the most difficult to read. In most of what Hume writes, it is clear that he wants to take a position, and it is clear where to find the position he wants to take. Hume is also usually clear about the positions he finds untenable, and he normally puts forth arguments to establish their untenability. The *Dialogues* does not share these characteristics. That Hume wants to take a position in this work is made difficult to establish by the fact that he never speaks in his own person when arguments are put forth; he never speaks in his own person when arguments are criticized; certain views, particularly the articulate Voice and Living Vegetable Library Analogies in Part III, do not appear to be assessed adequately; the final dictum regarding natural religion – that statement toward which the entire book has been progressing – is expressed in a hypothetical statement ("If the whole of natural theology ..." p. 227) and is regarded as a statement which "some people seem to maintain"; when the three principal speakers' positions are assessed, it is done by the character Pamphilus (a student of Cleanthes'), the one who is relaying the conversation which he audited, but whose (philosophical) credentials and relation to Hume we are never told; Pamphilus assesses "the principles" of the various speakers, but does not tell us what these principles are, and he entirely neglects to tell us whether proper inferences have been drawn from these principles.

The positions which Hume himself finds untenable, are also obscured by the fact that we are told in the Introduction that one reason why natural religion is a subject "to which dialogue-writing is peculiarly adapted, and where it is still preferable to the direct and simple method of composition" is that it is a question of philosophy "which is so *obscure* and *uncertain*, that human reason can reach no fixed determination with regard to it; ... Reasonable men may be allowed to differ, where no one can reasonably be positive."[1] In the next paragaraph, the question of the being of a God is contrasted with that concerning the nature of the Divine Being. This again leads to uncertainty as to which positions, if any, Hume finds tenable: "What

---

[1]   D. 128.

truth so obvious, so certain, as the *being* of a God... But in treating of this obvious and important truth; what obscure questions occur, concerning the *nature* of that divine Being; his attributes, his decrees, his plan of providence? These have always been subjected to the disputations of men: Concerning these, human reason has not reached any certain determination ... nothing but doubt, uncertainty, and contradiction, have, as yet, been the result of our most accurate researches."[2]

To add to the difficulty, the following peculiar situation exists. The main concern of the *Dialogues* is the Argument from Design which seeks to establish, on the basis of certain resemblances between the world and machines, that the cause of the design of the world resembles human intelligence. From Part II through VIII we find one of the speakers, Philo, arguing against this position. For the most part, we are convinced of Philo's commitment to the soundness of his criticisms. However, when dealing with the topic of God's moral Attributes in Parts X and XI, Philo admits that his objections against the intelligence claim are "mere cavils and sophisms":

Formerly, when we argued concerning the natural atttitudes of intelligence and design, I needed all my sceptical and metaphysical sublety to elude your grasp. In many views of the universe, and of its parts, particularly the latter, the beauty and fitness of final causes strike us with such irresistible force, that all objections appear (what I believe they really are) mere cavils and sophisms; nor can we then imagine how it was ever possible for us to repose any weight on them.[3]

Earlier, at the end of Part VIII, when explaining that victory in argument against all religious systems requires an offensive war, Philo accounts for the complete victory of the sceptic by saying: "And if every attack, as is commonly observed, and no defence, among theologians is succesful; how complete must be *his* victory, who remains always, with all mankind, on the offensive, and has himself no fixed station or abiding city, which he is ever on any occasion, obliged to defend?"[4] The word 'his' in this passage, which Hume has italicized, is significant. It shows that Philo does not identify himself at this point with the sceptic, even though he is the one who has offered the critique of the Argument from Design, and even though complete victory is declared for the sceptic. Why Philo disassociates himself from the sceptical arguments developed in Parts II through VII obviously needs to be explained. But how Philo can maintain both that the sceptic triumphs when doing battle offensively, and two sections later, that all sceptical arguments are "mere cavils and sophisms" at least when directed against claims regarding God's natural attributes, must also be explained.

Early in Part II, prior to Cleanthes' presentation of the Argument from Design (the sole defender of this argument in the book), Philo maintains that

[2]   D. 128. These words are spoken by Pamphilus.
[3]   D. 201–202.
[4]   D. 187.

we need not have recourse to an extreme sceptical position in order to show – what he subsequently does attempt to show through the use of sceptical arguments – that "we ought never to imagine that we comprehend the attributes of this divine Being, or to suppose that his perfections have any analogy or likeness to the perfections of a human creature."[5] To make his point, he employs Hume's doctrine of impressions and ideas:

... there is no need of having recourse to that affected scepticism, so displeasing to you, in order to come at this determination. Our ideas reach no farther than our experience: We have no experience of divine attributes and operations: I need not conclude my syllogism: You can draw the inference yourself.[6]

If this argument is decisive, then why was the extreme sceptical position needed at all? And if this argument is not decisive, where, if anywhere, does Hume indicate this? We can also ask whether Hume believed that this argument, although not a sceptical one, is to be included in those which are "mere cavils and sophisms."

After six pages of almost uninterrupted narrative by Philo in Part XII, he asserts that what he has just said constitutes "my unfeigned sentiments on this subject; and these sentiments, you know (Cleanthes), I have ever cherished and maintained."[7] Are we then to believe that Philo does have a "fixed station," but one which is such that no sceptical attack can be victorious with respect to it? But if Philo does have such a "fixed station," why is it not clear on page 227 (the penultimate paragraph of the book) that it is Philo himself who holds to the proposition which "the whole of natural theology ... resolves itself into ..." Tied in with this is the fact that in the first eight sections of the book, Philo denies both that we have any ideas of divine perfections and that God's attributes have any resemblance to ours. On the other hand, in Part XII he appears to hold that we are justified in believing that there is some analogy between God and us. To cite just one passage in Part XII: "That the works of nature bear a great analogy to the productions of art is evident; and according to all the rules of good reasoning, we ought to infer, if we argue at all concerning them, that their causes have a proportional analogy."[8]

The Argument from Design, the central argument in the *Dialogues*, is first stated by Cleanthes.[9] Demea, the third speaker in the debate, immediately objects to the proof on two grounds. First, he disagrees with the conclusion of the argument inasmuch as it maintains the similarity of the deity to human intelligence. In other words, Demea rejects anthropomorphism. But Demea also objects to the way Cleanthes offers his argument: Cleanthes' version is

[5] D. 142.
[6] D. 142–143.
[7] D. 241.
[8] D. 216–217.
[9] D. 143.

given as an analogical argument. Demea asserts: "What! No demonstration of the being of a God! No abstract arguments! No proofs *a priori*... Can we reach no farther in this subject than experience and probability?"[10] Several paragraphs later, Philo attempts to interpret Demea's worries in regard to Cleanthes' version of the argument: "But what sticks most with you (Demea), I observe, is the representation which Cleanthes has made of the argument *a posteriori*; and finding that the argument is likely to escape your hold and vanish into air, you think it so disguised that you can scarcely believe it to be set in its true light."[11] He then indicates that he "shall endeavour so to state the matter to you, that you will entertain no further scruples with regard to it,"[12] and he goes on to present a second version of the Argument from Design. Does Philo intend us to believe that Demea will be prepared to accept the Design Argument once it is given in the form provided by Philo? Or are we to conclude that Philo's version is only intended to present Demea with the best version of the argument, even though it will not hold up under Philo's criticisms any better than did the Cleanthean version? Of course, we must also ask whether the second argument adds anything to the version offered by Cleanthes, and whether the criticisms which affect one equally affect the other.

This brief discussion indicates some of the difficulties facing the serious reader of Hume's *Dialogus concerning Natural Religion*, and it points out the need for a systematic investigation of this book. The present study is concerned with Hume's examination of the Argument from Design insofar as this argument makes the claim that the cause of the design of the world resembles human intelligence. This book, therefore, deals with the first eight Parts of the *Dialogues*, and Part XII, the final section of the book.

The central thesis of the present study is that the *Dialogues* is a book which contains a framework, the elements of which Hume endeavoured throughout his philosophical life to analyze and understand. The following constitute this framework: a) The differences between deductive and inductive arguments; b) Hume's analysis of causality and his use of the principle 'like effects prove like causes'; c) His views on scepticism (its different forms and uses) and his belief in the proper method for philosophy; d) and his views on what have come to be called 'natural beliefs'. Before turning our attention to the *Dialogues*, a discussion of these topics will be offered.

[10] D. 143.
[11] D. 145.
[12] D. 145.

When I am present, therefore, at any dispute, I always consider with myself whether it be a question of comparison or not that is the subject of controversy; and if it be, whether the disputants compare the same objects together, or talk of things that are widely different.

From Hume's essay "Of the Dignity or Meanness of Human Nature."

It seems evident, that the dispute between the sceptics and dogmatists is entirely verbal, or at least regards only the degrees of doubt and assurance, which we ought to indulge with regard to all reasoning: And such disputes are commonly at the bottom, verbal, and admit not of any precise determination. No philosophical dogmatist denies, that there are difficulties both with regard to the senses and to all science: and that these difficulties are in a regular, logical method, absolutely insolveable. No sceptic denies, that we lie under an absolute necessity, notwithstanding these difficulties, of thinking, and believing, and reasoning with regard to all kind of subjects, and even of frequently assenting with confidence and security. The only difference, then, between these sects, if they merit that name, is, that the sceptic, from habit, caprice, or inclination, insists most on the difficulties; the dogmatist, for like reasons, on the necessity." (D. 219)

The only passage in the *Dialogues* in which Hume speaks in his own person.

The Philosophic Background to the *Dialogues*

HUME'S VIEWS ON REASONING[1]

Hume believed that given the way in which the world presents itself to us, nothing about the world appears necessary. Since a deductive argument, or demonstration as he usually refers to it, seeks to draw a conclusion which makes a claim about what is necessary, Hume held that demonstrations cannot provide us with factual knowledge. Necessary knowledge is always relational knowledge (although, of course, the converse is not true, namely, that all relational knowledge is necessary). In the *Treatise of Human Nature*,[2] where Hume provides his most extensive discussion of relations, he points out that of the seven which he lists, (resemblance, identity, relations of space and time, proportion in quantity or number, degrees in any quality, contrariety, and causation) only four are such that the relation depends entirely on the contents of the ideas compared. Therefore, only in the case of these four relations – resemblance, contrariety, degrees in any quality, and proportions in quantity or number – can we make claims about what is necessarily the case. Examples of necessary and contingent relations are in order. We can begin with necessary relations. If you think of two different shades of a given colour, or of ten units of a given item as compared with five units of that item, you learn that the two shades resemble, or that the ten units of X are greater than the five units of X. Now, at the moment and perhaps forever after, these colours may not be found anywhere in the world, and the given item with different sets of units may not exist anywhere. Hume's point is that although the existence of the particulars is a contingent matter, the relations in question are not also contingent, since the relations between these ideational contents cannot be other than they are, given that the ideational contents are what they are.

On the other hand, merely thinking of two objects (even though you know they exist) cannot disclose whether they are near each other or far from each other, since how things are actually related spatially can only be apprehended

---

[1] On Hume's account of reasoning, see also the third chapter of my *Reason and Conduct in Hume and His Predecessors*, Martinus Nijhoff, The Hague, 1974.

[2] T. 13–15, 69–73.

by obtaining data as to where each is located. The ideational contents of objects are compatible with the objects being near or far: hence, from the ideational contents no awareness of where they are with respect to each other can be learned. Spatial relations between objects, therefore, are contingent.

Like relations in space between objects, causal relations between objects are, according to Hume, ones which are never necessary.[3] For a causal relation to be a necessary relation, it would have to be possible to discover the relation merely from the ideational contents of the objects deemed cause and effect (as one can do with resemblances between shades of colours), or from a discernment of the power in the object deemed the cause which is adequate to the production of the effect. Hume holds that the ideational contents of objects never disclose a causal relation, and no examination of an object ever reveals its causal power. Causal relations, therefore, are ones which are discerned only through having certain experiences, viz. in learning of a causal relation, we must observe objects to be constantly conjoined. Seeing the objects constantly conjoined generates a habit in the mind, which subsequently leads us to expect the effect whenever we observe the cause. This habit, according to Hume, serves to make us believe that what we observed to be conjoined, are really causally connected. Causal reasoning requires seeing an object believed to be a cause and inferring what the effect of the cause will be, or seeing an effect and inferring its cause. The *Dialogues* confines itself to the latter task: regarding the design of the world as an effect, the question is raised whether anything can be known about the cause of its design.

In ordinary cases, where we reason from effects to causes, we utilize the principle 'like effects prove like causes'. Having seen objects of one sort constantly conjoined with objects of another sort, when presented with an additional example of the type of object believed to be the effect, we conclude that its cause is of the sort with which we have seen objects of this type constantly conjoined. Having seen these sorts of objects constantly conjoined gives us assurance that our causal claims are trustworthy. Hume holds that the principle 'like effects prove like causes' operates reliably if the following conditions are met. First, the effect under consideration about whose cause we want to learn, must bear a sufficient resemblance to certain effects previously observed, to enable us to classify it as belonging to the same class. Second, we must be familiar with the cause of effects of this type. This requires observing such effects constantly conjoined with a given kind of object. Reasoning from effects to causes, our highest assurance would occur

---

[3]   Hume's most extensive discussion of causality appears in the *Treatise of Human Nature*, Book I, Part III, Sections I–XIV. See also his *Enquiry Concerning Human Understanding*, Sections IV–VII.

in cases where what is regarded as the cause is both sufficient and necessary for the production of the effect.

Reading the *Dialogues* reveals that one of the claims which Hume seeks to make is that the Argument from Design fails because the two conditions just cited cannot be met in the case of God and the design of the world. It is a mistake, however, to conclude that this is all that Hume seeks to show regarding the employment of this principle in the case of God and the world. The constructive element in Hume's analysis, as I will show later, is to determine the extent to which the principle 'Like effects prove like causes' can be utilized in the the case of God and the world while granting that the two conditions cited cannot be satisfied.

SCEPTICISM

That the Argument from Design does not succeed is shown by Philo through his role as sceptic. Accordingly, if we are to understand the nature of the exchange between Philo and Cleanthes, attention must be paid to the types of scepticism which the *Dialogues* utilizes.

Although it is obvious at certain points throughout the *Dialogues* that scepticism is being used,[4] the precise strategy employed by Philo has not, in my opinion, been properly understood. It is this, I submit, which has given rise to the well-known complaints about Part XII. Furthermore, without a proper understanding of the role of scepticism with the *Dialogues*, it is difficult to determine whether Philo and Cleanthes are ever brought to a common position. Or alternatively, the understanding one has of the role of scepticism within the *Dialogues* will influence the view one comes to have regarding the positions which Philo and Cleanthes ultimately adopt. For example, Philip Stanley[5] maintains that "Philo of the *Dialogues* is an excessive sceptic, a Pyrrhonist. Cleanthes is a mitigated sceptic. The two join forces long enough to oust a dogmatist (Demea) then split to argue their respective positions when he is gone. No conclusion is given." James Noxon[6] in his article on Hume's Agnosticism, states that because the nature of Philo's scepticism differs from Hume's, Philo's position cannot be taken as Hume's position:

---

[4]   See, for example, Philo's comments at the end of Part VIII, and his admission of scepticism at the end of Part X.

[5]   Philip Stanley, "The Scepticisms of David Hume," *Journal of Philosophy* (32) 1935, p. 423.

[6]   James Noxon, "Hume's Agnosticism," *Philosophical Review*, Volume LXXIII, (1964), reprinted in *Hume: A Collection of Critical Essays*, edited by V.C. Chappell, Anchor Books, Garden City, New York, 1966. My references are from Chappell.

4

... the significance of Philo's recantation in the final dialogue is quite plain and in perfect
accordance with Hume's usual strictures on a certain type of skeptic. Philo was a skeptic and
Hume was a skeptic, but Philo's skepticism was of a different type from Hume's, and of the type
that Hume consistently repudiated and condemned: Philo's skepticism is excessive skepticism, or
Pyrrhonism, a position which it is impossible to maintain consistently... What then, was the
nature of Hume's own skepticism? He called it a 'mitigated skepticism'...[7]

Noxon's account takes it for granted that for Hume Pyrrhonism has no
constructive role to play in inquiry, and that those sections in which Philo
takes the side of the sceptic have no positive contribution to make to the
discussion in Part XII. In the ensuing discussion, I will show that from what
Hume has to say about Pyrrhonism, we learn that it was not "consistently
repudiated and condemned" by him; that, in fact, he allowed it could have
a significant role to play in our investigations. Consequently, the fact that
pyrrhonistic arguments are put forth does not by itself show that Hume sees
no role for them in arriving at the position which he calls 'mitigated
scepticism'.

Hume's most extensive discussion of scepticism is provided in Section XII
of the *Enquiry Concerning Human Understanding.* He begins with a
discussion of a form of scepticism which he calls 'antecedent scepticism':

It recommends an universal doubt, not only of our former opinions and principles, but also of
our very facilities; of whose veracity, say they, we must assure ourselves, by a chain of reasoning,
deduced from some original principle, which cannot possibly be fallacious or deceitful.

His critique of this form of excessive scepticism is brief:

But neither is there any such original priciple, which has a prerogative above others, that are self-
evident and convincing: or if there were, could we advance a step beyond it, but by the use of
those very faculties, of which we are supposed to be already diffident.[9]

And he concludes that excessive antecedent scepticism cannot be upheld:

The Cartesian doubt, therefore, were it ever possible to be attained by any human creature (as
it plainly is not) would be entirely incurable; and no reasoning could ever bring us to a state of
assurance and conviction upon any subject.[10]

He does suggest, however, that antecedent scepticism does have something of
value to offer, provided that it is accepted in a less extreme form. In fact,
Hume speaks of this type of scepticism, when moderate, as "a necessary
preparative to the study of philosophy, by preserving a proper impartiality in
our judgements, and weaning our mind from all those prejudices, which we

---

[7] Chappell, p. 380–381.
[8] E. 149–150.
[9] E. 150.
[10] E. 150.

may have imbibed from education or rash opinion."[11] Moderate antecedent scepticism makes the following recommendations:

To begin with clear and self-evident principles, to advance by timorous and sure steps, to review frequently our conclusions, and examine acurately all their consequences.[12]

Although antecedent scepticism, when moderate, is a necessary preparative to the study of philosophy, Hume held that more was necessary before philosophy could be on a solid foundation, since we require some means of knowing whether we are following the recommendations of this type of scepticism. It is not enough *to believe* that our principles are clear and self-evident, and that we are advancing by timorous and sure steps, etc.: there must be some means whereby this can be established or confirmed. To do so, Hume recommends another version of extreme scepticism, which he calls 'consequent scepticism.'[13] This form of scepticism differs from excessive antecedent scepticism in that it functions once arguments are put forth, rather than prior to their presentation.

There is another species of scepticism, *consequent* to science and enquiry, when men are supposed to have discovered, either the absolute fallaciousness of their mental faculties, or their unfitness to reach any fixed determination in all those curious subjects of speculation, about which they are commonly employed. Even our very senses are brought into dispute, by a certain species of philosophers; and the maxims of common life are subjected to the same doubt as the most profound principles or conclusions of metaphysics and theology.[14]

It is clear from this passage (and other in the same section) that Hume believes that sceptical arguments can be brought forth which challenge claims about our capacity to achieve truth in general or in regard to particular topics, which challenge the reliability of the senses, and the maxims of common life.[15] These sceptical arguments are not easily refuted through additional argumentation, and he allows that we may not be able to refute them at all:

These principles may flourish and triumph in the schools; where it is, indeed, difficult, if not impossible to refute them.[16]

---

[11]   E. 150.
[12]   E. 150. It was precisely the absence of these features in previous philosophers which Hume criticized in the Introduction to the *Treatise*: "Tis easy for one of judgement and learning, to perceive the real foundation even of those systems, which have obtained the greatest credit, and have carried their pretensions highest to accurate and profound reasoning. Principles taken upon trust, consequences lamely deduced from them, want of coherence in the parts, and of evidence in the whole, these are everywhere to be met and with in the systems of the most eminent philosophers, and seem to have drawn disgrace upon philosophy itself." (T. xvii).
[13]   E. 150.
[14]   E. 150.
[15]   We can omit discussion here of the various sceptical arguments which Hume considers in the *Enquiry*.
[16]   E. 159.

6

When consequent scepticism is simply destructive in nature, that is, when its only use is to provide arguments against our mental faculties, our senses, and the maxims of common life, Hume does condemn it:

For here is the chief and most confounding objection to *excessive* scepticism, that no durable good can ever result from it; while it remains in its full force and vigour. We need only ask such a sceptic, *What his meaning is? And what he proposes by all those curious researches?* He is immediately at a loss, and knows not what to answer... a Pyrrhonian cannot expect, that his philosophy will have any constant influence on the mind: or if it had, that its influence would be beneficial to society. On the contrary, he must acknowledge, if he will acknowledge anything, that all human life must perish, were his principles universally and steadily to prevail.[17]

Pyrrhonism in its destructive form poses no real threat to us:

The great subverter of *Pyrrhonism* or the excessive principles of scepticism is action, and employment, and the occupations of common life.[18]

Nature is always too strong for principle. And though a Pyrrhonian may throw himself or others into a momentary amazement and confusion by his profound reasonings; the first and most trivial event in life will put to flight all his doubts and scruples, and leave him the same, in every point of action and speculation, with the philosophers of every other sect, or with those who never concerned themselves in any philosophical researches. When he awakes from his dream, he will be the first to join in the laugh against himself, and to confess, that all his objections are mere amusement, and can have no other tendency than to show the whimsical condition of mankind, who must act and reason and believe; though they are not able, by their most diligent enquiry, to satisfy themselves concerning the foundation of these operations, or to remove the objections, which may be raised against them.[19]

Pyrrhonism, therefore, finds its refutation in the necessity we all stand under to trust our mental faculties, our senses, and the maxims of common life.

As a destructive device, Pyrrhonism is not defensible. But Hume does believe that Pyrrhonism can be of value to philosophy insofar as it can be useful in teaching us to avoid errors in our inquiries. In this way, then, it can be of service to moderate antecedent scepticism. Hume writes:

There is, indeed, a more mitigated scepticism or academical philosophy, which may be both durable and useful, and which may, in part, be *the result* of this Pyrrhonism, or excesssive scepticism, when its *undistinguished* doubts are, in some measure, corrected by common sense and reflection.[20]

Mitigated scepticism, or academic philosophy, is the kind of scepticism to which Hume himself subscribes: we now learn that it results from excessive scepticism when the 'undistinguished doubts' of the latter are corrected by

[17]   E. 159–160.
[18]   E. 158–159.
[19]   E. 160.
[20]   E. 161. Italics in text omitted; italics present inserted.

'common sense and reflection'. The difficulty here is to determine what he means by the expression 'the result of this Pyrrhonism'; what he regards as the latter's 'undistinguished doubts'; and how the corrections leading to mitigated scepticism are effected by 'common sense and reflection'.

Mitigated scepticism is contrasted by Hume with dogmatism; and it is Pyrrhonism which can turn the dogmatist into a mitigated sceptic. Hume's meaning, therefore, is that a dogmatist can be converted to a position of mitigated scepticism, and this conversion requires that the dogmatist be presented with certain pyrrhonistic arguments. This is what Hume means when he speaks of mitigated scepticism as being 'the result of this Pyrrhonism':

The greater part of mankind are naturally apt to be affirmative and dogmatical in their opinions; and while they see objects only on one side, and have no idea of any counterpoising argument, they throw themselves precipitately into the principles, to which they are inclined; nor have they any indulgence for those who entertain opposite sentiments. To hesitate or balance perplexes their understanding, checks their passion, and suspends their action. They are, therefore, impatient till they escape from a state, which to them is so uneasy: and they think, that they could never remove themselves far enough from it, by the violence of their affirmations and obstinacy of their belief. But could such dogmatical reasoners become sensible of the strange infirmities of human understanding ... such a reflection would naturally inspire them with more modesty and reserve, and diminish their fond opinion of themselves, and their prejudice against antagonists.[21]

In an earlier passage in the first *Enquiry*, Hume develops his concern regarding the one-sidedness of the dogmatist:

The passion for philosophy, like that for religion, seems liable to this inconvenience, that, though it aims at the correction of our manners, and extirpation of our vices, it may only serve, by imprudent management, to foster a predominant inclination, and push the mind, with more determined resolution, towards that side which already *draws* too much, by the bias and propensity of the natural temper.[22]

Dogmatism among the learned is to be dealt with in the same way as it is in the case of the vulgar:

The illiterate may reflect on the disposition of the learned, who amidst all the advantages of study and reflection, are commonly still diffident in their determinations: and if any of the learned be inclined, from their natural temper, to haughtiness and obstinacy, a small tincture of Pyrrhonism might abate their pride, by showing them, that the few advantages, which they may have attained over their fellows, are but inconsiderable if compared with the universal perplexity and confusion, which is inherent in human nature.[23]

What emerges from Hume's discussion of dogmatism is that we are liable to

[21] E. 161.
[22] E. 40.
[23] E. 161.

err in our reasoning if we are not impartial, or in other words, if our reasonings are intended to support a particular bias or inclination. To effect such impartiality in our reasonsings, Hume urges exposure to the arguments of the pyrrhonian – arguments designed to counter-balance (Hume's term is 'counterpoising') those of the dogmatist. The effect of these counter-balancing arguments, when directed against the arguments of the dogmatist, is to produce a suspense of judgment: its is not reasonable to assent to the conclusion of an argument when counter-arguments appear to have equal force and provide conclusions which conflict with the conclusion of the original argument. Dogmatism, therefore, falls prey to Pyrrhonism.

At this stage, Pyrrhonism provides us with 'undistinguished doubts' because the Pyrrhonian does not confine his attack to the actual errors in the dogmatist's reasoning. Accordingly, the suspension of judgment which Pyrrhonism attempts to bring about can be accomplished only be casting doubt on all elements involved in the dogmatist's reasoning.

Once exposed to the Pyrrhonian's counter-arguments, the dogmatist will realize that his previous confidence and obstinancy were unjustified; but before he can adopt the position of mitigated scepticism, he must be freed from the suspense of judgment into which the pyrrhonian arguments have placed him. It is at this stage that the 'undistinguished doubts' of the Pyrrhonian are to be corrected by 'common sense and reflection'. The 'common sense corrections' are effected through Nature itself:

The *imagination* of man is naturally sublime, delighted with whatever is remote and extraordinary, and running, without control, into the most distant parts of space and time in order to avoid the objects, which custom has rendered too familiar to it. A correct *judgment* observes a contrary method, and avoiding all distant and high enquiries, confines itself to common life, and to such subjects as fall under daily practice and experience; leaving the more sublime topics to the embellishment of poets and orators, or to the arts of priests and politicians. To bring us to so salutary a determination, nothing can be more serviceable, than to be once thoroughly convinced of the force of the Pyrrhonian doubt, and of the impossibility, that anything, but the strong power of natural instinct, could free us from it.[24]

The suspense of judgment into which the dogmatist is thrown by the pyrrhonian is broken, therefore, through the necessity we all stand under to trust our mental faculties, our senses, and the maxims of common life in dealing with the affairs of common life; in short, the suspense of judgment is broken through the force of our instinctive beliefs. Since natural instinct can alone free us from the pyrrhonian doubts, and since natural instinct, according to Hume, only has reference 'to common life and to such subjects as fall under daily practice and experience,' it follows that whenever our arguments go beyond common life and experience, the arguments of the

---

[24] E. 162.

Pyrrhonian will retain their force. This distinction between those cases where pyrrhonian doubts retain their force and where they do not, is not made by the Pyrrhonian *qua* Pyrrhonian.

The role of 'reflection' in correcting the 'undistinguished doubts' of the Pyrrhonian can also be made clear. Instinct breaks the hold of Pyrhonism, and guides us to confine our inquiries to common life. Nevertheless, even if our inquiries are so confined, errors are still possible. Accordingly, when Hume recommends 'reflection' to assist in correcting the 'undistinguished doubts' of Pyrrhonism, he is urging that we scrutinize our empirical investigations to avoid errrors there as well:

Those who have a propensity to philosophy, will still continue their researches; because they reflect, that, besides the immediate pleasure, attending such an occupation, philosophical decisions are nothing but the reflections of common life, methodized and corrected.[25]

Hume's account of impression and ideas, and his Experimental Method are the key elements advocated for avoiding errors when dealing with matters of common life.[26]

Without the one-sidedness which characterizes the dogmatist, and mindful of the force of pyrrhonian objections, the mitigated sceptic is, for Hume, the one most likely to succeed in his inquiries:

There is ... one species of philosophy which ... strikes in with no disorderly passion of the human mind, nor can mingle itself with any natural affection or propensity; and that is the Academic or Sceptical philosophy. The academics always talk of doubt and suspense of judgement, of danger in hasty determinations, of confining to very narrow bounds the enquiries of the understanding, and of renouncing all speculations which be not within the limits of common life and practice. Nothing, therefore, can be more contrary than such a philosophy to the supine indolence of the mind, its rash arrogance, its lofty pretensions, and its superstitious credulity. Every passion is mortified by it, except the love of truth; and that passion never is, nor can be, carried to too high a degree.[27]

From our discussion of Hume on scepticism, we can offer an initial assessment of the positions taken by Stanley and Noxon, and we can offer our own hypothesis regarding the nature of the *Dialogues*. The confirmation of what I am about to say will have to await my analysis of the *Dialogues*.

From Part XII of the first *Enquiry*, it is highly inlikely that Stanley is correct in holding that a Pyrrhonian will join forces with a mitigated sceptic to oust a dogmatist. Hume's view is rather that a dogmatist must be exposed to pyrrhonistic arguments if he is to become a mitigated sceptic. Philo's

[25]   E. 162.
[26]   How these are involved will be discussed when we come to examine actual instances with which Hume deals. See also my *Reason and Conduct in Hume and His Predecessors*. Chapters 1 and 2.
[27]   E. 40–41.

pyrrhonistic arguments are not directed against Demea, but against Cleanthes. Following Part XII of the first *Enquiry*, it is likely that Cleanthes is the dogmatist, and that it is he who must be turned to mitigated scepticism. Part XII of the *Dialogues* would, on this account, contain the thoughts of Philo and Cleanthes once they are able to achieve a common position – that of mitigated scepticism. Philo's stand in Part XII now ceases to be enigmatic: having by this time taken Cleanthes through certain pyrrhonistic arguments, which generate sufficient doubt to cause a suspense of judgment regarding the natural attributes of the cause of the design of the world, Philo is able to offer his own position in Part XII by correcting the 'undistinguished doubts' of his sceptical arguments. Once again, basing our views on the first *Enquiry*, a change in Philo's position in Part XII is something which we ought to expect. If the use of sceptical arguments against Cleanthes' position has been successful, we should also expect an alteration in Cleanthes' position in Part XII as well. Both Cleanthes and Philo ought to emerge with a position which the Pyrrhonian cannot attack, inasmuch as it contains no more than the empirical data warrant.

If my position on Philo is borne out by the text, then Noxon's account can also be seen to be defective. Philo's pyrrhonistic arguments in the earlier parts of the text are needed to turn Cleanthes from dogmatism to mitigated scepticism. Hence, Philo's Pyrrhonism is not of the type which – to use Noxon's words – "Hume consistently repudiated and condemned": Philo is not a destructive sceptic. Philo, being a mitigated sceptic in Part XII, is mindful of his earlier sceptical arguments and presents his position in Part XII in a manner which avoids the possibility of a further attack by the Pyrrhonian. And if Cleanthes has, by Part XII, also been rendered a mitigated sceptic, then he too can express Hume's views. Any disagreement which remains among Philo, Cleanthes, and Hume, would be of the sort which is allowed by the mitigated sceptic: disagreement may persist in certain cases, because the data are not sufficient to allow for a clear judgment.

NATURAL BELIEFS

The *Dialogues* is, for the most part, concerned with assessing the Argument from Design. In certain passages (to be examined later) it seems as though Hume holds that the belief in an intelligent designer of the universe can be counted as a 'natural belief'. Although no commentator denies that there is such a doctrine in Hume's philosophy, problems surrounding this doctrine are far from settled: no section in Hume's writings offers a systematic account of this topic, and consequently, nowhere does Hume set out the features a belief must possess, if it is to be classified as a 'natural belief.'

A proper examination of 'natural belief' in the *Dialogues* requires a preliminary examination consisting of two parts: we must know the essential features of natural beliefs; and we must know what difference it makes whether or not a belief is a natural belief.

Hume's discussion of belief (in the *Treatise of Human Nature*, and the first *Enquiry*) shows that he holds that the following are areas where belief can occur: 1) impressions of the outer senses, and internal impressions or impressions of reflection (our passions, emotions, and sentiments) are normally attended with belief; 2) memory perceptions are contrasted with imaginings in terms of the fact that the former are attended with belief and the latter are not;[28] 3) intuition and demonstration, if valid, are 'irresistible,' and therefore, must be believed once they are entertained;[29] 4) ideas which are inferred causally are believed, and part of Hume's effort in Part III of the first Book of the *Treatise* is spent accounting for the belief attending these ideas; and 5) natural beliefs – the focus of the present section.

Those beliefs falling under 1), 2), and 4) are explicated in terms of force and vivacity,[31] an aspect of all perceptions which can vary in degree. Vivacious perceptions, or those which can be made so, are assented to; those perceptions which are languid are not assented to. Therefore, we do not believe that these latter perceptions either represent matters of fact (which we do in those cases where an idea is believed) or are matters of fact (this occurs where an impression is believed). Wherever belief is due to enlivening the perception in question, what we believe is not under our control.[32] Those beliefs falling under 3) are concerned with establishing *a priori* whether an equality or inequality exists between two ideas in virtue of a common property.[33] Hume's point is that if the equality (or inequality) can be established merely through an examination of the contents of the ideas involved, then to deny what is true, is equivalent to asserting that equals are unequal, or unequals are equal, and these denials cannot be thought. Hence, belief in the case of intuition and demonstration occurs through the 'irresistibility' of the belief: once the statement is established through intuition or demonstration, we find that the

---

[28]   T. 8–10.

[29]   T. 31; T. 95.

[30]   See T. 94–117; T 623–629.

[31]   For a close textual analysis of Hume's account of impressions and ideas, see my *Reason and Conduct in Hume and His Predecessors*, Chapter 2.

[32]   "... the mind has the command over all its ideas, and can separate, unite, mix and vary them as it pleases; so that if belief consisted merely in a new idea, annex'd to the conception, it would be in a man's power to believe what he pleased. We may, therefore, conclude, that belief consists merely in a certain feeling or sentiment; in something that depends not on the will, but must arise from certain determinate causes and principles, of which we are not masters." (T. 623-624).

[33]   See Chapter 3 of my *Reason and Conduct in Hume and His Predecessors*.

denial of such statements is inconceivable.[34]

The members of the class of beliefs held to be 'natural beliefs' by Hume are, with the exception of the belief in an intelligent designer of the world, easy to identify: the belief in the continued and independent existence of objects; the belief in the Principle of Causality; and the belief each of us holds in personal identity. As noted earlier, Hume nowhere sets out in a systematic way the essential features of such beliefs. Nevertheless, these features can be elicited by focussing our attention on the accepted members of this class of beliefs.

1. A Belief Classified as a Natural Belief cannot be One Which can be Fully Analyzed in Terms of Hume's Account of Perceptions, or Impressions and Ideas

To get clear on this, it is best to begin with a case where the belief is fully analyzed in this way. At one point in the *Treatise*, Hume writes: "We cannot form to ourselves a just idea of the taste of a pine-apple, without having actually tasted it."[35] In this case, there is an impression of sensation, which causes the idea or thought of the taste of pine-apple; Hume insists that without the experience or impression of the taste of pineapple, the thought of this taste would be inaccessible to us. Hence, any belief we hold in the taste of pineapple is to be analyzed solely through impressions and ideas: i) the thought of the taste of pineapple derives entirely from the impression of such a taste, and ii) the taste of pineapple is held to be nothing but the taste which we experience. Compare this to Hume's words regarding the belief in personal identity:

There are some philosophers, who imagine we are every moment intimately conscious of what we call our SELF, that we feel its existence and its continuance in existence, and are certain, beyond the evidence of a demonstration, both of its perfect identity and simplicity. The strongest sensation, the most violent passion, say they, instead of distracting us from this view, only fix it more intensely, and make us consider their influence on *self* either by their pain or pleasure... Unluckily all these positive assertions are contrary to that very experience, which is pleaded for them, nor have we any idea of *self*, after the manner it is here explained. For from what impression cou'd this idea be deriv'd? This question 'tis impossible to answer without a manifest contradiction and absurdity; and yet 'tis a question which must necessarily be answer'd, if we

---

[34]   "... Wherein consists the difference betwixt believing and disbelieving any proposition? The answer is easy with regard to propositions, that are prov'd by intuition or demonstration. In that case, the person, who assents, not only conceives the ideas according to the proposition, but is necessarily determin'd to conceive them in that particular manner, either immediately or by the interposition of other ideas. Whatever is absurd is unintelligible; nor is it possible for the imagination to conceive any thing contrary to a demonstration." (T. 95).

[35]   T. 5.

wou'd have the idea of self pass for clear and intelligible. It must be some one impression, that gives rise to every real idea. But self or person is not any one impression, but that to which our several impressions and ideas are suppos'd to have a reference. If any impression gives rise to the idea of self, that impression must continue invariably the same, thro' the whole course of our lives; since self is suppo'd to exist after that manner. But there is no impression constant and invariable. Pain and pleasure, grief and joy, passions and sensations succeed each other, and never all exist at the same time. It cannot, therefore, be from any of these impressions, or from any other, that the idea of self is deriv'd; and consequently there is no such idea.[36]

The force of Hume's argument here is not only that there is no impression which can give rise to the belief in personal identity, but that there cannot be such an impression. Accordingly, Hume holds that a different causal explanation is relevant to the belief in personal identity.

Relying on introspection, Hume offers the following account of the mind:

The mind is a kind of theater, where several perceptions successively make their appearance; pass, re-pass, glide away, and mingle in an infinite variety of postures and situation. There is properly no *simplicity* in it at any one time, nor *identity* in different; whatever natural propension we may have to imagine that simplicity and identity.[37]

We hold a belief in the mind's identity, but cannot provide an impression from which this belief arises. Introspection supports the failure of the impressional test, by revealing the theatre-like character of the mind's perceptions. Therefore, whereas the taste of pineapple is regarded as nothing more than the experienced taste, "the identity, which we ascribe to the mind of man, is only a fictitious one."[38]

For a belief to be fully analyzable in terms of impressions and ideas, it must satisfy two conditions: what is believed must be derived entirely from a correspondent impression, and the content of such a belief must be held to be the same as the impression which gave rise to it. The belief in personal identity, as we have seen, fails to satisfy both conditions.

The belief in the continued and independent existence of body also fails to satisfy these conditions. For the first condition to be satisfied, the senses would have to provide the relevant impression, and Hume argues that they never can. The senses are incapable of providing the impression of the continued existence of an object "for that is a contradiction in terms, and supposes that the senses continue to operate, even after they have ceas'd all manner of operation";[39] they cannot offer their impressions as images of something distinct "because they convey to us nothing but a single perception, and never give us the least intimation of any thing beyond."[40] Since the first

[36] T. 251–252.
[37] T. 252.
[38] T. 259.
[39] T. 188.
[40] T. 189. Hume has additional arguments to offer in this regard, but they need not concern us here. See T. 189–193.

condition cannot be met, the second one cannot be met either: Hume therefore holds that the belief in the continued and independent existence of body is a "fiction."[41]

It might be thought that the belief in causality will prove to be an exception among natural beliefs to the point being argued here. Unlike the case of personal identity and physical objects, Hume holds that there is an impression – the habit or determination of mind – from which the belief in causal connections derives. Nevertheless, an examination of the text shows that the belief in causality accords with what has been said of the other natural beliefs.

The impression of reflection which Hume identifies as involved in our belief in causal connections (namely, the habit or determination of the mind which is itself generated by observing objects constantly conjoined) gives us no insight whatsoever into the actual connection between objects. Hume repeatedly urges that there is no perception of power available to us. Therefore, the belief in causal connections, although derived from an impression, is not derived from an impression of such a connection. It follows that the case of causality does not satisfy either condition set down by Hume for beliefs which are fully analyzable in terms of impressions and ideas. The belief in causal connections does not derive from the impression of such connections (hence the first condition is not satisfied), and since we regard the connection to be in objects and do not confine our belief in casuality to the habit which is generated, the belief in causal connections is not held to be exhausted in the content of the impression which gives rise to it (and so the second condition fails to be satisfied).

2. Because a Natural Belief Goes Beyond the Data of Experience, the Awareness Accompanying a Natural Belief is Always a Substitute for the Putative Object of that Belief

In the case of causality, the awareness we require is that of power or necessary connection. Since there is no impression of power, and since the idea of power is not obtainable through intuition or deduction, it follows from Hume's account of perceptions, that there is no awareness – call it a proper awareness – of power. What is substituted for this awareness is the determination of mind or habit, which follows our observation of objects constantly conjoined, and which the mind is able to "spread"[42] on external objects. The habit,

---

[41]   T. 209.

[42]   " 'Tis a common observation, that the mind has a great propensity to spread itself on external objects, and to conjoin with them many internal impression, which they occasion, and which always make their appearance at the same time that these objects discover themselves to the senses... (This) propensity is the reason, why we suppose necessity and power to lie in the

which is really a connection between perceptions, comes to be regarded as an awareness of power in objects.[43]

When speaking of the substitution involved in natural belief, Hume speaks of the activity of the mind as "feigning," and it is the resultant awareness which is the fiction mentioned earlier.

3. In the Case of a Natural Belief, We are Unable to Explicate the Putative Referent of the Belief

In holding a given natural belief, we are not aware of how we came to hold this belief, nor of what is before the mind, nor of the alleged feature to which the natural belief supposedly has reference. Hence, a further feature of a natural belief is that through it we are unable to explicate the putative referent of the belief. We do not know, therefore, what a causal connection between objects really is, we do not understand how the self comes to have an identity, and we do not understand the nature of an object which possesses a continued and independent existence.

4. What We Believe Naturally May not Be at All

Because we have no direct experience of what we believe naturally, and cannot prove the existence of what we believe naturally, those matters which fall under 'natural belief' may not *be* at all. There may not be causal connections between objects, there may not be a proper identity to the self, and there may not be objects which possess a continued and independent existence. Nevertheless, Hume makes it clear that the 'natural belief' is unaffected by whatever is actually the case with respect to these matters, given that our assent is not based on genuine insight.

5. A Natural Belief is Unavoidable and Therefore Universal

(a) A natural belief is held in spite of our ignorance of the matter believed (point 3) and without regard to the existence or non-existence of the matter believed (point 4). Therefore, these beliefs are not reasonable in the sense that

---

objects we consider, not in our mind, that considers them; not withstanding it is not possible for us to form the most distant idea of that quality, when it is not taken for the determination of the mind, to pass from the idea of an object to that of its usual attendant." (T. 167).

[43] For Hume's discussion of the substitutions in the case of physical objects and personal identity see T. 207–208, t. 254, T. 259–260.

they are based upon appropriate and sufficient evidence. Now, although these beliefs lack a proper evidential base, Hume maintains their unavoidability and, therefore, their universality: we cannot but hold these beliefs. What, then, makes these beliefs unavoidable and universal?

At the beginning of 'Of Scepticism with regard to the Senses,' Hume speaks of the sceptic continuing to reason and believe, even though a defense of reason cannot be provided by reason. Turning next to body, he writes: "... and by the same rule he must assent to the principle concerning the existence of body, tho' he cannot pretend by any arguments of philosophy to maintain its veracity. Nature has not left this to his choice, and has doubtless esteem'd it an affair of too great importance to be trusted to our uncertain reasonings and speculations."[44] It is this peculiar lack of choice – the element of choice removed by Nature – which renders a natural belief unavoidable. How is this done? The most direct answer to this appears in "Of Scepticism with regard to the Senses." Having shown that neither the senses nor reason can produce the opinion of continued and distinct existence, Hume concludes that this opinion must arise through the imagination. Impressions, according to Hume, "are internal and perishing existences and appear as such";[45] therefore, "the notion of their distinct and continu'd existence must arise from a concurrence of some of their qualities with the qualities of the imagination; and since this notion does not extend to all of them, it must arise from certain qualities peculiar to some impressions."[46] In the case of the belief in body, the qualities the impressions must possess are constancy and coherence.[47] For the belief in causality, the quality impressions must possess is constant conjunction. The same type of analysis is what Hume sought to provide in the section on "Personal Identity."[48] To speak of a natural belief as unavoidable, therefore, means that given certain perceptions with certain specifiable characteristics, the imagination will generate the awareness or belief in question – a belief which experience alone can never yield.

(b) Although unavoidable and universal, a natural belief is a ready target for the Pyrrhonian because its lacks an adequate evidential base. Hume holds that pyrrhonistic arguments levied against natural beliefs cannot be countered by reason.[49] The refutation of Pyrrhonism comes through "action and employment, and the occupations of common life. These principles may flourish and triumph in the schools – But as soon as they leave the shade, and by the presence of real objects, which actuate our passions and sentiments, are

44 T. 187.
45 T. 194.
46 T. 194.
47 T. 194–195.
48 See T. 259–263.
49 E. 159.

put in opposition to the more powerful principles of our nature, they vanish like smoke, and leave the most determined sceptic in the same condition as other mortals."[50] Elsewhere in "Of Scepticism with regard to the Senses," Hume speaks of removing sceptical doubts through "carelessness and in-attention."[51] We can see, therefore, that the unavoidability and universality of a given natural belief can be made manifest by showing the influence of instinct (Nature), and therefore, the impotence of sceptical arguments, in regard to this belief. This is the same influence of 'common sense' as occurs when pyrrhonian arguments are directed against our mental faculties, our senses, and the maxims of common life.[52]

6. A Natural Belief is Always One Which is "an Affair of too Great Importance to be Trusted to Our Uncertain Reasonings and Speculations"[53]

Natural beliefs are so important to us that they cannot await a foundation in reason, nor can they be vulnerable, in a lasting manner, to the attack of the sceptic. The great importance of natural beliefs is seen in two respects. First, natural beliefs provide the basis for certain types of empirical knowledge. In the case of the habit involved in causality, Hume writes: "Without the influence of custom, we should be entirely ignorant of every matter of fact beyond what is immediately present to the memory and senses... There would be an end at once ... of the chief part of speculation."[54] Just as we should have no awareness of causal connections without the influence of custom, without the natural belief in body, we should hold no beliefs about objects, and without the natural belief in personal identity, there would be no awareness of selfhood, and therefore, no beliefs about the self.

The second important function assigned to natural beliefs is to be found in

---

[50]   E. 159.

[51]   "This sceptical doubt, both with respect to reason and the senses, is a malady, which can never be radically cur'd, but must return upon us every moment, however we may chace it away, and sometimes may seem entirely free from it. 'Tis impossible upon any system to defend either our understanding or senses; and we but expose them farther when we attempt to justify them in that manner. As the sceptical doubt arises naturally from a profound and intense reflection on those subjects, it always encreases, the farther we carry our reflections, whether in opposition or conformity to it. Carelessness and in-attention alone can afford us any remedy. For this reason I rely entirely upon them; and take it for granted, whatever may be the reader's opinion at this present moment, that an hour hence he will be persuaded there is both an external and internal world." (T. 218).

[52]   The belief in causality is a natural belief, and the principle of causality is one the maxims of common life which Hume has in mind.

[53]   T. 187.

[54]   E. 145.

the fact that they provide us with essential ways of approaching our experiences in order to get on in the world. Of the natural belief in causality, Hume writes:

Here, then in a pre-established harmony between the course of nature and the succession of our ideas; ... Custom is that principle, by which this correspondence has been affected; so necessary to the subsistence of our species, and the regulation of our conduct, in every circumstance and occurrence of human life. Had not the presence of an object, instantly excited the idea of those objects, commonly conjoined with it, all our knowledge must have been limited to the narrow sphere of our memory and senses; and we should never have been able to adjust means to ends, or employ our natural powers, either to the producing of good or avoiding of evil...[A]s this operation of the mind, by which we infer like effects from like causes, and *vice versa*, is so essential to the subsistence of all human creatures, it is not probable, that it could be trusted to the fallacious deductions of our reason...[55]

The case of body and the self are too manifest to require any elaboration here.

These, then, are the features which distinguish natural beliefs from our other beliefs. We are now in a position to decide what difference it makes whether or not the belief in an intelligent designer of the world is a natural belief. Such a natural belief must influence the way we approach the world, and the way we act in it; it must be central to both. The belief itself would have a peculiar character in that, although it would be the belief in an intelligent designer, and therefore, present itself as falling under anthropomorphism, no explication of the divine nature would be possible (as no explication of power is possible by us). Not only would there be this duality in the case of God, wherein we both hold to his intelligence and find that we cannot unpack the divine nature, the same would be true of the world, namely, the world must present itself as though it is the product of an intelligent designer, and yet it should not be possible to explicate its nature. Nevertheless, just as our belief in causal connections between objects is compatible with however it is that change occurs, so our belief in the world as the product of an intelligent artificer must be compatible with whatever the true nature of the world, and with its origin of design (if it was designed).

To say that a belief in an intelligent designer of the world is a natural belief is not to rule out all reasoning about this matter: insofar as the Argument from Design employs data as evidence for its conclusion, it is permissible a) to determine whether the data support the conclusion offered, and b) to

---

[55]   E. 55. See also E. 45. Of our natural or instinctive behaviour generally, Hume writes:

Nature is always too strong for principle... [Pyrrhonism] can have no other tendency than to show the whimsical condition of mankind, who must act and reason and believe; though they are not able, by their most diligent enquiry, to satisfy themselves concerning the foundation of these operations, or to remove the objections, which may be raised against them (E. 160).

determine whether the data support *any* conclusion. In the last chapter, I will show that this is the procedure which Hume follows in regard to all natural beliefs – this procedure being the 'reflective' element which is employed to correct the 'undistinguished doubts' of the Pyrrhonian. For Hume, the claim that a belief is a natural belief is compatible with *some* reasoning on the same subject: we can determine what position the available data can support in regard to these beliefs. However, using Hume's results in the case of the other natural beliefs, we can anticipate that only insofar as the belief is instinctive or natural is it action-guiding and essential to our well-being. It is the natural belief which nature has not left to our choice, because it is deemed an affair of too great importance to be entrusted to our uncertain reasonings. Therefore, provided it can be shown that belief in an intelligent designer of the world is a natural belief, it is not to be expected that any conclusion of reason on the topic of the cause of the design of the world can be action-guiding. If such conclusions of reason could be action-guiding, then nature would have done something in vain – given us a natural belief to organize our experience and guide our actions.

CHAPTER 2

Introduction and Part I of the *Dialogues*

INTRODUCTION

When the *Dialogues* opens, it does so with comments by Pamphilus to Hermippus. Like all the characters in the *Dialogues*, Pamphilus is one who is not easy to understand. He speaks in three places: in the Introduction, at the end of Cleanthes' presentation of the Articulate Voice and Living Vegetable Library analogies in Part III, and at the end of the book at which point he assesses the position of Philo, Cleanthes, and Demea, the three people involved in the debate. The literature is far from unanimous on how trustworthy his remarks are, particularly those at the end of the book, and on how to interpret what he says. The position to be adopted here is that Pamphilus' remarks are to be regarded as trustworthy – setting aside the problem of how they are to be interpreted – provided that nothing in the text indicates that we should not do so.

It has not hitherto been noticed that although Pamphilus speaks in the Introduction, nowhere in that section are his own views given. In the first five paragraphs he is reporting to Hermippus what "has been remarked," although we are not told whose views are being expressed. The sixth paragraph, also spoken by Pamphilus, makes known that he overheard the substance of the dialogue while spending part of the summer with Cleanthes, and it contains a succinct account of the speakers. The account, however, is not Pamphilus': it is Hermippus'. It is Hermippus who "opposed the accurate philosophical turn of Cleanthes to the careless scepticism of Philo, or compared either of their dispositions with the rigid inflexible orthodoxy of Demea."

What, then, are we to make of the Introduction? The first five paragraphs do not pose a problem since the main point made, namely, the suitability of dialogue form to an inquiry into the existence and nature of God, appears to be borne out by the text. The dialogue form is advocated where the topic is both "obvious" and "important," or where the question raised is so "obscure and uncertain" that we can reach no fixed determination with regard to it.[1] It is consistently maintained by all the speakers that the existence

[1]   D. 128.

of God is obvious and important, and as we will see, the text bears out that the question of the nature of God does remain obscure and uncertain. Besides, it would be strange for Hume to attempt to mislead us on the form the book should take.

It is the sixth or last paragaraph which presents us with problems in interpretation, for what are we to make of the accounts given of the various speakers? If we accept the accounts in a non-technical way, that is, without reference to Hume's philosophy, it is easy to conclude that Cleanthes is the strongest thinker of the three, and therefore has the strongest position: this is, I think, the most natural interpretation of the phrase "the accurate philosophical turn of Cleanthes."[2] The use of the phrase "careless scepticism" in describing Philo can, in the same spirit, be regarded as an indication of an inferior brand of scepticism.[3] Finally, Demea's "rigid inflexible orthodoxy" can be regarded as a religious position which is unaffected by any of the arguments which are brought forth during the discussion.

I have no opposition to regarding Demea's position as outlined above, provided it is understood that orthodoxy in his case is of the mystical variety, which maintains the essential unknowability and incomprehensibility of the deity.[4] I think, however, that a re-examination of the accounts given of Cleanthes and Philo is in order.

[2] There are many defenders of this position in the literature on the *Dialogues*. The position is made particularly attractive in virtue of the fact that in the final paragraph of the book, Pamphilus' assessment of the three speakers reveals that he holds Cleanthes has the best of the debate. An indication of the extent of the agreement in the literature with Pamphilus' assessment can be got from Kemp Smith's commentary on the *Dialogues*, p. 58–59.

[3] On this point A.E. Taylor writes: "Nor is Philo, I think, ... a very worthy spokesman of scepticism... His is what Pamphilus justly describes as a 'careless' scepticism; Cleanthes hardly goes too far when he speaks of it as 'rambling'. His business is not to bring his opponent's 'experimental' theology to the test of confrontation with assured principles of reason, but merely to throw out a succession of objections which are, or can be temporarily made to look, plausible without much concern for their compatibility with one another... The scepticism which can so lightheartedly contradict itself can hardly be very formidable to the believer." ("The Present Day Relevance of Hume's *Dialogues Concerning Natural Religion*," *Proceedings of the Aristotelian Society*, Suppl. Col. 18, 1939, p. 184–185.

[4] In the opening paragraph of Part II, Demea asserts:
The question is not concerning the *being* but the *nature* of God. This, I affirm, from the infirmities of human understanding, to be altogether incomprehensible and unknown to us. The essence of that supreme mind, his attributes, the manner of his existence, the very nature of his duration; these and every particular, which regards so divine a Being, are mysterious to men. Finite, weak, and blind creatures, we ought to humble ourselves in his august presence, and conscious of our frailties, adore in silence his infinite perfections, which eye hath not seen, ear hath not heard, neither hath it entered into the heart of man to conceive them. They are covered in a deep cloud from human curiosity: It is profaneness to attempt penetrating through these sacred obscurities: And next to the impiety of denying his existence, is the temerity of prying into his nature and essence, decrees and attributes.
Demea does not alter this position throughout the discussion of the Argument from Design.

Let us begin with the characterization of Philo as a 'careless sceptic'. When discussing Hume's views on natural belief and Pyrrhonism, we saw that the sceptical doubts raised by the Pyrrhonian are spoken of as being removed through 'carelessness and in-attention'.[5] The term 'carelessness', therefore, can be employed by Hume as a technical (non-pejorative) term which carries important philosophical significance, inasmuch as it characterizes the move from Pyrrhonism to Mitigated Scepticism. Hence, when Philo is characterized as a 'careless sceptic', some weight ought to be given to reading this in the spirit of Hume's own views on natural belief and Pyrrhonism. The fact that the term 'careless' is used to modify 'sceptic' tends to support my reading. What I have said above does not by itself *prove* that my reading is the correct one. But it points the way to an interpretation of Philo which is drawn from Hume's established views.

Of the three main speakers in the *Dialogues*, only Demea is given a religious characterization; Cleanthes and Philo are referred to in philosophical terms. We are given the impression in the account of Demea that he is the one most aptly spoken of as a dogmatist: a dogmatist cannot be more accurately described than as 'rigid' and 'inflexible'. It is this type of consideration which led Philip Stanley to speak of Demea as a dogmatist. Since Cleanthes and Demea do not hold similar positions in the *Dialogues*, it is easy to conclude that Cleanthes cannot be a dogmatist. Philip Stanley writes: "Cleanthes is your open-minded religious scientist, cautious, unable to reject the evidence for a something implied in the ordered beauties of his proper field."[6] Earlier in the article, Stanley refers to Cleanthes as a 'mitigated sceptic'.

Now, is it true that if we agree that Demea is a dogmatist – which I want to allow – that Cleanthes cannot be regarded as one as well? I think not. Demea is a *religious* dogmatist. But this leaves open the possibility that Cleanthes (at least for a time in the *Dialogues*) is a *philosophical* dogmatist. Philosophical dogmatists, as we saw earlier, are those who "see objects only on one side, and have no idea of any counter-poising argument" with the result that "they throw themselves precipitately into the principles, to which they are inclined."[7] Hence, there is a great deal of assurance and obstinacy in the philosophical dogmatist. We also saw the need for sceptical arguments to turn the dogmatist from this position with a view to arriving at mitigated scepticism. The reference to "the accurate philosophical turn of Cleanthes," I submit, may be a reference to the philosophical conversion which the dogmatist undergoes to achieve the position of mitigated scepticism. The

---

[5]   T. 218.
[6]   Philip Stanley, "The Scepticisms of David Hume," p. 430.
[7]   E. 161.

"accuracy" of the turn on this account would characterize the success with which it is made.

As with my thesis regarding Philo at this early stage of our analysis of the *Dialogues*, so with my treatment of Cleanthes: much more evidence is required to confirm the view put forth. In any case, if I am correct, then the Introduction contains important clues to our understanding of the roles of the three characters within the *Dialogues*.

PART I: PRELIMINARY DISCUSSION: CAN THERE BE A NATURAL THEOLOGY?

Of all the sections in the *Dialogues*, Part I is that which is most consistently either ignored or summarized in a few sentences. To pass over this section is a serious error, since it provides us with insights into the positions which Philo and Cleanthes will attempt to defend in subsequent sections. Philo, as I will now show, adopts the role of a moderate antecedent sceptic in Part I. In his response to Philo, Cleanthes reveals that he lacks an understanding of Philo's use of scepticism, and that he is closely allied with the Humean notion of the dogmatist.

Philo opens the philosophic aspect of the discussion with the following warning:

Let us become thoroughly sensible of the weakness, blindness, and narrow limits of human reason: Let us duly consider its uncertainly and needless contrarieties, even in subjects of common life and practice: Let the errors and deceits of our very senses be set before us; the insuperable difficulties, which attend first principles in all systems; the contradictions, which adhere to the very ideas of matter, cause and effect, extension, space, time, motion; and in a word, quantity of all kinds, the object of the only science, that can fairly pretend to any certainty or evidence. When these topics are displayed in their full light, as they are by some philosophers and almost all *divines*; who can retain such confidence in this frail faculty of reason as to pay any regard to its determinations in points so sublime, so abstruse, so remote from common life and experience? ... with what assurance can we decide concerning the origin of worlds, or trace their history from eternity to eternity?[8]

We are told by Pamphilus that in Cleanthes he could "distinguish an air of finesse; as if he perceived some raillery or artificial malice in the reasonings of Philo."[9] Cleanthes ensuing remarks indicate that he regards Philo's position to be representative of excessive scepticism, and he provides Philo with Hume's answer (in the first *Enquiry*) to this position:

You propose then, Philo, said Cleanthes, to erect religious faith on philosophical scepticism; and

[8] D. 131–132.
[9] D. 132.

you think that if certainty or evidence be expelled from every other subject of enquiry, it will all retire to these theological doctrines, and there acquire a superior force and authority. Whether your scepticism be as absolute and sincere as you pretend, we shall learn bye and bye, when the company breaks up: We shall then see, whether you go out at the door or the window; and whether you really doubt, if your body has gravity, or can be injured by its fall; according to popular opinion, derived from our fallacious senses and more fallacious experience. And this consideration, Demea, may, I think, fairly serve to abate our ill-will to this humorous sect of the sceptics. If they be thoroughly in earnest, they will not long trouble the world with their doubts, cavils, and disputes: If they be only in jest, they are, perhaps, bad raillers, but can never be very dangerous, either to the state, to philosophy, or to religion.[10]

In this passage, Cleanthes shows that he misunderstands Philo's meaning. Philo's remarks are not offered as a version of excessive scepticism. He is not advocating the cessation of all inquiry: he is rather making the claim that because of known difficulties with our faculties and concepts even in regard to what is most familiar to us, we cannot proceed with assurance in those matters which are beyond common life and experience. This is not excessive scepticism, but what Hume in the first *Enquiry* spoke of as 'mitigated scepticism'. Furthermore, since Philo's sceptical considerations are offered prior to the consideration of any particular arguments, his scepticism at this point is 'antecedent scepticism'. In short, Philo, in the passage quoted earlier, represents antecedent scepticism 'when more moderate'; and this, it will be recalled, Hume characterized as reasonable, and as " a necessary preparative to the study of philosophy."[11]

Two questions arise at this point: (1) How is Philo attempting to provide the "necessary preparative to the study of philosophy," and (2) Why does Cleanthes require it? Turning initially to the second question raised, it seems, from Cleanthes' other remarks in Part I, that he does not, in fact, require such a preparative: he appears to be well prepared to do philosophy according to Humean standards of preparedness. Toward the end of Part I, Cleanthes appeals to the need for settling problems through the evidence available to us:

But I observe, says Cleanthes, with regard to you Philo, and all speculative sceptics, that your doctrine and practice are as much at variance in the most abstruse points of theory as in the conduct of common life. Wherever evidence discovers itself, you adhere to it, notwithstanding your pretended scepticism; and I can observe, too, some of your sect to be as decisive as those who make greater professions of certainty and assurance... These sceptics, therefore, are obliged on every question, to consider each particular evidence apart and proportion their assent to the precise degree of evidence which occurs. This is their practice in all natural, mathematical, moral and political science. And why not the same, I ask, in the theological and religious.[12]

The only plausible answer, in Humean terms, as to Cleanthes' lack of preparedness is that, although he appeals to the need for evidence in deciding

[10]   D. 132.
[11]   E. 150.
[12]   D. 136–137.

issues, he will err, or is likely to err, in dealing with the data he has. But why should this be so? The answer can be constructed by examining the other passages in Part I in which Cleanthes speaks.

The passages which are most helpful here are those in which Cleanthes attacks scepticism. In some passages[13] he once again calls attention to the fact that sceptics accept evidence in other sciences, and that there is in sceptics a general trust of our cognitive faculties in spite of the acknowledged difficulties with them. He concludes from this that the sceptics are "a sect of jesters or railliers."[14] And he goes on: "But for my part, whenever I find myself disposed to mirth and amusement, I shall certainly choose my entertainment of a less perplexing and abstruse nature. A comedy, a novel, or at most a history, seems a more natural recreation than such metaphysical subtleties and abstractions."[15] The point to reaize is that Cleanthes does not, like Philo and Hume, see a role for scepticism in inquiry. From a Humean point of view, Cleanthes could be a mitigated sceptic or a dogmatist. The fact that he does not acknowledge a useful role for scepticism, which is an essential aspect of being a mitigated sceptic, leads to the conclusion that he is a dogmatist.

Cleanthes argues that if there is a difference between theology and the other sciences, the advantage falls on the side of the former. For scientific arguments are difficult to comprehend, whereas the religious hypothesis "is founded on the simplest and most obvious arguments, and unless it meet with artificial obstacles, has such easy access and admission into the mind of man."[16] Cleanthes shows no concern that facility in accepting an argument does not necessarily constitute evidence that it is a good argument. Or, at least, he does not argue that facility in accepting his argument establishes, or assists in establishing, its correctness. Cleanthes does make reference to the fact that the religious hypothesis is based "on the simplest and most obvious arguments," but the context makes it clear that he regards "easy access and admission into the mind of man" to be the effect of apprehending "the simplest and most obvious arguments." Therefore, for Cleanthes, the former is a sign of the latter, although nowhere does he attempt to prove – what he must prove – that this procedure is reliable, at least so far as the "religious hypothesis" is concerned. Unlike Hume, who holds that it is an awareness of sceptical objections and their correction through common sense and reflection which should assist in the evaluation of arguments, Cleanthes regards sceptical objections to the religious hypothesis as 'artificial obstacles' possessing no value at all. Increasingly, therefore, Cleanthes begins to fit Hume's description of the dogmatist: "... while they see objects only on one

---

[13]   D. 137.
[14]   D. 137.
[15]   D. 137.
[16]   D. 138.

side, and have no idea of any counterpoising arguments, they throw themselves precipitately into the principles, to which they are inclined; nor have they any indulgence for those who entertain opposite sentiments."[17] As such, he leaves himself vulnerable to error.

In an additional passage, Cleanthes puts it beyond doubt that he has no sympathy whatever for scepticism:

And it is now, in a manner, avowed, by all pretenders to reasoning and philosophy, that atheist and sceptic are almost synonymous. And as it is certain, that no man is in earnest, when he professes the latter principle; I would fain hope that there are as few, who seriously maintain the former.[18]

What is also significant about this passage is that Cleanthes is content to group all sceptics together, and therefore, he does not draw a distinction between mitigated scepticism (as Philip Stanley regards Cleanthes) and excessive scepticism or Pyrrhonism.

In the last paragraph in Part I, Cleanthes asserts:

It is very natural ... for men to embrace those principles, by which they find they can best defend their doctrines; nor need we have any recourse to priestcraft to account for so reasonable an expedient. And surely, nothing can afford a stronger presumption, that any set of principles are true, and ought to be embraced, than to observe, that they tend to the confirmation of true religion, and serve to confound the cavils of atheists, libertines, and freethinkers of all denominations.[19]

Cleanthes does not indicate what he means by 'true religion'. But this much is clear: he believes that the religious argument he has to offer should be accepted because it tends to confirm what he regards as the true religion. Cleanthes, therefore, begins the dialogue without the features which the mitigated sceptic holds "ought for ever to accompany a just reasoner," namely, "a degree of doubt, and caution, and modesty."[20] Furthermore, he begins without the type of impartiality in judgment and lack of prejudice which Hume holds is a necessary preparative to the study of philosophy.[21] Cleanthes condones the procedure – he calls it reasonable – whereby principles are accepted because, through them, a favored doctrine can be defended. Hume, on the other hand, as we have seen, regards this as an "inconvenience."[22] Therefore, Cleanthes does not begin the *Dialogues* with the philosophic disposition which Hume holds we require if we are to achieve accuracy in our reasonings.

[17] E. 161.
[18] D. 139.
[19] D. 140.
[20] E. 162.
[21] D. 150.
[22] E. 40.

We can now turn to the first question raised, namely, how is Philo
attempting to provide Cleanthes with the necessary preparative to the study
of philosophy? As we shall see, Philo's efforts accord with Hume's views on
this matter.

The major passages given to Philo in Part I are sparked by Cleanthes'
misunderstanding of Philo as a destructive Pyrrhonian. Cleanthes insists that
Pyrrhonians can renounce all belief and opinion for only short periods of
time,[23] but then asks why anyone would want to make such a renunciation.[24]
And the last point which he makes before Philo speaks is to compare
Pyrrhonism with Stoicism, pointing out what he regards as an error in each;

... [B]oth of them (i.e. Stoicism and Pyrrhonism) seem founded on this erroneous maxim, that
what a man can perform sometimes, and in some dispositions, he can perform always, and in
every disposition. When the mind, by Stoical reflections, is elevated into a sublime enthusiasm
of virtue, and strongly smit with any *species* of honour or public good, the utmost bodily pain
and sufferance will not prevail over such a high sense of duty; and it is possible, perhaps, by its
means, even to smile and exult in the midst of tortures. If this sometimes may be the case in fact
and reality, much more may a philosopher, in his school, or even in his closet, work himself up
to such an enthusiasm, and support in imagination the acutest pain or most calamitous event
which he can possibly conceive. But how shall he support this enthusiasm itself? The bent of his
mind relaxes, and cannot be recalled at pleasure: Avocations lead him astray: Misfortunes attack
him unawares: And the *philosopher* sinks by degrees into the *plebeian*.[25]

Philo agrees with Cleanthes' comparison between Stoics and Sceptics. But he
maintains that Cleanthes has failed to note the lingering effect of each. In the
case of Stoicism, Philo points out that "though the mind cannot ... support
the highest flights of philosophy, yet even when it sinks lower, it still retains
somewhat of its former disposition; and the effects of the Stoic's reasoning
will appear in his conduct in common life, and through the whole tenor of his
actions."[26] In regard to Scepticism, Philo asserts:

In like manner, if a man has accustomed himself to sceptical considerations on the uncertainty
and narrow limits of reason, he will not entirely forget them when he turns his reflections on other
subjects; but in all his philosophical principles and reasoning, I dare not say, in his common

---

[23]   "In reality, Philo, continued he, it seems certain, that though a man, in a flush of
humour, after intense reflection on the many contradictions and imperfections of human reason,
may entirely renounce all belief and opinion; it is impossible for him to persevere in this total
scepticism, or make it appear in his conduct for a few hours. External objects press in upon him:
Passions solicit him: His philosophical melancholy dissipates: and even the utmost violence upon
his own temper will not be able, during any time, to preserve the poor appearance of scepticism."
(D. 132).
[24]   "And for what reason impose on himself such a violence? This is a point on which it
will be impossible for him ever to satisfy himself, consistently with his sceptical principles." (E.
132–133).
[25]   D. 133.
[26]   D. 133.

conduct, he will be found different from those, who either never formed any opinions in the case, or have entertained sentiments more favourable to human reason.[27]

Philo is not a destructive sceptic: rather, he is indicating that an appreciation of the force of sceptical considerations in regard to reason is vital to those attempting to do philosophy. In elaborating on this point, Philo shows himself to be entirely in accord with Hume's views.

The lesson which scepticism offers, according to Philo, is that inquiry·must be confined within experience; he explains that sceptical arguments against reason and the senses show us the uncertainties present in both, but such sceptical arguments "are not able to counterpoise the more solid and more natural arguments, derived from the senses and experience."[28] Once we leave the empirical realm, however, pyrrhonistic arguments are able to counterbalance our arguments: the victory of the sceptic is to be found in the suspense of judgment which this counterbalancing brings about:

But it is evident, whenever our arguments lose this advantage, and run wide of common life, that the most refined scepticism comes to be upon a footing with them, and is able to oppose and counterbalance them. The one has no more weight than the other. The mind must remain in suspense between them; and it is that very suspense or balance, which is the triumph of scepticism.[29]

Philo's point here is that Nature will not assist in deciding controversies which go beyond common life. Hence, here we lack a decision procedure to determine which, if any, of the arguments presented are acceptable – or more acceptable – than others which are presented.

We can now understand how Philo is attempting to provide the necessary preparative to the study of philosophy which is advocated by Hume: if we understand the limits of human knowledge, we will not attempt to gain understanding which exceeds these boundaries. Philo is clearly indicating that the topic of God goes beyond what we can know, and he is therefore urging Cleanthes to refrain from an inquiry into the divine nature. Philo is confident that an inquiry such as Cleanthes is suggesting will result in a victory for the sceptic.

We can now see how commentators have been misled in dealing with Part I. Since Philo stresses sceptical considerations and Cleanthes emphasizes the need for evidence in deciding issues, Philo is interpreted as a Pyrrhonian, and Cleanthes is regarded as the one with the greater philosophic ability. My inquiry has shown that Philo, not Cleanthes, is the one who, from a Humean point of view, possesses the necessary preparative to the study of philosophy, because of his awareness of sceptical considerations on the uncertainty and

[27] D. 134.
[28] D. 135.
[29] D. 135–136.

narrow limits of reason. Cleanthes is now seen as a dogmatist in the Humean sense, and therefore, as one who, despite his insistence on the need for evidence, will likely err in the use he makes of the data he presents. Judging from Part I, therefore, it is Philo, and not Cleanthes, who will provide the necessary guidance throughout the discussion.

If, as I have maintained above, Philo is to provide the necessary guidance to the discussion, what form will this guidance take? Before examining the subsequent sections, only a tentative answer can be provided. Assistance in this matter is again to be sought from the first *Enquiry* (Section XII). The only cure for dogmatism, according to Hume, is to be exposed to the arguments of the sceptic. At this stage a suspense of judgment should follow, and it is then possible to decide – through impartiality in judgment and the removal of prejudice – what we ought to believe by correcting the 'undistinguished doubts' generated by the sceptical arguments. Once the corrections are made, the position which is held is that of the mitigated sceptic. If this is, in fact, the procedure followed by Philo in the *Dialogues*, then we should encounter sceptical arguments which oppose the arguments of the dogmatist; we should encounter a suspense in judgment in the discussion; and we should then find an attempt to sort out those points and arguments against which the sceptical arguments will always retain their force, and those against which the sceptical arguments are seen to be ineffective. Furthermore, we should find an admission by Philo that those arguments which he uses to produce a suspense of judgment are themselves in need of correction since they generate 'undistinguished doubts', that is, they are directed against claims which we should reject, as well as those which we should accept. The move from Pyrrhonism to mitigated scepticism is effected through distinguishing between these claims.

CHAPTER 3

Hume's *Dialogues*: Part II

THE ARGUMENT FROM DESIGN IS PRESENTED

As Part II opens, Demea, addressing himself to Cleanthes, makes the distinction between the existence of God and the nature of God, maintaining that the former is certain and self-evident, while the latter is incomprehensible and unknown:

> I must own, Cleanthes, said Demea, that nothing can more surprise me, than the light, in which you have, all along, put this argument. By the whole tenor of your discourse, one would imagine that you were maintaining the being of a God, against the cavils of atheists and infidels; and were necessitated to become a champion for that fundamental principle of all religion. But this, I hope, is not by any means a question among us. No man; no man, at least, of common sense, I am persuaded, ever entertained a serious doubt with regard to a truth so certain and self-evident. The question is not concerning the *being* but the *nature* of God. This, I affirm, from the infirmities of human understanding, to be altogether incomprehensible and unknown to us.[1]

Demea's basis for this view is religious.[2] Philo agrees with Demea's claim concerning the being and nature of God, but his support is philosophical:

> ... where reasonable men treat these subjects, the question can never be concerning the *being*, but only the *nature* of the Deity. The former truth, as you well observe, is unquestionable and self-evident. Nothing exists without a cause: and the original cause of this universe (whatever it be) we call God.

Ronald J. Butler maintains that although the distinction between God's existence and God's nature is consistently held throughout the *Dialogues*, in Hume's non-theological writings no distinction whatsoever is allowed between

---

[1]   D. 141.

[2]   John Laird ("The Present Day Relevance of Hume's Dialogues," p. 207) makes the point that the *Dialogues* "are in the main between Cleanthes and Philo. Demea, in principle, does not count." There is already a sense in which Demea does count: in the opening paragraphs of Part II, Hume is attempting to show, in fact to insist, that Philo's view of the unknowability and incomprehensibility of the divine nature is identical to that held by "all divines almost, from the foundation of Christianity, who have ever treated of this or any other theological subject, and in particular, to that held by Demea, the orthodox religionist in the discussion. Reason, therefore, and religion arrive at the same, rather than different, views regarding the divine nature.

something's existence and its nature.[3] Butler claims that what is strange about Hume's view is that, in the religious context, "we can have a belief in the existence of something, and *ipso facto* an idea of the something that exists, without being able to say *anything* about the nature of what it is that exists."[4] Now, Butler is mistaken in holding that in Part II Philo believes that we have an idea of God. In at least two passages he insists that we have no idea of God:

... as all perfection is entirely relative, we ought never to imagine, that we comprehend the attributes of this divine Being, or to suppose, that his perfections have any analogy or likeness to the perfections of a human creature ... let us beware, lest we think, that our ideas any wise correspond to his perfections, or that his attributes have any resemblance to these qualities among men.[5]

In reality, Cleanthes, ... there is no need of having recourse to that affected scepticism, so displeasing to you, in order to come to this determination. Our ideas reach no farther than our experience: We have no experience of divine attributes and operations: I need not conclude my syllogism: You can draw the inference yourself.[6]

Philo's point, therefore, is that we cannot say anything about God's nature because we do not have an idea of God. Although Philo maintains that we have no ideas of divine attributes, and therefore, no ideas which correspond to the divine nature, he does not hold that there is nothing before the mind when we think of God. His point, again, however, is that the ideas before the mind are not ideas of divine attributes:

Wisdom, thought, design, knowledge; these we justly ascribe to him; because these words are honourable among men, and we have no other language or other conceptions, by which we can express our adoration of him. But let us beware, lest we think, that our ideas any wise correspond to his perfections, or that his attributes have any resemblance to these qualities among men. He is infinitely superior to our limited view and comprehension...[7]

Philo's position no longer appears strange, since the thought of God's existence is, consistent with the doctrine in the *Treatise*, seen to be "the very same with the idea of what we conceive to be existent": that nothing can be said about the nature of what it is that exists stems from the fact that the ideas

---

[3]   R. J. Butler "Natural Belief and the Enigma of Hume," *Archiv für Geschichte der Philosophie*, 42, 1960, p. 94. Butler quotes the following to support his position: "The idea of existence, then, is the very same with the idea of what we conceive to be existent. To reflect on any thing simply, and to reflect it as existent, are nothing different from each other. That idea, when conjoined with the idea of any object, makes no addition to it. Whatever we conceive, we conceive to be existent. Any idea we please to form is the idea of a being; and the idea of a being is any idea we please to form." (T. 66–67).

[4]   Butler, p. 94–95.

[5]   D. 142.

[6]   D. 143.

[7]   D. 142.

before the mind do not accurately reflect the divine nature.

What is most perplexing about Philo's comments is his admission that there is an original cause of this universe, and that the claim of the existence of God is 'unquestionable and self-evident'. It was Philo who, in Part I, urged us to become "thoroughly sensible of the weakness, blindness, and narrow limits of human reason" and to "duly consider its uncertainty and needless contrarities, even in subjects of common life and practice" with a view to seeing that no one can "retain such confidence in this frail faculty of reason as to pay any regard to its determinations in points so sublime, so abstruse, so remote from common life and experience." It was also Philo in Part I who warned that "when we look beyond human affairs and the properties of the surrounding bodies: When we carry our speculations ... (for example) ... into the creation and formation of the universe ... we must be far removed from the smallest tendency to scepticism not to be aprehensive, that we have here got quite beyond the reach of our faculties." How, then, can Philo now maintain that the existence of an original cause of the universe is unquestionable and self-evident?

One answer is to maintain that, granting our belief in the Principle of Causality ('Nothing exists without a cause'), the causal claim about the universe is subsumed under a general law of reason, and in this sense the claim is unquestionable and self-evident. However, this answer appears to be unsatisfactory. For even if it is true that Hume holds that the causal principle cannot be questioned by any reasonable person, certainly the *unity* of the universe which would lead to the requirement of an original cause can be questioned. In fact, one of the criticisms which Cleanthes levies against Demea's argument for a First Cause is precisely the point that the world can be explained by offering a causal explanation for each of its parts without the need for an original cause:

In such a chain too, or a succession of objects, each part is caused by that which preceded it, and causes that which succeeds it. Where then is the difficulty? But the *whole*, you say, wants a cause. I answer, that the uniting of these parts into a whole, like the uniting of several distinct counties into one kingdom, or several distinct members into one body, is performed merely by an arbitrary act of the mind, and has no influence on the nature of things. Did I show you the particular causes of each individual in a collection of twenty particles of matter, I should think it very unreasonable, should you afterwards ask me, what was the cause of the whole twenty. This is sufficiently explained in explaining the cause of the parts.[8]

Philo concurs with all Cleanthes' criticisms regarding the need for an original cause of the universe, and adds a number of his own criticisms.

There are two other possibilities open to us in explaining Philo's position in this passage. One is to say that he is here simply being inconsistent with his

8   D. 190–191.

views in Part I and elsewhere in the *Dialogues*. I believe that this alternative ought to be adopted only if we cannot offer an account which accords with Philo's position in other parts of the book. But there is such an account which renders Philo's position consistent. In Part I, Philo warned against 'reasoning' beyond common life and experience; however, this is compatible with holding 'beliefs' which have no empirical referent. An analogous situation occurs in Hume's analysis of cause. Although we cannot reason to what (if anything) actually connects objects in the relation of cause and effect, we still hold a belief that objects are connected in this relation, and Hume holds, it is reasonable for us to do so. The same is true of our belief in physical objects and the self. The vulgar consciousness finds all three beliefs imposed upon it, and all three appear unquestionable and self-evident.[9]

Philo's position in the passage under consideration can be taken as indicating that there is a natural belief in regard to the cause of the universe, a belief which is unquestionable and self-evident as are our other natural beliefs. Nothing which Philo says in Part I or elsewhere is incompatible with claims of natural belief, and, as we have seen, Philo adopts a position which stresses the importance of instinct. On the account offered, we can also explain Philo's assertion that God exists, and his denial regarding our knowledge of the nature of God. A natural belief is never founded on perceptions which correspond accurately to the reality to which the belief refers or is about. Hence, in speaking of the original cause of the universe as 'whatever it be', he is calling attention to this feature of a natural belief. Philo, it will be recalled, in his discussion of the similarity between Stoics and Sceptics, urged that once a person has accustomed himself to the relevant sceptical considerations, he will not entirely forget them in all his philosophical principles and reasoning, and common conduct. I am suggesting that this influence of Pyrrhonism is precisely what is evident in Philo's reference to the original cause as 'whatever it be'.[10] Hence, early in Part II, Philo appears to be adopting a position on God which bears great

---

[9]   In regard to causality, Hume writes: "'Tis a general maxim in philosophy, that *whatever begins to exist, must have a cause of existence*. This is commonly taken for granted in all reasonings, without any proof given or demanded." (T. 78–79). Similarly, concerning our belief in physical objects, he writes: (the sceptic) must assent to the principle concerning the existence of body, though he cannot pretend by any arguments of philosohpy to maintain its veracity... We may well ask, *What causes induce us to believe in the existence of body*? but 'tis in vain to ask, Whether there *be body or not*. That is a point, which we must take for granted in all our reasonings." (T. 187).

[10]   This is compatible with Philo's assertion early in Part XII that the original cause is intelligent, for this is what the natural belief leads us to believe. But just as we believe in a necessary connection between cause and effect and cannot explain what this connection is, so we believe in an intelligent cause but cannot explain what this intelligence is. It is important to realize that Philo can speak in these two ways consistent with the doctrine of natural belief, just as Hume can speak of necessary connection in two ways consistent with his views on natural belief.

similarity to Hume's treatment is his other works of what we are led to believe naturally. It is evident that what I have set forth is not a proof that natural belief is present in the *Dialogues*. What I am suggesting is that Hume is putting forth this position, and will later develop and argue for it.

Cleanthes does not believe that by inquiring into the nature of God, we can uncover God's 'powers'. In fact, he appears to allow that God's powers are not knowable by us. Two passages in Part IV make this point:

The Deity, I can readily allow, possesses many powers and attributes, of which we can have no comprehension. (D. 158)

... the Deity possesses attributes, of which we have no comprehension ... (D. 159)

Cleanthes appears rather to want to establish that certain ideas which we do have can be applied to God, namely, our ideas of those features pertaining to an intelligent being:

It seems strange to me, said Cleanthes, that you, Demea, who are so sincere in the cause of religion, should still maintain the mysterious, incomprehensible nature of the Deity, and should insist so strenuously, that he has no manner of likeness of resemblance to human creatures ... if our ideas, so far as they go, be not just and adequate, and correspondent to his real nature, I know not what there is in this subject worth insisting on.[11]

For though it be allowed, that the Deity possesses attributes of which we have no comprehension; yet ought we never to ascribe to him any attributes, which are absolutely incompatible with that intelligent nature, essential to him. A mind, whose acts and sentiments and ideas are not distinct and successive; one, that is wholly simple, and totally immutable; is a mind which has no thought, no reason, no will, no sentiment, no love, no hatred; or in a word, is no mind at all. It is an abuse of terms to give it that appellation; and we may as well speak of limited extension without figure, or of number without composition.[12]

Hence, the central dispute is a dispute regarding the adequacy of our ideas of an intelligent being to characterize the divine nature.

Cleanthes will argue analogically that the ideas we already possess of what a mind is can be used to characterize the nature of God. If this is done successfully, then Cleanthes will have shown that there is a 'specific resemblance' between the human mind and God. Philo, as we have seen, maintains the incomprehensibility of the divine nature. Now, in order for Philo to be victorious, he must prove that Cleanthes is mistaken in holding to the claim of a 'specific resemblance' between our mind and God. He does not have to prove that there is no resemblance whatsoever between our mind and God. A 'specific resemblance' exists when the similarities between the items compared are adequate to include both in the same class. Hence, Philo

---

[11]   D. 158.
[12]   D. 159.

will have succeeded if he can prove that there is no justification for including God in the class of 'intelligent beings'.

(We can now understand why Philo's syllogism which immediately precedes Cleanthes' version of the Argument from Design[13] does not appear as a stumbling block to Cleanthes. Cleanthes effort is designed to show that the ideas *we already have* are sufficient to give us insight into the nature of God.)

THE TWO VERSIONS OF THE ARGUMENT FROM DESIGN

Cleanthes' version of the Argument from Design reads as follows:

> Look round the world: Contemplate the whole and every part of it: You will find it to be nothing but one great machine, subdivided into an infinite number of lesser machines, which again admit of subdivisions, to a degree beyond what human senses and faculties can trace and explain. All these various machines, and even their most minute parts, are adjusted to each other with an accuracy, which ravishes into admiration all men who have ever contemplated them. The curious adapting of means to ends, throughout all nature, resembles exactly, though it much exceeds, the productions of human contrivance; of human design, thought, wisdom, and intelligence. Since therefore the effects resemble each other, we are led to infer, by all the rules of analogy, that the causes also resemble; and that the Author of nature is somewhat similar to the mind of man; though possessed of much larger faculties, proportioned to the grandeur of the world, which he has executed. By this argument *a posteriori*, and by this argument alone, we do prove at once the existence of a Deity, and his similarity to human mind and intelligence.[14]

George J. Nathan[15] correctly points out that Cleanthes is making two points with his argument, namely, that the cause of the design of the world is intelligent, and that the cause of design is external to the design. This is confirmed by the fact that all Philo's criticisms are directed against one or other of these claims. We must now get clear on the premises for Cleanthes' argument.

Since the argument begins with a reference to finding the world 'to be nothing but one great machine, subdivided into an infinite number of lesser machines', it is tempting to hold that the claim that the world is a machine is a premise in this argument.[16] However, this is not a correct reading of Cleanthes' argument. First, when Philo criticizes Cleanthes, he makes the point that there is not sufficient resemblance between human artifacts and the universe to argue that they are effects of the same kind:

[13] "Our ideas reach no further than experience: We have no experience of divine attributes and operations: I need not conclude my syllogism: You can draw the inference yourself." (D. 142–143).

[14] D. 143.

[15] Chappell, p. 319.

[16] This is the position Nathan adopts in his paper.

If we see a house, Cleanthes, we conclude, with the greatest certainty, that it had an architect or builder; because this is precisely the species of effect, which we have experienced to proceed from that species of cause. But surely you will not affirm, that the universe bears such a resemblance to a house, that we can with the same certainty infer a similar cause, or that the analogy is here entire and perfect. The dissimilitude is so striking, that the utmost you can here pretend to is a guess, a conjecture, a presumption concerning a similar cause...[17]

Cleanthes, however, does not appear bothered by this; he has recourse to the adaptation of means to ends and coherence of parts which are present in all machines and in the design of the world to support his claim:

It would surely be very ill received, replied Cleanthes; and I should be deservedly blamed and detested, did I allow that the proofs of a Deity amounted to no more than a guess or conjecture. But is the whole adjustment of means to ends in a house and in the universe so slight a resemblance? The oeconomy of final causes? The order, proportion, and arrangement of every part?[18]

Second, the principle employed within the Argument from Design to establish the resemblance between the deity and us is 'like effects prove like causes'. And when Philo puts forth his version of the Argument from Design two pages later (Cleanthes acknowledges that Philo's version provides a fair representation of Argument) he states clearly that "the adjustment of means to ends is alike in the universe, as in a machine of human contrivance." By this statement, he is acknowledging that the comparison within the argument is between the means to ends relations and coherence of parts present in the design of machines and the world, and not simply between machines and the world.[19]

Stated formally, Cleanthes' argument can be put in the following way:

Argument I

$P_1, P_2, P_3...P_n$ (human artifacts)	have	A (means to ends relations), B (coherence of parts).
Q (the universe)	has	A (means to end relations), B (a coherence of parts).
$P_1, P_2, P_3...P_n$ (human artifacts)	have	C (have mind or intelligence as their cause of design).
∴ Q (universe)	also has	C (has mind or intelligence as its cause of design).

[17] D. 144.
[18] D. 144–145.
[19] The significance of the difference in these two positions will be developed as we proceed.

Argument II

$P_1, P_2, P_3...P_n$ (human artifacts)	have	C (have mind or intelligence as their cause of design).
Q (universe)		has C (has mind or intelligence as its cause of design).
$P_1, P_2, P_3...P_n$ (human artifacts)		have D (an external cause of design).
$\therefore$ Q (universe)		also has D (an external cause of design).

Because he believes that Cleanthes is making reference to the machine-like character of the world in the second part of his argument, George Nathan argues that the second part of the argument begs the question: "The second point is that because both artifacts and the universe are machines they both have external causes. However, this second point does not hold since we never observe directly that something is a machine. This is an inference from the experience of agents producing artifacts. In the present instance, it would be begging the question to call the universe a machine, because the inference from the particular order of the universe to an external orderer is precisely the issue in dispute. The inference, if valid, would justify calling the world a machine, but calling it a machine does not justify the inference."[20]

On my interpretation, Cleanthes is not begging the question in the second part of the argument, since the externality of the cause is concluded, not from the claim of the machine-like character of the world, but from the conclusion of the first part of the Argument, namely, that the universe has mind or intelligence as its cause of design. In the second version of the Argument from Design, we find the claim[21] that if matter contains the source or spring of order within itself then the cause of design is internal, whereas if the source or spring of the design of the world is mind than the cause of design is external to the world. Hence, the externality of the cause is seen to follow from the fact that the cause in intelligent, and not from the fact that the product is a machine (although, of course, if the product is a machine, then the cause of

---

[20] Chappell, p 399–400.
[21] The passage reads: "For aught we can know *a priori* matter may contain the source or spring of order originally, within itself, as well as mind does; and there is no more difficulty in conceiving, that the several elements from an internal unknown cause, may fall into the most exquisite arrangement, than to conceive that their ideas, in the great universal mind, from a like internal, unknown cause, fall into that arrangement" (D. 146).

design is external to it). My reading of Cleanthes' argument makes clear that the machine-like character of the world is a *conclusion* which the argument as a whole supports, rather than a *premise* which is employed in the argument. Cleanthes' argument is not an argument from the machine-like character of the world: it is an argument to it. It is only upon knowing that the adaption of means to ends has resulted from intelligence that the characterization of an object as a machine is countenanced.

The first criticism to Cleanthes' version of the Argument from Design comes not from Philo, but from Demea.

I shall be so free, Cleanthes, said Demea, as to tell you, that from the beginning, I could not approve of your conclusion concerning the similarity of the Deity to man; still less can I approve of the mediums, by which you endeavour to establish it. What! No demonstration of the being of a God! No abstract arguments! (D. 143)

Philo agrees with Demea's position regarding "the adorable mysteriousness of the divine nature,"[22] in opposition to Cleanthes' attempt to establish the similarity between the deity and ourselves through the design argument, but he claims that Cleanthes "has fairly represented that argument."[23] Nevertheless, he agrees to restate the argument in a form more acceptable to Demea. It reads as follows:

Were a man to abstract from every thing which he knows or has seen, he would be altogether incapable, merely from his own ideas, to determine what kind of scene the universe must be, or to give the preference to one state or situation of things above another. For as nothing, which he clearly conceives, could be esteemed impossible or implying a contradiction, every chimera of his fancy would be upon an equal footing; nor could he assign any just reason, why he adheres to one idea or system, and rejects the others, which are equally possible.

Again; after he opens his eyes, and contemplates the world, as it really is, it would be impossible for him, at first, to assign the cause of any one event; much less, of the whole of things or of the universe. He might set his fancy a rambling; and she might bring him in an infinite variety of reports and representations. These would all be possible; but being all equally possible, he would never, of himself, give a satisfactory account for his preferring one of them to the rest. Experience alone can point out to him the true cause of any phenomenon.

Now according to this method of reasoning, Demea, it follows (and is, indeed, tacitly allowed by Cleanthes himself) that order, arrangement, or the adjustment of final causes is not, of itself, any proof of design; but only so far as it has been experienced to proceed from that principle. For aught we can know *a priori*, matter may contain the source or spring of order originally, within itself, as well as mind does; and there is no more difficulty in conceiving, that the several elements, from an internal unknown cause, may fall into the most exquisite arrangement, than to conceive that their ideas, in the great, universal mind, from a like internal, unknown cause, fall into that arrangement. The equal possibility of both these suppositions is allowed. By

---

[22] D. 145.
[23] D. 145.

experience we find (according to Cleanthes), that there is a difference between them. Throw several pieces of steel together, without shape or form; they will never arrange themselves so as to compose a watch: Stone, and mortar, and wood, without an architect, never erect a house. But the ideas in a human mind, we see, by an unknown, inexplicable oeconomy, arrange themselves so as to form the plan of a watch or house. Experience, therefore, proves that there is an original principle of order in mind, not in matter. From similar effects we infer similar causes. The adjustment of means to ends is alike in the universe, as in a machine of human contrivance. The causes, therefore, must be resembling. (D. 145–146)

For purposes of analysis, it is useful to set out Philo's version of the argument in a more rigorous form, adding steps which make explicit some of the conclusions which Philo appears to want to draw on Cleanthes' behalf:

(1) Experience or observing objects constantly conjoined can alone show us the true cause of any event.

(2) (from (1)) Therefore, the presence of order, arrangement, or the adjustment of final causes does not by itself prove that the principle of the design is mind or intelligence.

(3) (from (1)) A priori, matter may contain the source or spring of order originally within itself, as well as mind.

(4) If matter contains the source or spring of order of the universe, then the source or spring of design is internal to the design; and if mind or intelligence contains the source or spring of order of the universe, then the source or spring of design is external to the design.

(5) By experience, or observing objects constantly conjoined, we find (according to Cleanthes) a principle of order in mind, and no principle of design in matter.

(6) (from (1) and (5)) Therefore, mind or intelligence, contains a principle of order; matter does not.

(7) (from (6)) Therefore, design is evidence of mind as the principle of design.

(8) The universe everywhere shows signs of design.

(9) (from (7) and (8)) Therefore, the principle of design in the universe is mind.

(10) (from (4) and (9)) Therefore, the principle of design of the universe is external to the universe.

(11) Like effects prove like causes.

(12) In machines of human contrivance, we find an adjustment of means to ends (i.e. a design of a certain kind).

(13) In the universe, we find a adjustment of means to ends (i.e. a design of the same kind).

(14) (from (11), (12), and (13)) Therefore, the cause of the design of the universe resembles the cause of the design of machines of human contrivance.

(15) The cause of the design of machines of human contrivance is human intelligence.

(16) (from (14) and (15)) Therefore, the cause of the design of the universe resembles human intelligence.

In setting out the argument in this way, we are able to see the complex nature of Cleanthes' commitment. For this rendering shows us that Cleanthes actually holds to two points regarding mind or intelligence. From step six we learn that Cleanthes holds that all design must stem from mind or intelligence, since we cannot find an alternative cause of order in matter itself. But he is not, according to this argument, committed to holding that *all* order is the result of something resembling *human* intelligence: this is something which requires additional argumentation through the principle (step (11)) that like effects prove like causes. Hence, the two points which the argument makes regarding mind are that all order or design is the product of intelligence, and to show that the particular intelligence in question is like ours requires the use of the principle 'Like effects prove like causes'. It is possible to disagree with the first claim, and yet to hold to the second, i.e. although denying mind as the cause of all order, it is possible to claim that a particular event has a cause which resembles human intelligence. It is important to realize, therefore, that Philo's version of Cleanthes' argument lends itself to the possibility of accepting a part of the total argument, while rejecting the other part. As I have set the argument out, the crucial point in the argument comes between steps (10) and (11). It is possible to accept steps (11) through (16) without also accepting steps (6), (7), (9) and (10).

The longer version of the argument also makes explicit the various points which must come under scrutiny. They are:

a) Is intelligence always responsible for order or arrangement?

b) Is an external cause always responsible for order or arrangement?

c) Is there a resemblance between the universe and machines of human contrivance sufficient for claiming that their respective causes resemble each other?

d) Is the claim of resemblance between the causes of the world and machines of human contrivance (assuming that a positive answer can be given to question c)) sufficient to justify the claim that the cause of the design of the world is external to the world itself?[24]

In examining Philo's criticisms, it is important, if we are to understand the dialogue as a whole, to make a sympathetic case for Cleanthes. The *Dialogues* does not end at the end of Part II, and it is important to try to understand why Cleanthes consents to continue the discussion in the face of Philo's

---

[24]   Question d) is required, since it is not the case that any claim of resemblance in answer to c) will justify calling the cause external.

criticisms. My point here is not that of Kemp Smith who holds that since Cleanthes is the one advocating the Argument from Design "the reader's respect for Cleanthes must be maintained to the very close of the *Dialogues*, otherwise their dramatic balance would be upset."[25] The dramatic balance of the *Dialogues* is not what sustains the discussion: it is rather the case that Cleanthes at first believes that Philo's criticisms can be refuted (Part III), he is then affected by the cumulative effect of Philo's criticisms (Parts IV–VIII), and in Part XII he, along with Philo, appears willing to assess and modify his position in the light of these criticisms. The interpretation presented here will show that this can best be understood as the conversion of the dogmatist to mitigated scepticism.

PHILO'S INITIAL CRITICISMS OF THE ARGUMENT FROM DESIGN

I now turn to Philo's criticisms in Part II. His first criticism centers around the principle 'like effects prove like causes'. This principle works best where the cases are exactly similar. "Every alteration of circumstances occasions a doubt concerning the event, and it requires new experiments to prove certainly, that the new circumstances are of no moment or importance."[26] However, how can Cleanthes maintain "that his usual phlegm and philosophy have been preserved in so wide a step as [he] you have taken, when [he] you compared to the universe houses, ships, furniture, machines; and from their similarity in some circumstances infered a similarity in their causes.?" [27] Hence, Cleanthes must provide experiments to show that the differences in the case of the world and machines are of no consequence here, or he must admit that their causes of design are different.

In this initial criticism, we begin to see Philo's meaning when he says that he is arguing with Cleanthes 'in his own way'.[28] For Philo, while not challenging the principle 'like effects prove like causes', demands that it be employed in a certain way. The principle, Philo maintains, can be used with maximum confidence where the object into whose cause we are inquiring bears so close a resemblance to other objects whose cause is known, that it can be classified as an object of that type.

---

[25]   D. 64. In a related passage Kemp Smith writes: "Philo is permitted to make his points; but however cogent and conclusive they may be, something must always be done to preserve Cleanthes' dignity and to cover over this failure to make any effective reply" (D. 64). I will show that Kemp Smith's interpretation fails to explain Philo's 'constructive pyrrhonism', and its uses in dealing with Cleanthes' Argument.

[26]   D. 147.

[27]   D. 147.

[28]   D. 145.

Cleanthes would not find Philo's criticism to have any relevance because he believes that the differences discovered between machines of human contrivance and the universe are of no consequence to the force of his argument. We have already examined a passage[29] in which Cleanthes discounts the differences between the world and machines, and focuses instead on the resemblances which are found: the adaptation of means to ends and coherence of parts found throughout the design of machines and the world – these are the features from which like causes can be inferred. Again, at the end of Part V, after having listened to additional criticisms from Philo, Cleanthes asserts:

These suppositions I absolutely disown, cried Cleanthes: They strike me, however, with no horror; especially, when proposed in that rambling way in which they drop from you. On the contrary, they give me pleasure, when I see, that, by the utmost indulgence of your imagination, you never get rid of the hypothesis of design in the universe; but are obliged, at every turn, to have recourse to it. To this concession, I adhere steadily; and this I regard as a sufficient foundation for religion.

It is important to understand that Philo's initial criticism cannot be considered decisive, or even effective, as stated, inasmuch as no attention is given to Cleanthes' position, and the relevance of the similarities between the world and machines which his argument utilizes. This lack of regard for the similarities between the world and machines may also give us insight into the 'undistinguished doubts' which Philo's Pyrrhonism is generating in regard to Cleanthes' argument. What Philo's initial criticism does accomplish is to reveal the source of the disagreement between Philo and Cleanthes: Philo insists that a classification of the world as a machine of a given sort whose cause is known must precede the employment of the principle 'like effects prove like causes'; Cleanthes insists that the presence of means to ends relations and a coherence of parts is all the resemblance required between a given item and machines to countenance employment of the principle 'like effects prove like causes'. Further argumentation is required to determine the force of each position.

(2) Thought or intelligence, as we understand it, is but one principle within the universe. How then do we justify transferring a conclusion from parts to the whole? Does not the great disproportion between machines and the world bar all comparison and inference?

This criticism goes further than the first in that it makes explicit the reality of additional springs and principles within the world itself. The question to raise is why Cleanthes is not moved by this to the point of questioning his own argument. The answer is that Philo's criticism, as it is formulated in Part II, does not prove that other springs and principles, by themselves, are capable

---

[29]   D. 144.

of producing effects which manifest means to ends relations and a coherence of parts. All that Philo has established is that the principles which he mentions – heat and cold, attraction and repulsion – and those to which he alludes, are similar to thought in that they are active causes "by which some particular parts of nature, we find, produce alterations on other parts."[30] Philo has not established that any principle other than thought is capable of yielding a design such as we find in the world. Hence, Cleanthes is not troubled by Philo's point regarding additional springs and principles in the world.

The third, fourth, fifth, and sixth criticisms are all amenable to a similar analysis. (3) The third criticism asks how we select reason or intelligence as the principle of design of the world, even if we could use the origin of one part of nature as the basis for the inference concerning the origin of the whole. (4) In the fourth, Philo points out that not only cannot one part of nature form the basis for a conclusion concerning the whole, the operations of one part of nature often do not provide the basis for an inference concerning another part. (5) Philo's fifth criticism questions whether we can justly attribute thought as the principle of design of the whole world in its embryo-state, even if it were the only principle of design discovered in the world once it has achieved its given constitution and arrangement. (6) As a sixth criticism, Philo points out the multiplicity of springs and principles we discover in the world, and he raises the possibility of Nature using "new and unknown principles" in "so new and unknown a situation as that of the first formation of a universe." (D. 149)

In each of these criticisms, Philo pays no heed to the likenesses apparent in the design of the world and machines of human contrivance which Cleanthes' argument incorporates; he does not show that any other principle could plausibly be suggested as capable of designing a world such as the present one; therefore, he has not disproved Cleanthes' claim that on the basis of the exact resemblance between the world and machines in terms of means to ends relations and a coherence of parts, thought or intelligence is the only principle capable of producing a design such as we find in the world. Accordingly, Cleanthes continues to hold that his analogical argument is convincing. Philo's criticisms here are not compelling: to constitute a challenge to Cleanthes' position, Philo's criticisms must establish, with at least as much plausibility as the Argument from Design possesses, that a design such as we find in the world could have been caused by springs and principles other than thought.

(7) In his last criticism, Philo recalls the importance of seeing two species of objects constantly conjoined when we engage in causal reasoning. "But how this argument can have place, where the objects, as in the present case,

---

[30]   D. 147.

are single, individual, without parallel or specific resemblance, may be difficult to explain. And will any man tell me with a serious countenance, that an orderly universe must arise from some thought and art, like the human; because we have experience of it? To ascertain this reasoning, it be requisite, that we had experience of the origin of worlds; and it is not sufficient surely, that we have seen ships and cities arise from human art and contrivance..."[31]

George Nathan regards Philo's attack here as a criticism of the claim that the world has an external designer.[32] In fact, however, the criticism is directed against the claim of intelligence: Philo asks whether any one can in all seriousness maintain 'that an orderly universe must arise from some thought and art, like the human'. Of course, the intelligence of the cause – if this can be made out – will lead analogically to the claim of externality. But here Philo's criticism is directed specifically against the claim of intelligence. Nathan interprets Philo as arguing that in "order for Cleanthes to call the universe a machine it is necessary that he have experience of worlds being ordered by an external agent... Experience must be the judge of whether the universe had an external agent as cause and obviously experience can tell us nothing of the origin of the universe."[33] In point of fact, however, this is not Philo's argument. His concern centers around the lack, as he sees it , of a specific resemblance between the world and anything else, and God and anything else. In short, he claims that neither the world nor God are members of species, and therefore, the principle 'Like effects prove like causes' is inapplicable in the case of each.

The criticism, as it is presented, is inappropriate. First, it merely asserts that God and the world are not members of classes – no proof is offered – and therefore the point is not stronger than Cleanthes' claim that God and the world can be so classified. The classification of the world as a machine is not the crucial classification for Cleanthes'case: this claim, as I showed earlier, is a conclusion to which the Argument from Design leads, and not a premise of the Argument. The crucial classification of the world and machines is in terms of the adaptation of means to ends and coherence of parts which each exhibits. Philo' criticism, therefore, is making – but not arguing – the point that the principle 'like effects prove like causes' is inapplicable to God and the design of the world.

Also, as with the other criticisms which Philo advances in Part II, no weight is given to the resemblance between the effects. The criticism is phrased as though the principle 'like effects prove like causes' is entirely inapplicable in the present discussion. Philo does not show that this is so, nor does 'he

---

[31] D. 149–150.
[32] Chappell, p. 400.
[33] Chappell, p. 400.

examine how the principle might be applied, given the resemblance which does exist between the world and a machine.

Summing up, we are now able to see why Philo's criticisms cannot be taken as decisive in the manner in which they are presented in Part II, and we are able to understand why Cleanthes is unwilling at this point to give up or modify his initial position. We are also in a position to grasp how it is that Philo's criticisms begin to raise 'undistinguished doubts': none of the criticisms which he puts forth takes into account the resemblance which does exist between the world and machines of human contrivance. Accordingly, he does not allow at this stage for the use of the principle 'like effects prove like causes' to the extent that this might be justified by the resemblance which does exist. This must await Philo's success in showing that the resemblance cannot be used to classify the world and machines of human contrivance as members of the same species.

CHAPTER 4

Hume's *Dialogues*: Part III

CLEANTHES' ILLUSTRATIVE ANALOGIES

At the close of Part II, Cleanthes seeks to reply to Philo's claim that to prove that an orderly universe must arise from an intelligent being requires having experience of the origin of the worlds. Cleanthes replies that "to prove by experience the origin of the universe from mind is not more contrary to common speech than to prove the motion of the earth from the same principle. And a cavallier might raise all the same objections to the Copernican system, which you have urged against my reasonings. Have you other earths, might he say, which you have seen to move? Have ..."[1] Philo exclaims that, in fact, we have other earths which we have seen move, namely, all the planets and moons contained in our hemisphere. Philo explains that Galileo showed that there was no essential difference between the earth and the other celestial bodies: "But Galileo, beginning with the moon, proved its similarity in every particular to the earth ... After many instances of this kind, with regard to all the planets, men plainly saw, that these bodies become proper objects of experience; and that the similarity of their nature enabled us to extend the same arguments and phenomena from one to the other."[2] Philo asks Cleanthes whether he can make an equally strong case with respect to the world and machines of human contrivance.

Cleanthes' answer to Philo appears in Part III. He remarks that Copernicus undertook to prove the similarity of celestial bodies to the earth only because some had denied this similarity. But there is no need to prove the similarity of the works of nature to machines of human contrivance "because this similarity is self-evident and undeniable [.] The same matter, a like form: what more is requisite to show an analogy between their causes, and to ascertain the origin of all things from a divine purpose and intention?"[3] Philo's objections in Part II, are like those of philosophers who denied motion "and ought to be refuted in the same manner, by illustrations, examples, and

---

[1] D. 150.
[2] D. 151.
[3] D. 152.

instances, rather than by serious argument and philosophy.''[4]

The two illustrations which Cleanthes puts forth concern an 'Articulate Voice' speaking from the clouds, and a 'Living Vegetable Library'. No reply to these illustrations is made by Philo in Part III. At the end of Cleanthes' presentation, Pamphilus speaks and tells Hermippus:

Here I could observe, Hermippus, that Philo was a little embarrassed and confounded: But while he hesitated in delivering an answer, luckily for him, Demea broke in upon the discourse, and saved his countenance.[5]

Now in seeking to evaluate the two analogies, we must bear in mind that our account must be compatible with, and in fact assist in explaining, why Philo is 'embarrassed and confounded'. Two interpretations are possible. One account of Philo's response is that Cleanthes' illustrations, rather than strengthening his case, actually weaken it. Hence, Philo is embarrassed by Cleanthes' weak attempt, and confounded regarding the particular selection of examples he employs. This is the spirit of the account offered by Kemp Smith:

Though Hume has made every effort to dignify the part assigned to him [i.e. Cleanthes] there are somewhat narrow limits to what can be done in this regard. Cleanthes has so little aptitude for philosophical analysis that he is unable to appreciate, much less to meet, Philo's criticisms. This is shown, in particular, by the illustrations which he employs in Part III of the *Dialogues*, in his reply to Philo's comments upon his assertion that the similarity of the works of nature to those of human art are "self evident and undeniable." These illustrations are indeed illustrative; but mainly of the difficulties which stand in the way of Cleanthes' thesis; and so far from helping to obviate Philo's objections, they serve only to reinforce them.[6]

On the other hand, if Philo is embarrassed and confounded, this could be due to a weakness or weaknesses in his own critical position which he will have to acknowledge (although not in Part III). This interpretation appears to be more in keeping with Hume's views on the matter. In the off-quoted letter which Hume wrote to Gilbert Eliot (March 10, 1751) he says of Cleanthes' analogies:

The instances I have chosen for Cleanthes are, I hope, tolerably happy, and the confusion in which I represent the sceptic seems natural.

This letter begins with the words: "You would perceive by the sample I have given you, that I make Cleanthes the hero of the Dialogue." This strenthens the claim that Philo's embarrassment and confusion cannot be regarded as a

---

[4]   D. 152.
[5]   D. 155.
[6]   D. 63.

result of the overall weakness of Cleanthes' illustrations.[7]

Kemp Smith holds, as we have seen, that Cleanthes' analogies do nothing to support his case.[8] Nevertheless, he agrees that the way in which Pamphilus speaks to Hermippus, it is suggested that Cleanthes' analogies do strengthen his position:

As Hume has suggested in his letter to Gilbert Elliot, Cleanthes has shot his both by the close of Part III, and nothing which he advances later in any way substantially increases the force of his main contentions. It was necessary, therefore, if the dramatic interest of the remaining nine Parts was to be maintained, that Cleanthes' arguments should make as strong and favourable an impression upon the reader as possible; and even that it be suggested that they are little likely to be overthrown. Accordingly, at this point (the close of Part III) Pamphilus, the narrator of the *Dialogues*, is permitted one of his few interventions.[9]

But, says Kemp Smith, the suggestion is not to be taken seriously:

The careful reader can hardly, however, fail to note that in the immediately preceding passages, Cleanthes, so far from replying to the very damaging criticisms that Philo has already made, has by his mode of restating his positions presented them anew in a form to which these criticisms even more forcibly apply. This restatement of Cleanthes' position has, indeed, been determined throughout, not by any expectation, on Hume's part, of *strengthening* them ... but for the quite contrary purpose of leading on to the even more damaging criticisms which Philo still has in reserve.[10]

If Cleanthes' is to be the 'hero' of the *Dialogues*, it is difficult to accept that Kemp Smith's account above is correct. Also, if the illustrations offered by Cleanthess are 'tolerably happy' then it is difficult to see how Kemp Smith can be correct. The letter to Eliot contains a postscript which confirms the view that Hume is more sympathetic to certain elements in Cleanthes' position that Kemp Smith allows. Hume writes:

He [i.e. Cleanthes] allows, indeed, in Part 2, that all our inference is founded on the similitude of the works of nature to the usual effects of mind. Otherwise they must appear a mere chaos. The only difficulty is, why the other dissimilitudes do not weaken the argument. And indeed it would seem from Experience and Feeling, that they do not weaken it as much as we might naturally expect. A theory to solve this would be very acceptable.

Nothing in Hume's letter to Eliot indicates that he is favorably disposed to Cleanthes' *Argument* from Design. It is the illustrations in Part III which are 'tolerably happy', and it is these same illustrations which make Philo's confusion 'seem natural'. Cleanthes is said to be the 'hero' of the Dialogue.

---

[7]   Hume does ask Eliot to assist him in supporting Cleanthes' case, but it does not follow from this that Hume believed Cleanthes' illustrations were so weak as to add nothing to his position.

[8]   We will look at the details of Kemp Smith's argument when we examine the two analogies.

[9]   D. 65.

[10]   D. 65–66.

But what reason does Hume offer for this? It is that Cleanthes recognizes, as does Hume, that our belief in an intelligent designer of the world is not weakened 'as much as we might naturally expect' by the dissimilarities between the world and machines. Now, at one point in Part III Cleanthes tells Philo:

Some beauties in writing we may meet with, which seem contrary to rules, and which gain the affections, and animate the imagination, in opposition to all the precepts of criticism, and to the authority of the established masters of art. And if the argument for theism be, as you pretend, contradictory to the principles of logic: its universal, its irresistible influence proves clearly, that there may be arguments of a like irregular nature. Whatever cavils may be urged; and orderly world, as well as a coherent, articulate speech, will still be received as an incontestable proof of design and intention.[11]

It is through Cleanthes' recognition of these irregular or maverick arguments, particularly in natural religion, that Hume regards him as the 'hero' of the work.

From what has been presented, we should, therefore, expect two elements in Cleanthes' illustrations in Part III, namely, support for the (analogical) Argument from Design, and support for the (irregular) argument for theism. As we will see, Hume held that of these two approaches, only the former is unacceptable. It is through Philo's Pyrrhonism that Cleanthes will be made to see that an intelligent cause for the design of the world cannot be defended through analogical argumentation. Cleanthes' continued support for the analogical argument will substantiate his classification as a dogmatist. The irregular argument for theism will be dealt with in Part XII.

THE ARTICUALTE VOICE ILLUSTRATION

Cleanthes' first illustrative analogy concerns an articulate voice heard in the clouds. We are asked to suppose that "this voice were extended in he same instant over all nations, and spoke to each nation in its own language and dialect"; the words spoken "not only contain a just sense and meaning, but convey some instruction altogether worthy of a benevolent Being, superior to mankind"; in the next paragraph we are told that what is heard is "a rational wise coherent speech." Now Cleanthes asks:

Could you possibly hesitate a moment concerning the cause of this voice? And must you not instantly ascribe it to some design or purpose? Yet I cannot see but all the same objections ... which be against the system of theism, may also be produced against this inference. Might you not say, that all conclusions concerning fact were founded on experience: That when we hear an articulate voice in the dark, and hence infer a man, it is only the resemblance of the effects, which

[11]   D. 155.

leads us to conclude that there is a like resemblance in the cause: But that this extraordinary voice, by its loudness, extent, and flexibility to all languages, bears so little analogy to any human voice, that we have no reason to suppose any analogy in their causes... You see clearly your own objections in these cavils; and I hope too, you see clearly, that they cannot possibly have more force in the one case than in the other.[12]

Cleanthes appears to be maintaining that the articulate voice heard from the clouds can be held to have an intelligent designer or cause as a result of the resemblances which we find between ordinary human voices and this voice speaking from the clouds. If so, then establishing that the cause of the articulate voice is an intelligent being takes exactly the form as Cleanthes' attempt in Part II to show that the cause of the design of the world is an intelligent being. In both cases, the arguments are based on noted resemblances. To the extent that this is the position which Cleanthes is defending, his position can be schematized as follows:

$$\frac{1.\ \text{Ordinary voices (effects)}}{\text{Intelligent beings (causes)}} = \frac{3.\ \text{Works of human contrivance}}{\text{Intelligent beings}}$$

$$\frac{2.\ \text{Articulate Voice (effect)}}{\text{Superior Intelligent Being (cause)}} \qquad \frac{4.\ \text{Works of Nature}}{\text{Superior Intelligent Being}}$$

Since 4 is alleged to stand to 3 as 2 is held to stand to 1, if we deny 4 even granting 3, then we must deny 2 even granting 1. But since we do not want to deny 2, we cannot deny 4.

The obvious attack on this position is to establish some fundamental difference between 1 and 2 on the one hand, and 3 and 4 on the other, which would enable us to accept 2 on the basis of 1, while rejecting 4 on the basis of 3. It can be argued that the characteristics appealed to in the case of what is heard from the clouds are sufficient to classify what is heard as a voice, and since voices are found constantly conjoined with intelligent beings as their cause, we can reason by analogy regarding the intelligence of the cause of what is heard from the clouds. However, Philo's criticisms in Part II make reference to alternative principles of order; hence, he questions whether, in fact, the world is machine-like. To know that the world is a machine requires knowing of an intelligent cause of design, whereas knowing of an articulate *voice* does not require knowing that the cause is intelligent. Therefore, we can reason analogically from the voice to an intelligent designer, whereas to call

[12] D. 152.–153.

the world a machine requires knowing of an intelligent designer. However, Cleanthes' argument focuses on means to ends relations and a coherence of parts in order to make the inference to an intelligent designer, and not with whether we can begin with the classification of the world as a machine. A re-appraisal of Cleanthes' illustrative analogy is therefore in order.

In the two paragraphs in Part III in which Cleanthes expounds his views on the Articulate Voice and the relevance of this discussion to the case of God and the design of the world, he appears to be making two different points. The first deals with the possibility of reasoning analogically from the observed resemblances in the effects to resembling causes. However, within these two paragraphs, and scattered throughout his entire discussion in Part III and in Part XII, mention is also made by Cleanthes of an immediate or instantaneous inference to an intelligent cause of design:

Could you possibly hesitate a moment concerning the cause of this voice? And must you not instantly ascribe it to some design or purpose?[13]

Consider, anatomize the eye: Survey its structure and contrivance; and tell me from your own feeling, if the idea of a contriver does not immediately flow in upon you with a force like that of a sensation. The most obvious conclusion surely is in favour of design; and it requires time, reflection and study, to summon up those frivolous, though abstruse, objections, which can support infidelity.[14]

On page 154 (the second last line) he refers to such arguments as 'natural' arguments. He acknowledges that such arguments have an irregularity to them, since they appear to contravene the principles of logic:

And if the argument for theism be, as you pretend, contradictory to the principles of logic: its universal, its irresistible influence, proves clearly, that there may be arguments of a like irregular nature. Whatever cavils may be urged; an orderly world, as well as a coherent, articulate speech, will still be received as an incontestable proof of design and intention.[15]

According to this passage, Cleanthes believes that the inference to an intelligent cause for the Articulate Voice and the inference to an intelligent cause for the world are both contained within such 'natural' or 'irregular' arguments.

In seeking to understand 'natural arguments' we can begin by asking for their form. And this is easily answered. Cleanthes holds that such arguments proceed directly from the data to a conclusion, without the need for constant conjunction to link the data and conclusion. The conclusion strikes us as obvious, given the data, and the requirement for causal claims, namely, that the items be observed constantly conjoined, is waived in this case. When

---

[13] D. 101.
[14] D. 152.
[15] D. 155.

Cleanthes began Part III, he indicated that Philo's objections ought to be refuted as one would refute those who denied motion, namely, by illustrations, examples, and instances. Part of Cleanthes' meaning in this is now clear. The Articulate Voice analogy helps to deal with Philo's objections in Part II, inasmuch as Cleanthes is now presenting an argument form where the requirement for constant conjunction can be left out. One of Philo's objections in Part II made the point that to know the nature of the cause of the design of the world, worlds would have to be formed under our eyes. Cleanthes' position in Part III suggests that there are other causal inferences to an intelligent cause of design (e.g. the Articulate Voice, the eye) where this requirement of constant conjunction is waived, and he is further suggesting that the case of God and the world is another instance ot this. In short, Cleanthes seeks to show that not all causal claims are based, or need be based, on constant conjunction.

Is the evidence which we have for inferring an intelligent cause for the voice the same as the evidence for inferring an intelligent cause for the world? Pike thinks not:

For Cleanthes, on the the other hand, the evidence we have for the existence of another finite mind (sensible and articulate speech) is not the same as the evidence we have for the existence of God (order and contrivance in nature), but the *evidential relation* between the premise and the conclusion in each of the cases is the same.[16]

Although I agree with Pike that the evidential relation in both cases is the same, I disagree with his claim that the evidence in the two cases is different. What I will now show is that in seeking to deal with Philo's objections in Part II, Cleanthes, in offering us the Articulate Voice, is not only offering an argument form which seems to meet Philo's objection about the need for constant conjunction, he also shows that the evidence employed to establish an intelligent designer of the world *is precisely the kind of evidence* where the requirement for constant conjunction can be waived. The Articulate Voice analogy is regarded by Cleanthes as appropriate, since the evidence employed is identical to that used in Part II.

Certain considerations will prove that this must be Cleanthes' considered opinion on the question of evidence. To begin with, it should be kept in mind that his original argument employed means to ends relations and a coherence of parts as evidence for an intelligent cause of the design of the world, and Philo's criticisms in Part II sought to deny, or at least question, a knowledge of this cause based only on the aforementioned characteristics in he effect. Hence, the challenge to Cleanthes is one of showing how *these* characteristics support a belief in an intelligent designer. Second, after Cleanthes has offered

16 Pike, p. 230.

the two illustrative analogies in Part III, he again calls attention to the adaptation of means to ends, and indicates that this has been his central focus:

> Who can behold the male and female of each species, the correspondence of their parts, and instincts, their passions and whole course of life before and after generation, but must be sensible, that the propagation of the species is intended by nature. Millions and millions of such instances present themselves through every part of the universe; and no language can convey a more intelligible, irresistible meaning, than the curious adjustment of final causes. To what degree, therefore, of blind dogmatism must one have attained, to reject such natural and such convincing arguments?[17]

His point clearly is that natural arguments are arguments which employ 'the adjustment of final causes' as evidence for an intelligent cause of design, and in the next paragraph, he asserts that the case of the world and the case of the Articulate Voice are instances of natural arguments. Therefore, Cleanthes intends those very characteristics employed in the Design Argument to be employed in the illustrations used in Part III.

This position is precisely what we should expect Cleanthes to maintain. At the beginning of Part III, he characterized his problem in convincing Philo about an intelligent cause of design of the world as similar to those philosophers who had difficulty establishing the existence of motion. And, as we saw, he claims that Philo's objections ought to be refuted in the same way as those who held there was motion defended their claim – through illustrations, examples, and instances. What we should expect in the case of motion is to have this feature pointed out to us in a variety of objects and situations. The objects and situations might all be different; but the characteristic, motion, would be that to which attention is drawn. Now, employing the treatment of motion as a guide, we should expect to find a variety of objects and situations brought to our attention, and we should be made to see that in all these cases the inference is precisely the one Cleanthes seeks to establish – from the adaptation of means to ends and coherence of parts to an intelligent cause of design. Also, of course, if Cleanthes is following what Pike maintains, that the argument form is the same in the case of the world and in the case of the Articulate Voice but that the evidence is different, then Cleanthes cannot make his case, since the differences in evidence could be urged as an obstacle to drawing the same conclusion in both cases. He can suceed only if he can show that the Articulate Voice illustration and the case for the world involve identical argument forms, and identical evidence.

We must now ask whether it can be established that the characteristics in

---

[17]   D. 154.

the two cases are identical, namely, means to ends relations and a coherence
of parts. The Voice is regarded as 'rational, wise, and coherent'. Now, at least
part of rationality and wisdom consists in the proper adaptation of means to
ends, and the feature of coherence indicates that all such adaptations of
means to ends work together as well as individually, precisely the point made
of the means to ends relation in the world. The words delivered contain a just
sense and meaning, and convey some instruction altogether worthy of a
benevolent being. To convey 'a just sense and meaning' again indicates an
adaptation of means to ends: the words are the means whereby the just sense
and meaning are conveyed. But the coherence of parts must also be included
if the words are to function in concert in conveying this sense and meaning.
The words delivered 'convey some instruction altogether worthy of a
benevolent being', and it might be thought that here the comparison with the
world breaks down, since Hume maintains that the world does not appear to
be the product of a benevolent designer. However, this can be answered if we
take into account the type of benevolent instruction which Hume allows that
the world manifests, and which is articulated in the Principle of the
Uniformity of Nature, a principle which we believe holds of the world. By
experience we learn what causes what, and we are led to believe that causal
relations which obtained in the past will continue to obtain; therefore, the
world instructs us in regard to those matters which we should pursue and
those to be avoided. The instruction of the Voice discloses means to ends
relations; the message of nature discloses the very same thing.

Accordingly, all the characteristics which Cleanthes assigns to the
Articulate Voice are reducible to the characteristics which form the basis of
a claim about an intelligent designer of the world, namely, means to ends
relations and a coherence of parts. The full force of Cleanthes' use of the
Articulate Voice illustration can now be understood. Just as there is an
immediate inference from the means to ends relations and coherence of parts
in the Voice to an intelligent cause of design, so there should be a similar
inference to an intelligent designer of the world, given that the world also
manifests rational design through these characteristics. The illustration is also
significant in that it moves away from 'machine' examples, and seeks to
support the view that it is rational design, and not just rational design in
machines, which leads to the inference of an intelligent cause of design.

Does Cleanthes believe that natural arguments are rational arguments? On
this point, Pike answers affirmatively:

The inference does not involve consideration of an empirically established correlation between
classes ... of course, this is not to say that the existence of God is as much an exercise in reason
as is the inference from articulate and sensible speech to the existence of another mind. In both
cases, the process of inferring is a rational activity. In neither case, however, is it the *same kind*

of rational activity as is involved when one reasons from data to a conclusion by way of an "argument from experience."[18]

Pike does not discuss how this argument can be classified as rational in nature. In any case, the textual evidence goes against Pike's claim. First, in presenting the Articulate Voice illustration, Cleanthes is not so much concerned with establishing that it involves a rational inference as he is with emphasizing how we would react to such a voice.[19] In one passage he appears to be concerned with the rational character of natural arguments. This passage occurs after both analogies are offered, and he says: "Whatever cavils may be urged; and orderly world, as well as a coherent, articulate speech, will still be received as an incontestable proof of design and intention." However, he is speaking about how such arguments will be received, and not about their true nature. We believe that the proof offered is incontestable; he does not say that it is incontestable. Preceding the passage just quoted, and in the same paragraph, Cleanthes makes certain points which put it beyond question that he does not regard natural arguments as rational arguments. He remarks, by way of illustration, that "some beauties in writing we may meet with, which seem contrary to rules, and which gain the affections, and animate the imagination, in oppostion to all the precepts of criticism, and to the authority of the established masters of art." These maverick beauties, Cleanthes is holding, appeal to the affections and the imagination, not to reason. He continues that "if the argument for theism be, as you pretend, contradictory to the principles of Logic: its universal, its irresistible influence proves clearly, that there may be arguments of a like irregular nature," indicating that such maverick arguments also appeal to the affections and the imagination, not to reason.

Because Cleanthes compares natural arguments to certain maverick arguments in other fields, Pike urges that in Part III Cleanthes is retracting his support for the *Argument* from Design, that is, the argument presented in Part II.[20] That this position is mistaken can be seen from the following considerations. In Part XII Cleanthes emphasized that both routes – the analogical and natural arguments – as well as a third, education, lead to a belief in an intelligent designer for the world:

A false, absurd system, human nature, from the force of prejudice, is capable of adhering to with obstinacy and perseverance: But no system at all, in opposition to a theory, supported by strong

---

[18]   Pike, p. 231.

[19]   It will be recalled that he asks Philo: "Could you possibly hesitate a moment concerning the cause of this voice. And must you not instantly ascribe it to some design or purpose?" (D. 152).

[20]   Pike writes: "Cleanthes here seems to be *retracting* the claim that the "hypothesis of design" can be supported by an inference of the sort used in the sciences, i.e. an argument from experience." (Pike, p. 229).

and obvious reason, by natural propensity, and by early education, I think it absolutely impossible to maintain or defend.[21]

Further, if Pike is correct, this leaves unexplained why Philo continues to attack the analogical version of the argument – Pike himself acknowledges that in subsequent sections Philo's criticisms are directed against the argument from analogy – and why Cleanthes seeks to defend that argument at various stages throughout Philo's critique.

Why does Cleanthes continue to defend the version of the argument from design presented in Part II? Part of the answer can be gathered from his belief in the success of his illustrative analogy. We saw that in presenting the Articulate Voice analogy, Cleanthes suggests a possible line of criticism based on the dissimilarities between this voice and ordinary human voices. His position, however, is that the standard which this suggested criticism applies is greater than that normally employed in regard to analogical arguments; therefore, this line of criticism, in the voice example, does not move us to reject the argument about an intelligent cause. Cleanthes maintains that the suggested line of criticism against the voice example is on a par with Philo's objections to the Argument from Design. Therefore, he believes that Philo's criticisms in Part II are also setting a standard which is too high. That is, just as the dissimilarities between the voice from the clouds and ordinary human voices do not, according to Cleanthes, move us to reject the inference to an intelligent cause for the voice from the clouds, so the dissimilarities between the design of the world and machines of human contrivance should not be deemed relevant to rejecting the inference to an intelligent cause for the design of the world. The voice from the clouds exhibits design (means to ends relations and a coherence of parts) – the same design which is present in ordinary human voices – and this is held to countenance reasoning by analogy to an intelligent cause for this Voice; the world exhibits design (means to ends relations and a coherence of parts) – the same design which is present in machines – and, by a parity of reasoning, this should also be held to countenance reasoning by analogy to an intelligent cause for the design of the world. Both arguments, according to Cleanthes, meet the usual standards applied to analogical arguments. It is not that the Argument from Design cannot be criticized (the differences between the world and machines can always be emphasized); it is rather the case that it should not be criticized, any more than the Articulate Voice analogy should be criticized (the differences between the Articulate Voice and ordinary voices can be emphasized, but are not). Both arguments, according to Cleanthes, meet the usual standards applied to analogical arguments.

[21] D. 216.

The other reason why Cleanthes continues to defend the Design Argument has already been discussed in connection with Part II of the *Dialogues*. A close look at that section shows that although Philo introduces alternative principles of order, nothing which he says there proves that any principle of order can produce an effect like the effects known to stem from intelligence, namely, those displaying means to ends relations and a coherence of parts. In fact, this is only accomplished by the end of Part VIII.

THE LIVING VEGETABLE LIBRARY ILLLUSTRATION

Cleanthes' second illustration, that of the Living Vegetable Library, begins with two assumptions: "Suppose, that there is a natural, universal, invariable language, common to every individual of the human race; and that books are natural productions, which perpetuate themselves in the same manner with animals and vegetables, by descent and propagation."[22] With these assumptions in mind, he asks whether upon viewing these volumes containing 'the most refined reason and most exquisite beauty' you could "doubt that its original cause bore the strongest analogy to mind and intelligence[.] When it reasons and discourses; when it expostulates, argues, and enforces its views and topics; when it applies sometimes to the pure intellect, sometimes to the affections; when it collects, disposes, and adorns every considerations suited to the subject; could you persist in asserting, that all this, at the bottom, had really no meaning, and that the first formation of this volume in the loins of its original parent proceeded not from thought and design?"[23] Cleanthes continues by affirming that any difference betwen the case of the imagined vegetable library and the universe is to the advantage of the latter: "The anatomy of an animal affords many stronger instances of design than the perusal of Livy or Tacitus."[24] He also urges that the illustration of the Vegetable Library, which Cleanthes assumes Philo (and everyone else) will accept, is equally vulnerable to Philo's earlier objection regarding the cause of the design of the world: "Any objection which you start ... by carrying me back to so unusual and extraordinary a scene as the first formation of worlds, the same objection has place on the supposition of our vegetating library."[25] He concludes this second illustration by offering the following alternatives: "Choose, then, your party, Philo, without ambiguity or evasion: Assert either that a rational volume is no proof of a rational cause, or admit of a similar

---

[22] D. 153.
[23] D. 153.
[24] D. 154.
[25] D. 154.

cause to all the works of nature."[26]

The Vegetable Library analogy is usually criticized by commentators on two grounds. First, the Library example employs organisms to illustrate the force of the Design Argument, and, as commentators have repeatedly urged, this appeal cannot succeed. For example, Kemp Smith writes:

... what is peculiarly characteristic of the argument from design – at once its strength and its greates weakness – is that it has always professed to find its chief and most convincing evidence precisely in the field where the analogy to which it appeals is *least* applicable, namely, in the field of animal and vegetable life. The organic is not only organized; it is self-organizing. Organisms are self-developing, self-maintaining, self-regulating, self-propagating. Their 'form', that is to say, is as native and natural to them as is the 'matter' of which they are composed. In an artificial product, on the other hand, the form, so far from being native to it, depends for its existence on an external artificer.[27]

It would appear, then, that since organisms have internal unintelligent principles of order, the appeal to organisms is doomed to failure in seeking support for the Design Argument.

Secondly, the organic library example raises a question whether the object appealed to can be called a book. As Kemp Smith puts it:

... it is precisely the differences between 'project and forethought' as revealed in articulate speech, in a book, or in a machine, and 'order and final causes' as exhibited in plants and animals, that have to be reckoned with. In Cleanthes' illustration they are confounded together, not distinguished. If a book is really a book it is due to project and forethought, *not* to propagation; if, on the other hand, it is due to propagation it must be a vegetable or animal, and to term it a book is to insist on a resemblance while refusing the conditions which can alone make it relevant.[28]

To the extent that Cleanthes' illustration is intended to establish through analogical reasoning the similarity of the cause of the vegetable library to human intelligence, what form would the argument take, or more specifically, to what is the vegetable library being compared? On Kemp Smith's reading, Cleanthes' vegetable library would be compared to other vegetables, and this is what leads Kemp Smith to hold that this analogy is inapplicable, inasmuch as vegetables have internal unintelligent principles of order, and the Design Argument is intended to show that the cause of the design of the world is external to the world and intelligent.

However, it is an error to read Cleanthes' illustration in this way. What has repeatedly been overlooked is that Cleanthes recognizes that the library has as its *immediate* cause 'descent and propagation'. In other words, the way the

[26]   D. 154.
[27]   D. 102.
[28]   D. 103.

illustration is set up, the role of unintelligent internal principles of order is acknowledged. Now, at this point, it might be said that this simply shows Cleanthes' inability to recognize that, because it calls attention to alternative principles of order, the library example hurts his case. However, Cleanthes is attempting to make certain points which he believes will support his case about the world. First, in maintaining the inference to an intelligent cause for the vegetable library, Cleanthes does not focus on what the books are, namely, natural productions or organisms, but rather on what they do. It is when one of the books is opened and we discover that it reasons and discourses; that it expostulates, argues, and enforces its views and topics; that it applies sometimes to the pure intellect, sometimes to the affections; and that it collects, disposes, and adorns every consideration suited to the subject – it is then, according to Cleanthes, that the inference to an intelligent cause is justified.

Secondly, Cleanthes' concern is not with the immediate cause of design of the volumes. His concern is with the 'original cause', with 'the first formation of this volume in the loins of its original parent.' The basis for comparison, therefore, appears to be the rational activities of this vegetable library and identical rational activities in ordinary volumes. His argument would then be that since rational activities have always been observed to stem from intelligent beings, we can, by analogy, infer that the rational vegetable volumes also have an intelligent cause. The immediate cause of the volumes does not satisfy what experience has shown to be the cause of rational activity. Hence, the immediate cause cannot alone account for what the volumes do. The only way to account for what the volumes do is to distinguish between the immediate cause of a particular volume and the original parent, or that which so structured the processes of 'descent and propagation' that each volume has the capacity for rational activity.

But a further point must be made. In arguing analogically to an intelligent cause for the volumes, we do not require that we experience a constant conjunction between the original parent of the volumes and particular volumes. The reasoning appears satisfactory, even though we do not have access to the original cause. This accounts for Cleanthes' challenge to Philo: "And any objection which you start in the former case, by carrying me back to so unusual and extraordinary a scene as the first formation of worlds, the same objection has place on the supposition of our vegetating library... Assert either that a rational volume is no proof of a rational cause, or admit of a similar cause to all the works of nature."

Two questions should be raised: first, how does the inference from the activities of the volumes to an intelligent original cause, even if allowed, illustrate that the world had an intelligent cause of design; and, second, what reason does Cleanthes have for tying the activities in the example to organic volumes?

In addressing the first question, it is clear that the illustration will be successful provided that there are sufficient similarities between the activities of the volumes and the world to enable us to infer the cause of one through arriving at the cause of the other. How, then, do the activities of the volumes resemble the world? All the activities cited for the volumes can be reduced to the very characteristics used by Cleanthes in connection with seeking to establish that there is an intelligent cause for the design of the world, namely, means to ends relations and a coherence of parts. This is particularly evident in the reference to the volume insofar as it 'collects, disposes, and adorns every consideration suited to the subject', although it fits the other activities as well. 'To reason and discourse, to expostulate, argue, and enforce its views and topics' – all these activities involve the proper adaptation of means to ends and a coherence of parts. In applying 'sometimes to the pure intellect, sometimes to the affections', the volume puts itself forth as a means of dealing with these capacities.

Hence, the force of the illustration can be schematized as follows:

$$\frac{\dfrac{\text{Rational activity in ordinary volumes (Means to ends relations and a coherence of parts)}}{\text{Intelligent Principle of Order}}}{\dfrac{\text{Rational activity in the Vegetable Library (Means to ends relations and a coherence of parts)}}{\text{Intelligent Principle of Order}}} = \frac{\dfrac{\text{Rational activity in machines (Means to ends relations and a coherence of parts}}{\text{Intelligent Principle of Order}}}{\dfrac{\text{Rational activity in the world (Means to ends relations and a coherence of parts)}}{\text{Intelligent Principle of Order}}}$$

The second question raised was why the activities cited in the example are tied to organic volumes. One part of the answer lies in the fact that, if successful, we are made aware of the fact that the immediate cause may not suffice in accounting for design, and that we can reason by analogy to an original cause of design, even where we have not had any experience of such an original cause conjoined with the item in question. We have never seen a vegetable library designed by its original cause, but yet, Cleanthes claims, having seen rational volumes designed by intelligence, we can reason to the original cause of the organic volumes. But there is another part to the answer, and it is emphasized by Cleanthes himself:

But if there be any difference, Philo, between this supposed case and the real one of the universe, it is all to the advantage of the latter. The anatomy of an animal affords many stronger instances of design than the perusal of Livy or Tacitus.[29]

In other words, the organic volumes themselves display the same features of design which the activities of the volumes display (means to ends relations and a coherence of parts), and, therefore, the volumes *qua* organic existences require an intelligent original cause of design just as they require an intelligent original cause of design in virtue of their activities. Hence, animals and vegetables for Cleanthes can now be seen to require an intelligent original cause of design. The organisms in the world, therefore, can be used as evidence that the original cause of design is an intelligent being, and organisms do not appear to conflict with the thesis of the design argument.

It is now clear why Cleanthes would not be bothered by the first objection cited earlier by Kemp Smith regarding the self-organizing character of organisms, namely, Cleanthes holds that their design is evidence of an intelligent original designer. And it is also clear why Cleanthes would not be bothered by Kemp Smith's second criticism. For Cleanthes believes that the vegetable library example shows that no distinction can be made between the results of 'project and forethought' (the activities of the volumes) and 'order and final causes' (the structure of the organisms) which is adequate to establish that the causes of each are different. Means to ends relations and a coherence of parts, wherever these features are found, Cleanthes is saying, require an intelligent principle of order. Kemp Smith's point, therefore, that if a book is really a book it stems from project and forethought and not propagation, and if it is due to propagation it is not a book, would be regarded by Cleanthes as an assertion by someone who fails to distinguish between immediate and original causes. The immediate cause of the volumes, descent and propagation, enables us to regard what comes about as organic. But the original cause which is inferred is what enables us to regard the result as a book. Hence, for Cleanthes there is nothing odd in speaking of organic books.

We can now understand more fully why Philo's objections in Part II are not seen as effective criticisms by Cleanthes. For Cleanthes' position acknowledges alternative principles of design, and it requires that even where experience discloses a non-intelligent principle as the immediate cause of intelligent contrivance (means to end relations and a coherence of parts), we should not regard this principle as adequate for the production of the design; rather, we should, by analogy, insist on an intelligent original principle of order. This shows us that a refutation of Cleanthes' position cannot be accomplished by simply pointing to non-intelligent immediate causes for rationally designed effects.

[29]   D. 154.

Cleanthes' 'natural' or 'irregular' argument must also be examined.[30] As in the case of the Articulate Voice example, there is a direct inference from the data to the conclusion, and again here as in the former case, there is no appeal to constant conjunction. His position is that once the volumes are observed, we could not doubt that their original cause greatly resembles intelligence. If we are to be persuaded by his natural argument, there must be sufficient similarities not only in the argument forms employed in the case of the vegetable library example and the design of the world, but also in what is compared, namely, the organic volumes and the world. As shown earlier when discussing the vegetable library as an instance of analogical reasoning, the similarities which Cleanthes wants to emphasize are brought out in virtue of means to ends relations and a coherence of parts. The same features are emphasized with respect to the natural argument. The rational activities of the volume lead immediately to a belief in an intelligent original cause. Furthermore, the rational design of the volumes does exactly the same thing.

The natural argument has an additional point to make in the case of the organic volumes which shows how it can be used to supplement the natural argument employed for the Articulate Voice example in answering Philo's ciriticisms in Part II.

In Part II Philo had raised the issue of alternative principles of order, and he raised the question as to how, among the various principles of order, we are to choose thought as that principle of order by which the world achieved its design. The natural argument employed in the case of the Articulate Voice example maintains that the rational nature of the sounds leads immediately to a belief in an intelligent cause of design. However, it does not follow from this alone that we will immediately infer an intelligent cause of design *whenever* we observe or experience means to ends relations and a coherence of parts. In other words, we might naturally associate these features with a variety of designing principles. The Vegetable Library example offers principles, namely, generation and vegetation, as the immediate cause of design of the volumes. Hence, there is a sense in which the natural argument is confronted by alternative principles of design. But Cleanthes' point is that even where alternative principles of order are present, the natural tendency in accounting for the design of the volumes and their activities is to select intelligence. In the case of the organic volumes, generation and vegetation do not compete with intelligence in accounting for the means to ends relations and coherence of parts which are evident. The Vegetable Library example, therefore, helps to illustrate the point – which the Articulate Voice case does not illustrate – that intelligence is the natural choice in accounting for design, even when we are

[30]   See especially D. 154, the second paragraph, and D. 155 the first paragraph, where the natural argument aspect is emphasized by Cleanthes.

aware of other principles of order. Vegetables have never been observed to stem from intelligence, and yet, intelligence is our natural choice in accounting for their design. The presence of means to ends relations and a coherence of parts in design appears to rule out alternative original principles of order.

With this I have completed my analysis of the two illustrative analogies in Part III. I have shown why Cleanthes believes that they are appropriate, and what remains for Philo if he is to offer effective criticisms against the Design Argument. But the illustrative analogies have disclosed another aspect of Cleanthes' position, namely, that he also holds an instinctive account of belief in an intelligent designer of the world, and this was nowhere in evidence in Part II. It remains to be seen whether Philo accepts the instinctive account, but in any case, what Philo now has to deal with is considerably more complex than what he found in Part II.

Cleanthes now holds that there is more than one route to an anthropomorphic conception of the deity, and he believes that the very same evidence, namely, means to ends relations and a coherence of parts, supports both routes. According to Cleanthes, we can 'reason' analogically, or draw a 'natural' inference, from the presence of means to ends relations and a coherence of parts to an intelligent cause of design.

Before leaving Part III of the *Dialogues*, a further word about Cleanthes' introduction of 'natural' or 'irregular' arguments. Cleanthes' claim of a 'natural' argument for the intelligence of the deity contains some similarities to Hume's discussion of natural belief in connection with causality, physical objects, and the self. Cleanthes speaks of the natural argument for theism as 'universal' and possessing 'irresistible influence' – characteristics which Hume attributes to natural beliefs. Again, Cleanthes, as does Hume in his discussion, regards the resultant belief as instinctive, and as arising in the imagination. When Hume analyzes a natural belief, he seeks those qualities in our perceptions which, through a concurrence with certain qualities in the imagination, produce the belief in question. Cleanthes' emphasis on the observation of means to ends relations and a coherence of parts could answer to the relevant qualities in our perceptions which assist in the 'natural' belief in an intelligent designer of the world.

But Cleanthes' instinctive account in Part III omits discussion of, or denies, certain characteristics which Hume maintains hold of all natural beliefs. For example, Cleanthes does not mention how the instinctive belief in an intelligent designer is helpful – or better essential – in the acquisition of empirical knowledge, and with respect to getting on in the world. In line with Hume's doctrine of natural belief, Cleanthes regards the natural argument as universal, but in the next paragraph, he takes this back, and acknowledges that the belief in an intelligent designer of the world is not universal.[31] According to Cleanthes, the natural argument advances our knowledge of the attributes of the deity, but according to Hume, natural beliefs never advance our knowledge of the subject under investigation (e.g. the causal powers in objects). A natural belief alters our awareness of the perceptions involved in generating the natural belief. For example, in the case of causality, perception which are observed to be conjoined, come to be regarded as being necessarily connected. In the case of the self, perceptions which are distinct and separable, are supposed 'to be united by identity'. Now, if the belief in an intelligent designer is a natural belief which arises from the observation of means to ends relations and a coherence of parts in the world, then there should be some alteration in our regard for these perceptions analogous to the alteration mentioned in the case of the other natural beliefs. Cleanthes is entirely silent on this matter.

It is, therefore, far from obvious that Cleanthes' natural argument accords with Hume's analysis of natural belief. Whether Cleanthes' suggestion of a natural argument is taken over by Philo and altered in accordance with the doctrine of natural belief must await a study of Part XII.

[31]   D. 155.

CHAPTER 5

Hume's *Dialogues* : Part IV

THE FIRST 'INCONVENIENCE' OF ANTHROPOMORPHISM

With the completion of Cleanthes' two illustrative analogies, Hume makes it fall to Demea to reply to Cleanthes. His reply loses sight of whatever philosophical objections may be brought to bear on these analogies, and he concentrates on his own objections to anthropomorphism which amount to showing that anthropomorphism misrepresents the deity, since (for Demea) the deity is incomprehensible.[1] In other words, Demea only succeeds in showing that anthropomorphism is incompatible with mysticism! – a position which no one will deny. But Demea's reply has an important role to play in that it opens the way in Part IV of the *Dialogues* for the exchange between Cleanthes and Philo.

At the beginning of Part IV, Cleanthes answers Demea by defending anthropomorphism.

I can readily allow, said Cleanthes, that those who maintain the perfect simplicity of the supreme Being ... are complete mystics, and chargeable with all the consequences which I have drawn from their opinion. They are, in a word, atheists, without knowing it... A mind whose acts and sentiments and ideas are not distinct and successive; one, that is wholly simple, and totally immutable; is a mind which has no thought, no reason, no will, no sentiment, no love, no hatred; or in a word, is no mind at all. It is an abuse of terms to give it that appelation; and we may as well speak of limited extension without figure, or of number without composition.[2]

Philo, however, argues that all orthodox divines disagree with Cleanthes in his support of anthropomorphism:

Pray consider, said Philo, whom you are at present inveighing against. You are honouring with the appellation of atheist all the sound, orthodox divines almost, who have treated of this subject; and you will, at last, be yourself, found, according to your reckoning, the only sound theist in the world.[3]

Philo passes immediately from his attempt to emphasize that orthodoxy does

---

[1] See D. 155–157.
[2] D. 159.
[3] D. 159–160.

not approve of anthropomorphism to a philosophical objection regarding anthropomorphism:

But because I know you are not much swayed by names and authorities, I shall endeavour to show you, a little more distinctly, the inconveniences of that anthropomorphism, which you have embraced; and shall prove, that there is no ground to suppose a plan of the world to be formed in the divine mind, consisting of distinct ideas, differently arranged: in the same manner as an architect forms in his head the plan of a house he intends to execute.[4]

Philo begins by claiming that nothing is gained by Cleanthes' position whether it is assessed by 'reason' or by 'experience'. The judgment of reason is "that a mental world or universe of ideas requires a cause as much as does a material world or universe of objects; and if similar in its arrangement must require a similar cause. For what is there in this subject, which should occasion a different conclusion or inference? In an abstract view, they are entirely alike; and no difficulty attends the one supposition, which is not common to both of them."[5] Similarly, experience cannot "perceive any material difference in this particular, between these two kinds of world, but finds them to be governed by similar principles, and to depend upon an equal variety of causes in their operations.[6] Philo concludes that the type of argument employed by Cleanthes leads to an infinite regress:

How therefore shall we satisfy ourselves concerning the cause of that Being whom you suppose the Author of nature or, according to your system of anthropomorphism, the ideal world into which you trace the material? Have we not the same reason to trace that ideal world into another ideal world, or new intelligent principle.[7]

He then suggests, as though it will prove to be more satisfactory, that we should not go beyond the material world itself:

But if we stop, and go no farther; why go so far? Why not stop at the material world? How can we satisfy ourselves without going on in infinitum? And after all, what satisfaction is there in that infinite progression? ... If the material world rests upon a similar ideal world, this ideal world must rest upn some other;and so on without end. It were better never to look beyond the present material world.[8]

In suggesting that it is better never to look beyond the material world, what precisely is it that Philo is advocating? George Nathan maintains that "Cleanthes is unaware that Philo is trying to eliminate only the externality of

---

[4]   D. 160.
[5]   D. 160.
[6]   D. 161.
[7]   D. 161.
[8]   D. 161–162.

the cause. He is not trying to deny its intelligence."[9] Pike,[10] on the other hand, interprets Philo's position as eliminating the requirement for a causal account of the order present in the world: "If we introduce an ordered mind in an effort to explain the existence of an ordered world, must we not provide a similar explanation of the ordered mind? But if we accept this demand, we shall have to introduce yet another intelligent being as the creator of the first. This explanatory chain can end only in an infinite regress. We would probably do better to assume that order in the material world is an ultimate fact that does not require explanation. Once we take the first step down the explanatory trail we are committed to go on forever."[11] I will now examine critically the interpretations suggested by Nathan and Pike.

Certain questions suggest themselves regarding Nathan's position. First, what does Nathan mean by the intelligence of the cause? Second, what evidence is there that Hume does not want to deny the intelligence of the cause? And third, is Nathan correct in maintaining that Philo only wants to deny the externality of the cause, and not its intelligence?

To understand Nathan's sense of the terms 'rationality' and 'intelligence' (he treats these as synonyms in this context, see his article p.421) we must examine what he says in other parts of his paper. The first clue to Nathan's interpretation occurs when he discusses the Vegetable Library illustration. He points out that there is an essential ambiguity in the word "design" throughout the *Dialogues*: "At some stages the meaning of "design" is taken to be that of the rational or intelligent order which is produced by an external agent or the intentions and plans of that agent. However, "design" can also mean only the rational order itself without any further assumptions about external causes."[12] To determine whether an object has a rational order, Nathan suggests the following: "... just as we call a mind rational because of its particular order, and not because of its cause, likewise we determine whether any other thing has an intelligent order by examining its structure and not by looking for the cause. For Hume the way of determining such order is by comparing something to objects which are acknowledged to be rationally ordered and then ascertaining what points of analogy are present in both. If the aspects which are found in the ordered product are also found in the item in question, then we can pronounce that item rational. Of course, human artifacts suggest themselves as the obvious paradigm for such comparisons."[13] Nathan maintains that the rational order in human artifacts

[9]   Ch, 410.
[10]   Hume: *Dialogues Concerning Natural Religion,* edited and with commentary by Nelson Pike, the Bobbs-Merril Co. Inc., Indianapolis, New York, 1970.
[11]   Pike, 157.
[12]   Ch, 404.
[13]   Ch. 407–408.

derives from the fact that there are "parts which are related to each other by the reciprocal relation of cause and effect and which also contribute to some general purpose of the object as a whole."[14] Hence, on Nathan's reading of Hume, non-human products can be regarded as rationally ordered provided they also possess these features.[15] To be rationally ordered, therefore, there is no requirement of conscious design on the part of the cause. Nathan goes further and holds that where an effect displays the features which entitle us to regard it as rational or intelligently ordered, we can conclude that its cause is rational or intelligent, regardless of whether the cause is internal or external. Commenting on the effects of causal reasoning in man and similar results achieved through instinct in other animal (cases of external causes), Nathan writes: "Judging from the marvelous adaptation of means to ends which men evidence we must equally acknowledge a similar process on the part of animals. If man exhibits rationality, then so do other creatures. The fact of rationality is not diminished by the revelation that instinct is the cause of this amazing adaptive process. Rather, we are led to the conclusion that instinct possesses a rationality of its own."[16] Speaking in connection with the Vegetable Library illustration which Nathan maintains must be regarded as having internal ordering principles, he writes: "... even though the propagation of the natural volumes does not depend on conscious design, nevertheless the volumes are rational and are due to a rational cause. The character of the volumes remains unchanged, even if they did not have an external cause."[17]

Regarding the second question I raised in connection with Nathan's thesis, namely, is there evidence that Hume does not want to deny the intelligence or rationality of the cause of the design of the world, he argues as follows: "The ... principle which is responsible for the order in the universe has already been characterized as rational. It is rational or intelligent because its effects resemble the intelligently ordered objects of human artifice."[18] We are now able to see why he holds that in Part IV only the externality of the cause of the design of the world is being attacked: since Nathan holds that Hume ascribes rationality to causes the effects of which have a relation of parts to each other and to a general purpose, and since these features are not questioned in regard to the design of the world in Part IV, he concludes that nothing said by Philo in this part is critical of the rationality of the ordering cause. Now, although it is true that nothing said by Philo in Part IV challenges the claim that the world is rationally or intelligently ordered, this

---

[14]   Ch. 421.
[15]   Nathan's discussion of the topic of rationality appears in his paper p.405–408.
[16]   Ch. 407.
[17]   Ch. 407.
[18]   Ch. 421.

is not sufficient to confirm Nathan's position. For his argument is that Hume nowhere challenges the rationality of the cause of the design of the world, and therefore, Nathan's major effort is to show that Hume is arguing for a rational (in Nathan's sense) internal principle of order for the world. Therefore, I propose to turn to the third question raised in connection with Nathan's paper to determine whether Philo wants only to deny the externality of the cause. This is best approached by determining whether Philo ever criticizes the rationality or intelligence of the design of the world.

In proceeding with this problem I believe it best to advance in two stages. First, I will examine passages which are held by Nathan (and others) to establish that Philo accepts the rationality of the world, and therefore of its designing cause, and I will show that these passages do not support Nathan's view. In the second stage, I will turn to the text to show that there are passages in which Philo shows why the rationality of the design of the world and of its cause cannot be established. One more point before we begin. Nathan maintains, as we saw, (and I believe that this is correct), that for an effect to be considered rational, and, therefore, for the cause of that effect to be considered rational, the effect must be so ordered that it satisfies two conditions, namely, there must be a relation of parts to each other and to a general purpose. It is reasonable to hold that if the second condition is satisfied, then the first condition is also satisfied. That is, if the parts are so ordered that they lend themselves to some overall purpose, then the parts must be related to each other. Hence, claims of purposiveness allow us to conclude the existence of means to ends relations. Philo never denies that the design of the world exhibits mean to ends relations. However, it is far from obvious that the existence of means to ends relations allows us to claim that there is a general purpose to whatever possesses means to ends relations. As we shall see, it is this very point with which Hume is struggling in seeking to determine whether the order we find in the world is a rational order. Philo will deny that reason can ever establish that the design of the world is purposive.

The first passage quoted by Nathan appears in Part X. Philo asserts: "You ascribe, *Cleanthes* (and I believe justly) a purpose and intention to nature."[19] At first glance, this passage appears to support the view that the design of the world is a rational one. However, I believe that the situation is somewhat more complex, and to show this I want to return to a passage spoken by Philo in Part II in which he speaks – as he does in the passage from D.198 – of 'ascribing justly'. Philo there tells Demea and Cleanthes:

... as all perfection is entirely relative, we ought never to imagine, that we comprehend the attributes of this divine Being, or to suppose, that his perfections have any analogy or likeness

---

[19]   D. 198.

to the perfections of a human creature. Wisdom, thought, design, knowledge; these we justly ascribe to him; because these words are honourable among men, and we have no other language or other conceptions, by which we can express our adoration of him. But let us beware, lest we think, that our ideas any wise correspond to his perfections, or that his attributes have any resemblance to these qualities among men.[20]

At least in connection with divine attributes, 'justly ascribing' certain attributes to God does not involve any accuracy on our part in regard to such ascriptions: just ascription, in this case, is linked with a complete lack of comprehension of divine attributes, and a denial of any likeness between human perfections and those of God.

The passage spoken by Philo at D.198 in which he acknowledges a purpose and intention in nature is expressed in a manner similar to the way in which he expressed his views about divine attributes in Part II. And, therefore, in reading the passage in Part X, we should be open to the possibility that when Philo consents to a 'just ascription' of a purpose and intention to nature, he does not believe either that we understand the purpose and intention in nature, or that purposiveness as far as we understand it has any likeness to what is true of the world. In any case, the passage at D.198 cannot be taken *simpliciter* as evidence that Philo holds that there is a purpose and intention to nature.

The second passage quoted by Nathan occurs at the end of Part X:

In many views of the universe, and of its parts, particularly the latter, the beauty and fitness of final causes strike us with such irresistible force, that all objections appear (what I believe they really are) mere cavils and sophisms; nor can we then imagine how it was ever possible for us to repose any weight on them.[21]

In assessing this passage, the sentence preceeding what I have quoted is relevant. Philo tells Cleanthes that "formerly, when we argued concerning the natural attributes of intelligence and design, I needed all my sceptical and metaphysical subtilty to elude your grasp." The full point that Philo is making, therefore, is that in attacking the claim of intelligence and design, he employed sceptical (pyrrhonistic) arguments. However, often our perception of the world, particularly the adaptation of means to ends, strikes us so irresistibly that we can no longer deny the rationality of the world, even though we have been exposed to the sceptical arguments against the rationality of the world. In fact, the sceptical arguments now appear to us as mere cavils and sophisms (and are such).

The structure of Philo's point does not lend itself to interpreting him as holding that there are reasonable (or analogical) grounds for believing in a

[20] D. 142.
[21] D. 202.

purpose and intention to nature. Rather, what he says supports the view that a belief in purposiveness is an instinctive or natural belief. Notice that the concession to purposiveness follows the presentation of sceptical arguments. And notice futher that it is a particular view of the world 'striking' us with 'irresistible force' which gives rise to the belief in purposiveness. These are characteristics not of a reasonable belief, but of a natural one. [22]

A third passage relevant to our present discussion occurs in Part XII where Philo again appears to assent to the purposive nature of the world:

A purpose, an intention, or design strikes every where the most careless, the most stupid thinker.[23]

In understanding this passage it should be recalled that "carelessness" for Hume is a technical term which is used to characterize that state of mind which enables us to ignore the arguments of the sceptic and to be moved by our natural tendencies.[24] Hence, again here Philo is suggesting that a belief in purposiveness is natural, and not rational.

This passages we have examined lend themselves to the interpretation that a belief in the rationality of the design of the world is not something which reason can establish. It is usual with Hume in his effort to establish a belief as natural to show why reason is unable to establish the belief in question. I will now show that this standard practice of Hume's is also present in the case of the claim regarding the rationality of the design of the world.

The challenge to Philo to determine whether the world possesses a rational design is made by Cleanthes at the end of Part V: "... by the utmost indulgence of your imagination, you never get rid of the hypothesis of design in the universe, but are obliged, at every turn, to have recourse to it." Cleanthes' challenge is met by Philo in Part VIII. In this section, Philo proposes the following:

Suppose ... that matter were thrown into any position, by a blind, unguided force; it is evident that this first position must in all probability be the most confused and most disorderly imaginable, without any resemblance to those works of human contrivance, which along with a symmetry of parts, discover an adjustment of means to ends and a tendency to self-preservation. If the actuating force cease after this operation, matter must remain for ever in disorder, and continue an immense chaos, without any proposition or activity. But suppose, that the actuating force, whatever it be, still continues in matter, this first position will immediately give place to

---

[22]   I do not intend this to be taken as establishing conclusively that Hume regards the belief in purposiveness in the design of the world to be a natural belief: the full discussion of natural belief must await our analysis of Part XII of the *Dialogues*. My point here is that there is no support for Nathan's claim in the passages he cites that the world and its cause of design are rationally ordered.

[23]   D. 214.

[24]   See the discussion of 'natural belief' in Chapter I of this book. See also the conclusion of the section "Of Scepticism with regard to the Senses" in the *Treatise of Human Nature*.

a second, which will likewise in all probability be as disorderly as the first, and so on, through many succession of changes and revolutions ... Thus the universe goes on for many ages in a continued succession of chaos and disorder. But is it not possible that it may settle at last, so as not to lose its motion and active force ... yet so as to preserve an uniformity of appearance, amidst the continual motion and fluctuation of its parts? This we find to be the case with the universe at present. Every individual is perpetually changing, and every part of every individual, and yet the whole remains, in appearance, the same. May we not hope for such a position, or rather be assured of it, from the eternal revolutions of unguided matter, and may not this account for all the appearing wisdom and contrivance which is in the universe? Let us contemplate the subject a little, and we shall find, that this adjustment, if attained by matter, of a seeming stability in the forms, with a real and perpetual revolution or motion of parts, affords a plausible, if not a true solution of the difficulty.[25]

A blind unguided force – of the sort which this hypothesis postulates – could not be considered a rational designing principle in Nathan's sense. Now, if reason will always be confronted with the possibility that the cause of the design of the world is not a rational principle of order, and if only a rational principle of order can produce a rationally ordered effect, it follows that reason cannot establish that the world is a rationally ordered effect. The question we must now answer is why can reason not be convinced that the design of the world is a rational one.

Hume's answer to this must be that means to ends relations and a coherence of parts – features of the world which we can verify – do not ensure that there is a general purpose to whatever it is that possesses these features; for if they did, then their presence would rule out the possibility that the cause of design is a 'blind unguided force'. I believe that the point Hume is anxious to make is that purposiveness is not reducible to means to ends relations and a coherence of parts, nor do these features ensure purposiveness. If means to ends relations and a coherence of parts were either the same as a general purpose or features ensuring a general purpose, then these features would ensure that the object is rationally designed, and hence has a rational cause. But since we can deny the rationality of the cause even when these characteristics are present, it follows that a general purpose cannot be known or inferred merely from the presence of these features. If we take a machine or an organism as items which satisfy the requirements of a rational design, much can be learned about Hume's views on purposiveness and rational design. Machines and organisms all possess means to ends relations and a coherence of parts as well as a rational design, and therefore Hume's point is that it is a common error to confuse these characteristics with the notion of a general purpose, or to believe that these characteristics ensure a general purpose. Nathan himself has fallen into this confusion when he tells us that "for Hume the way of determining such rational order is by comparing

---

[25]   D. 184–185.

something to objects which are acknowledged to be rationally ordered and then ascertaining what points of analogy are present in both. If the aspects which are found in the ordered product are also found in the item in question, then we can pronounce that item rational. Of course, human artifacts suggest themselves as the obvious paradigm for such comparisons. For this reason Cleanthes' illustrations are especially apt. His comparison of the universe to machines, houses and books is useful because they all exhibit an intelligent structure.'' What Hume is trying to show is that the presence of means to ends relations and a coherence of parts is not sufficient to claim that an object possesses a rational structure and rational cause, and that, therefore, more is required before such a rational structure can be confidently affirmed. What more is needed?

A clue to answering this is provided by Hume in a passage in Part VIII which immediately follows the one we have been discussing. Philo asserts:

It is in vain, therefore, to insist upon the uses of the parts in animals or vegetables, and their curious adjustment to each other.I would fain know how an animal could subsist, unless its parts were so adjusted? Do we not find, that it immediately perishes whenever this adjustment ceases, and that its matter corrupting tries some new form? It happens, indeed, that the parts of the world are so well adjusted, that some regular form immediately lays claim to this corrupted matter: And if it were not so, could the world subsist? Must it not dissolve as well as the animal, and pass through new positions and situations; till in a great, but finite succession it fall at last into the present or some order.[26]

According to this passage, means to ends relations and a coherence of parts are necessary for an object's existence: without these features nothing can exist. Where an object comes into existence through a 'blind unguided force', the object and its particular set of causal relations are not brought into existence purposively. On the other hand, where an object and its particular set of causal relations come into existence through some guiding force (or principle), the resulting design is purposive. For the designing principle to bring about such an object, it is not necessary, according to Hume, that it be aware of the object it is designing:

A tree bestows order and organisation on that tree which springs from it, without knowing the order: an animal, in the same manner, on its offspring: a bird, on its nest: and instances of this kind are even more frequent in the world, than those of order, which arise from reason and contribance.[27]

What is required in order to say that the design is purposive is this: we must find the cause of design and the item designed constantly conjoined. It is precisely the absence of this constant conjunction in the case of God and the

---

[26] D. 185.
[27] D. 179.

design of the world which allows Philo to suggest a 'blind unguided force' as the origin of the design of the world. Therefore, we find ourselves returning to Philo's earlier objection in Part II: without seeing worlds formed under our eyes, it is impossible to comment on the cause of the design of the world – and this includes its rationality. Without the required constant conjunction, it will never be possible to answer the question, "Why does the world exhibit this particular set of means to ends relations?" Without an answer to this, the problem of the general purpose served by its design cannot be answered, with the result that we cannot establish the rationality of the design of the effect nor of its cause. In Part VIII Philo is suggesting that so long as we are unable to establish that the design of the world and its cause of design are both rational (in the sense discussed earlier) it will be impossible to determine if the question, "What is the purpose of the design we find in the world?" is well-formed, since there may not be a purpose to the design.[28]

It can now be seen, therefore, that Nathan is mistaken in holding that only the externality of the cause is being attacked by Hume, and not its rationality (in Nathan's sense of this term). The particular insight which Philo has revealed is that the presence of means to ends relations and a coherence of parts does not establish or guarantee a general purpose, and, therefore, these features alone cannot be used to establish the rationality of the effect and of the cause.

I turn now to the second suggested interpretation of Philo's position in advocating that 'it were better never to look beyond the present material world' in accounting for the design of the world. Pike interprets Philo as maintaining that we should eliminate the requirement for a causal account of the order in the world. By considering the present order as an ultimate fact, no explanation of it is required, and no regress is generated. The text, however, does not bear out Pike's interpretation.

First, the passage under consideration is amenable to more than one interpretation. When Philo says that 'it were better never to look beyond the present material world' he adds that 'by supposing it to contain the principle of its order within itself, we really assert it to be God'. Now, in saying this, Philo may either mean that order pertains to the very nature of the world, in which case the search for causes is removed, or he may mean that we should suppose that the world has an internal principle of order. It is only if Philo

---

[28]   This position does, of course, accord with Hume's view of regarding the lack of intelligibility of a natural belief. All natural beliefs – those generally accepted being the belief in causality, in a continuing self, and in body – are such that, despite their irresistibility and importance to us, they cannot be rendered intelligible. For example, the question "What is the nesessary connection between a cause and an affect of that cause?" may also not be well-formed, since there may not be such connections between objects. In any case, the habit generated in the mind which leads to the belief in a necessary connection between objects cannot be used to explain the necessary connection between objects – only the belief in such connections.

intends the former that he can be regarded as holding that the present order is not one requiring a causal explanation. To determine which of these Philo is maintaining, I will now examine other passages in which Philo is concerned with the infinite regress generated by Cleanthes' argument. I should add that the two positions outlined above allow for a *tertium quid*, namely, Philo may believe that neither position is actually defensible, in which case he is not committed to either position.

At D.162–163 Philo examines ways of stopping the regress in Cleanthes' position. His first attempt involves the suggestion that "the different ideas, which compose the reason of the supreme Being, fall into order of themselves, and by their own nature."[29] In assessing this, Philo asserts a) that this is "really to talk without any precise meaning"[30] and b) if it has meaning, he asks "why it is not as good sense to say, that the parts of the material world fall into order, of themselves, and by their own nature? Can the one opinion be intelligible, while the other is not so?"[31] Now, if Philo were opting for the claim that the parts of the material world fall into order by themselves through their own natures, then we could accept Pike's interpretation. For if the parts of the material world were self-ordering, there would be no distinction between what was ordered and what brought the order about: in this sense, the order in the world would be an ultimate fact. But this is not what Philo is maintaining. His aim in this passage is to argue that it is as plausible to hold to a self-ordering material world as it is to hold to a self-ordering divine reason, so that the one hypothesis has no advantage over the other. To adopt Pike's position requires believing that Philo holds that the notion of self-ordering phenomena can be given a precise meaning or be rendered intelligible, which he never acknowledges, and it requires believing that he holds that the hypothesis of a self-ordering material world is more defensible than that of a self-ordering divine reason, which he also does not acknowledge.

The second way in which Philo seeks to prevent the regress in Cleanthes' position is to examine the supposition that God's mind is a rational faculty, and that this is the cause of the order of the ideas in the divine mind:"... when it is asked, what cause produces order in the ideas of the supreme Being, can any other reason be assigned by you, anthropomorphites, than that it is a rational faculty, and that such is the nature of the Deity?"[32] But Philo again asks why, if this line is adopted with respect to the divine mind, a similar answer will not be equally satisfactory in accounting for the order of the world, without having recourse to any such intelligent Creator:"... It is only

[29] D. 162.
[30] D. 162.
[31] D. 162.
[32] D. 163.

to say, that *such* is the nature of material objects, and that they are originally possessed of a *faculty* of order and proportion.''[33] If Philo accepted this latter account, Pike's reading could be accepted. Philo, however, is quick to point out that "these are only more learned and elaborate ways of confessing our ignorance; nor has the one hypothesis any real advantage over the other, except in its greater conformity to vulgar prejudices.''[34] Philo concludes Part IV by emphasizing that neither hypothesis – that of a self-designing divine reason nor a self-designing material world – is either more intelligible or more plausible than the other in accounting for the design of the world:

An ideal system, arranged of itself, without a precedent design, is not a whit more explicable than a material one, which attains its order in a like manner; nor is there any more difficulty in the latter supposition than in the former.[35]

Nothing said by Philo in Part IV, therefore, supports Pike's position that to stop the regress Philo advocates assuming that order in the material world is an ultimate fact.

I mentioned earlier that Philo's comment 'that it is better never to look beyond the present material world in accounting for the design of the world, and that we should suppose it to contain the principle of its order within itself' is amenable to two interpretations: either the world should be regarded as though order pertains to its very nature, or else the world should be supposed to have an internal (as opposed to an external) principle of order. Since Philo refused to accept the former for the reasons discussed above, it might be thought that he is actually advocating acceptance of an internal principle of order for the world. This is the position which George Nathan argues Philo is willing to accept. I will now show that Nathan is mistaken in his reading, and that Philo is not prepared to accept, or better defend, an internal principle of order for the world.

In defence of his reading, Nathan argues as follows:

[1] Philo is defending the principle of an internal cause of order in the universe. [2]Cleanthes is positing an external cause which is itself internally ordered. [3]Both seek to avoid the infinite regress. To prevent the regress in which the order of the universe is explained by an external cause, etc. *ad infinitum*, it is necessary that there be an internal principle order somewhere in the series. [4]If the internal principle is necessary, then an external principle is impossible. [5]Since the internal principle is necessary for explanation, it is also sufficient. [6]Philo and Cleanthes agree that experience reveals an internal principle of order in the universe in plants, animals, and minds. Such things as watches and houses are observed to be the result of human minds which are themselves internally ordered. [7]Therefore because this internal principle exists in the universe, the universe has within it a necessary and sufficient explanation for its order.[8] As a result an external

[33]   D. 163.
[34]   D. 163.
[35]   D. 164.

principle of order for the universe is impossible. [9]Furthermore, if one external principle is impossible, an infinite series of such principles is equally impossible.[36]

To facilitate my discussion of this passage from Nathan's paper, I will refer to the superscripts which I have inserted.

The first sentence in this quotation is, of course, what Nathan is trying to establish, and therefore, our decision regarding it must await an appraisal of Nathan's argument. Sentence 2, however, can now be shown to reflect inaccurately Cleanthes' position. Although Cleanthes does want to hold that the cause of the design of the world is external to the world, he does not commit himself to holding that it is internally ordered. There is but one passage in the *Dialogues* wherein Cleanthes makes any response to Philo's charge of an infinite regress, and within it he shows himself to be without a proper answer:

> Even in common life, if I assign a cause for any event; is it any objection, Philo, that I cannot assign the cause of that cause, and answer every new question, which may incessantly be started? ... You start abstruse doubts, cavils, and objections: You ask me, what is the cause of this cause? I know not; I care not; that concerns not me. I have found a Deity; and here I stop my enquiry. Let those go farther, who are wiser and more enterprising.[37]

Even though Nathan is mistaken about Cleanthes in this regard, he may still, of course, be correct in his interpretation that Philo is defending an internal cause of order in the universe.

In the group of sentences numbered 3, Nathan wrongly accounts for how the infinite regres can be stopped. From the fact that an internal principle of order is posited somewhere in the series, it does not follow that there is no infinite regress. For it can still be asked of this internal principle of order, what it is that brought it about, and so on. In other words, the 'location' of the ordering principle is not all there is to the problem of the infinite regress, nor is it a complete solution to the problem. There are but two ways to stop the infinite regress which Philo has charged: either the thing designed must be such that order pertains to its very nature, or there must be an internal principle of order somewhere in the series of causer (as Nathan holds) which, for some specifiable reason,[38] does not itself require a causal explanation. If the former is true, i.e. if order pertains to the very nature of the world, then all external principles would be impossible, but, of course, so would all internal principles. To establish the necessity (and therefore sufficiency) of an

---

[36] Ch, 412–413.
[37] D. 163.
[38] This will be discussed shortly when we come to the passage in which Philo suggests how to stop the infinite regress charge.

internal principle of order for the world (Nathan's points 4 and 5), it must be shown that the nature of the world is such that order does not pertain to its very nature, and that the design of the world cannot be better explained by an external principle of order which is itself internally ordered and which does not itself require a causal explanation. Or alternatively, it must be shown that the evidence in favour of the hypothesis of an internal principle of order meets a satisfactory level of acceptability. According to Nathan, Hume held that this latter position can be upheld (Nathan's step 7). The evidence is given in 6, namely, by experience we find an internal principle of order in plants, animals, and minds. However, it does not seem likely that Hume would employ such evidence, since it is subject to the very same criticisms which Philo levied against Cleanthes in Part II, when Cleanthes sought to establish thought as the cause of the design of the world. In short, the problem still remains as to why we can accept what experience discloses about parts of the world to be applicable to the whole world. If Cleanthes has difficulty with this in his argument, it appears that Philo will have the same difficulty. If my point here is correct, then Nathan's steps 8 and 9, wherein it is concluded that Philo's evidence rules out all external causes of order for the world, cannot be accepted.

Thus far, I have stated how I believe that the regress can be stopped, and one way in which I do not believe that Philo would argue for an internal principle of order. However, it might be said that, textually, Nathan's position is accurate, even though we might disagree with Philo's arguments. I will now show that Philo does not adopt the position which Nathan puts forth in his behalf.

The one passage which is relevant to our present discussion appears toward the end of Part VI. Philo says:

And where I obliged to defend any particular system of this nature (which I never willingly should do), I esteem none more plausible than that which ascribes an eternal, inherent principle of order to the world; though attended with great and continual revolutions and alterations. This at once solves all difficulties; and if the solution, by being so general, is not entirely complete and satisfactory, it is, at least, a theory, that we must, sooner or later, have recourse to, whatever system we embrace. How could things have been as they are, were there not an original, inherent principle of order, somewhere in thought or in matter? And it is very indifferent to which of these we give the preference. Chance has no place, on any hypothesis, sceptical or religious. Everything is surely governed by steady, inviolable laws. And were the inmost essence of things laid open to us, we should then discover a scene, of which, at present, we can have no idea. Instead of admiring the order of material beings, we should clearly see that it was absolutely impossible for them, in the smallest article, ever to admit of any other disposition.[39]

Nathan quotes parts of this passage as evidence for his reading. However, it must be pointed out that there are certain peculiarities in Nathan's

[39]   D. 174–175.

presentation of it. First, he omits the bracketed portion in the first sentence in which Philo declares that he would never willingly defend what he is about to say.

Second, Nathan misquotes a portion of the first sentence, rendering 'eternal inherent principle of order to the world' as 'internal inherent principle of orderto the world'. Third, Nathan stops quoting the passage after the third sentence , thereby omitting Philo's claim that it is indifferent whether we opt for an original inherent principle in thought or in matter, and also omitting Philo's comments as to what we would find 'were the inmost essence of things laid open to us'.[40] Now, if the passage is read as Nathan has quoted it, it seems as though Philo is advocating an internal principle of order to the world. But even if the passage is rendered as Nathan has done, there is nothing supporting his step 6; that is, nothing said by Philo in this passage indicates that he accepts the existence of internal principles of order in the world as evidence that the principle of order of the world is also an internal one. In any case, once the entire passage is examined, it can be seen that Philo is not himself committed to an internal principle of order to the world.

Philo is making the following points:
(1) If he were to defend any theory, it would be that advocating an eternal inherent principle of order, but he would never willingly do it. This solution, by being so general, is not in a finished form nor wholly acceptable as it stands.
(2) An original inherent principle of order seems both necessary and sufficient for explaining the world, but we cannot determine whether this inherent principle is in thought (i.e. in an external principle of order) or in matter (i.e. in an internal principle of order).
(3) He suggests that if we could penetrate the essences of things, we would find that they cannot have any order other than the order they do have.

Each of these three points deserves some comment. In the case of (1), the inclusion of the term 'eternal' is important, for it shows that Philo realizes that the infinite regress cannot be stopped merely by positing an internal principle of order. On the other hand, if the cause is eternal, then the infinite regress criticism ceases to be effective: now it makes no sense to ask for the cause of this cause.

The hypothesis of an 'eternal inherent principle of order' avoids the problem of how the world is to be characterized (a criticism which Philo

---

[40] Nathan records the passage in question as follows: "And were I obliged to defend any particular system of this nature ... I esteem none more plausible than that which ascribes an internal, inherent principle of order to the world; though attended with great and continual revolutions and alterations. This at once solves all difficulties; and if the solution, by being so general, is not entirely complete and satisfactory, it is, at least, a theory, that we must sooner or later, have recourse to whatever system we embrace. How could things have been as they are, were there not an original, inherent principle of order somewhere in thought or in matter?"

brought against Cleanthes' Argument from Design), and it makes no reference whatever to what the ordering principle is. This explains Philo's assertion that the solution possesses too great a generality; this also explains why Philo denies completeness and full acceptability to this hypothesis. What Philo believes is that rather than offering a solution to the problem of the divine nature, he has, by asserting that the design of the world requires as its cause an eternal inherent principle of order, provided the 'form' which he regards the most plausible solution to possess.

If the world could be characterized as having a 'specific resemblance' to certain things found in the world, for example, if it could be characterized as machine-like, it would be possible to argue by analogy to the type of ordering principle it has, and this includes whether the ordering principle is internal or external. The claim of generality to the hypothesis in (1) coupled with Philo's claim in (2) that it is indifferent whether we opt for an internal or an external ordering principle establish that he believes that such a characterization of the world is not possible.

Even though we cannot, according to Philo, determine whether the ordering cause of the world is in thought or matter, it appears as though some succes has been obtained in the realization that no more plausible solution can be proposed to the problem of how the world achieved its design than that of an eternal inherent principle of order. Why, then, does Philo say that he would never willingly defend this position? In the passage under discussion, he says that the theory of an eternal inherent principle of order is one we must sooner or later have recourse to 'whatever system we embrace'. In other words, all systems of cosmogony are open to the criticism of an infinite regress, and, therefore, all must, in the end, posit an eternal inherent principle of order, for only in this way can the regress be stopped. But to argue in this way is to argue as Demea does in part IX: to explain the contingent, Demea argues, a modal jump is required to a necessarily existent being; otherwise, we become involved in an infinite regress, in which case no existent can be satisfactorily accounted for. I submit that Philo recognizes that to stop the regress to which all systems of cosmogony lead, we must have recourse to Demea's *a priori* argument in Part IX. However, since Philo holds that this argument is ill-grounded,[41] he is obviously unwilling to defend the claim of an eternal inherent principle of order to the world.

The third point raised by Philo in the passage under discussion, namely, that if we could penetrate the essences of things, we would find that they cannot have any order other than the order they have, can also be explained

---

[41]   We need not state his (and Cleanthes') criticisms here.

by turning to a passage in Part IX. Toward the end of this Part, Philo asserts:

> It is observed by arithmeticians, that the products of 9 compose always either 9 or some lesser product of 9; if you add together all the characters, of which any of the former products is composed ... To a superficial observer, so wonderful a regularity may be admired as the effect either of chance or design; but a skilful algebraist immediately concludes it to be the work of necessity, and demonstrates, that it must for ever result from the nature of these numbers. Is it not probable, I ask, that the whole oeconomy of the universe is conducted by a like necessity, though no human algebra can furnish a key which solves the difficulty? And instead of admiring the order of natural beings, may it not happen, that, could we penetrate into the intimate nature of bodies, we should clearly see why it was absolutely impossible, they could ever admit of any other disposition?[42]

This passage makes it clear that Philo is not claiming that the order in the world is necessary. What he is saying is that although we cannot establish the claim that the order of things in the world is necessary, it is also not possible to disprove it. And since this claim cannot be disproved (given that we cannot penetrate into the intimate nature of bodies) we will always be ignorant of whether a principle of order is required to account for the order in the world: the inclusion of principles of order presupposes that the order in the world is contingent, and that, therefore, the order arises from something other than the very nature of what is ordered.

I argued earlier that Philo refuses to defend the hypothesis of an eternal inherent principle of order to the world because this would involve him with the type of argument Demea employs in Part IX, and he holds this argument to be defective. We can now see an additional reason for his unwillingness to defend an eternal inherent principle of order to the world, namely, he would have to establish that the order in the world is contingent, and this he believes he cannot do.

To sum up, if the order in the world is contingent, then the ordering cause must be regarded as necessary to stop the infinite regress charge. And if not contingent, then the order must be necessary. In either case, our ignorance will continue, since we can neither understand nor demonstrate necessity as it relates to existence.

An ironic element in the debate between Philo and Cleanthes is apparent. Philo has shown that Cleanthes' Argument from Design ultimately rests on the *a priori* proof presented by Demea in Part IX. Yet, it is Cleanthes who offers the bulk of the critique against this *a priori* proof. By so doing, he shows that the 'inconvenience' of his Argument from Design, as developed by Philo, is something he cannot remedy.

---

[42]   D. 191.

CHAPTER 6

Hume's *Dialogues*: Part V

MORE 'INCONVENIENCES OF CLEANTHES' ANTHROPOMORPHISM

The 'inconveniences' of anthropomorphism which Philo began to develop in
Part IV are continued in Part V. Whereas Philo's argument in Part IV
concentrated on Cleanthes' attempt to establish an external principle of order
to the world, Philo's argument in Part V concentrates on the 'intelligence'
aspect of Cleanthes' position.

Philo begins by referring to 'the grandeur and magnificence of the works
of nature': he insists that the more we learn about the world through science,
the more Cleanthes' position is weakened:

Like effects prove like causes. This is the experimental argument; and this, you say too, is the
sole theological argument. Now it is certain, that the liker the effects are, which are seen, and
the liker the causes, which are inferred, the stronger is the argument. Every departure on either
side diminishes the probability, and renders the experiment less conclusive ... All the new
discoveries in astronomy, which prove the immense grandeur and magnificence of the works of
nature, are so many additional arguments for a Deity, according to the true system of theism:
But according to your hypothesis of experimental theism, they become so many objections, by
removing the effect still farther from all resemblance to the effects of human art and
contrivance.[1]

Philo insists that scientific discoveries reveal how dissimilar the world and
machines are.

But exactly what is Philo claiming through his references to science? Part
of what he is asserting is clear: his comment about 'the true system of theism'
is to be linked to his statement in Part II that "just reasoning and sound piety
here concur in the same conclusion, and both of them establish the adorably
mysterious and incomprehensible nature of the supreme Being."[2] In other
words, the discoveries in science complement philosophic reasoning and
orthodoxy (Demea's Mysticism) by pointing to the fact that the cause of the
design of the world is mysterious and incomprehensible. What is not clear in
Philo's discussion is why scientific discoveries lead to this conclusion.

[1] D. 165.
[2] D. 143.

The passage under examination might be taken as an argument for distinguishing the world from machines of human contrivance as a result of the complexity of the former in comparison to the latter. Other passages spoken by Philo lend support to this reading:

... when the bounds of nature are so infinitely enlarged, and such a magnificent scene is opened to us, then it is still more unreasonable to form our idea of so unlimited a cause from our experience of the narrow productions of human design and invention.[3]

Leaving aside the fact that it is far from clear that an argument for distinguishing the world from machines on the basis of complexity can be rendered successful, it can be shown that this is not the sort of argument which Philo is presenting.

It is in Part II that Philo provides his most detailed thoughts on analogical reasoning, and whenever his view is expressed, the same point is made: when reasoning by analogy, an *exact* resemblance must obtain between the items compared, and where differences do exist, they weaken the argument unless they can be shown to be irrelevant to the argument:

But observe, I entreat you, with what extreme caution all just reasoners proceed in the transferring of experiments to similar cases. Unless the experiments be exactly similar, they repose no perfect confidence in applying their past observation to any particular phenomenon. Every alteration of circumstances occasions a doubt concerning the event; and it requires new experiments to prove certainly, that the new circumstances are of no moment of importance.[4]

To establish that the resemblance is exact and the differences inconsequential, requires being able, on the basis of the similarities, to classify the items compared as being of the same kind. Causal knowledge, for Philo, requires seeing an object of one kind constantly conjoined with an object of another kind. His recurring complaint in Part II is that no observations of the world reveal it to be sufficiently like any of the items which we find in the world whose cause is known to enable us to classify the world as an object of that type. Hence, we lack the requisite constant conjunction for causal knowledge.[5]

I suggest that in the early paragraphs of Part V Philo is once again calling

---

[3] D. 166. In the next paragraph Philo says: "The discoveries by microscopes, as they open a new universe in miniature, are still objections, according to you; arguments, according to me. The farther we push our researches of this kind, we are still led to infer the universal cause of All to be vastly different from mankind, or from any object of human experience and observation.

[4] D. 147.

[5] "When two *species* of objects have always been observed to be conjoined together, I can *infer*, by custom, the existence of one wherever I *see* the existence of the other ... But how this argument can have place, where the objects, as in the present case, are single, individual, without parallel, or specific resemblance; may be difficult to explain." (D. 149)

attention to the fact that observation – including scientific observation – fails to disclose a sufficient resemblance between the world and particular machines to enable us to classify the world as a machine of a certain sort. And without this classification, there is no basis for engaging the principle 'like effects prove like causes.' Philo emphasizes that the problem is not that we have insufficient scientific observation and knowledge. It is rather that we have inductive support to the effect that the more we learn about the world, the greater the difficulty of establishing the requisite resemblance between the world and machines to employ the principle 'like effects prove like causes.' Hence, his inclusion in the second paragraph of Part V of the passages from Lucretius and Tully: older systems of science are at no disadvantage to more contemporary scientific systems with respect to natural theology, inasmuch as both old and new systems reveal the world to be unlike any machine with which we are familiar.

In the light of Philo's references to scientific discoveries in Part V, should Cleanthes yield to Philo's criticism regarding the issue of classification? That is, has Philo now shown that the argument which Cleanthes has presented in Part II cannot establish analogically that the cause of the design of the world is an intelligent being? I think not; and by developing this we will see why the *Dialogues* must continue beyond Part V if Cleanthes' argument is to be addressed fully.

To make the case that Philo's references to scientific discoveries in Part V effectively destroy Cleanthes' Argument from Design requires showing that the claim that the world is machine-like is a premise in Cleanthes' argument. For if Cleanthes begins with the claim that the world is machine-like, and then argues that the cause of the design of the world is an intelligent being since machines have been found constantly conjoined with intelligence as their cause of design, then, quite obviously, the appropriate criticism will center around proving that no observations of the world reveal that the design of the world resembles the machines we produce. We have encountered this criticism of Philo's when dealing with Part II. And Cleanthes responded at that time by calling attention to the exact resemblance between the world and machines in terms of means to ends relations and a coherence of parts.[6] This is the resemblance Cleanthes deems essential to his case. Therefore, when Philo argued in Part II that the world does not present itself to us as a machine of a certain sort, Cleanthes maintained that this does not affect his argument,

---

[6]   "It would surely be very ill received, replied Cleanthes; and I should be deservedly blamed and detested, did I allow that the proofs of a Deity amounted to no more than a guess or conjecture. But is the whole adjustment of means to ends in a house and in the universe so slight a resemblance? The oeconomy of final causes? The order, proportion, and arrangement of every part." (D. 144–145)

since he did not begin his argument with the claim that the world is machine-like.

We find the same pattern in Part V. Philo argues that science shows the world to be quite unlike the effects of human art and contrivance. And at the end of Part V, Cleanthes responds:

... by the utmost indulgence of your imagination, you never get rid of the hypothesis of design in the universe; but are obliged, at every turn, to have recourse to it. To this concession I adhere steadily; and this I regard as a sufficient foundation for religion.[7]

Philo has not yet established that the features of design which Cleanthes argues are evidence of an intelligent designing principle can arise from non-intelligent sources of order. From Cleanthes' point of view, the more instances we find of means to ends relations and a coherence of parts, the stronger the argument that the design of the world stems from mind. And this is precisely what science reveals. In response to Philo's question in Part V as to whether the discoveries in anatomy, chemistry, botany, etc. hurt the Design Argument, Cleanthes replies: "These surely are no objections ... they only discover new instances of art and contrivance. It is still the image of mind reflected on us from innumerable objects."[8]

The discussion in Part I of the *Dialogues* centers around the limits of human knowledge, and, more particularly, whether we can have knowledge which goes beyond what we can perceive. Cleanthes insists that we do have such knowledge in science, and that we can have it in theology; Philo insists that we cannot have it in theology. Our study has revealed the precise point of disagreement between Philo and Cleanthes on this matter. Cleanthes insists that as science advances, it continues to discover additional instances of design, and that this is sufficient to establish the intelligence of the cause of the design of the world; Philo maintains that the proper employment of the principle 'like effects prove like causes' requires a stricter classification of the world than that it exhibits means to ends relations and a coherence of parts, and that advances in science show this to be increasingly unlikely. It is important to realize, however, that nothing said by Philo in the opening paragraphs of Part V has established which of the disputants holds the correct view.

We have seen that Cleanthes believes his position to be untouched by Philo's objections in Part V in connection with discoveries in science; and I have shown that because of the evidential claim made by Cleanthes in Part II, he is justified in believing that *his* position has not been refuted. But within Part V, we also find Philo's *reductio ad absurdum* of anthropomorphism, and

[7] D. 169.
[8] D. 166.

I will now determine how effective this effort of Philo's is against Cleanthes' position.

Philo's *reductio* begins with Cleanthes' commitment to an anthropomorphic conception of God:

And what say you to the discoveries in anatomy, chemistry, botany ... these surely are no objections, replied Cleanthes: They only discover new instances of art and contrivance. It is still the image of mind reflected on us from unnumerable objects. Add, a mind like the human, said Philo. I know of no other, replied Cleanthes. And the liker the better, insisted Philo. To be sure, said Cleanthes.[9]

He now offers the first stage of his argument:

Now, Cleanthes, said Philo, with an air of alacrity and triumph, mark the consequences. *First*, by this method of reasoning, you renounce all claim to infinity in any of the attributes of the Deity. For as the cause ought only to be proportioned to the effect, and the effect, so far as it falls under our cognisance, is not infinite; what pretensions have we, upon your suppositions, to ascribe that attribute to the divine Being?[10]

It might be thought that Philo's argument is not permissible both because of his Pyrrhonism, and because of his (read Hume's) account of causality which does not allow for *a priori* knowledge of causes. In fact, however, the argument put forth by Philo does not represent his own view (hence, it is not in conflict with his Pyrrhonism), and to the extent that it involves a causal claim, Philo recognizes that it does so incorrectly. That this first step does not represent Philo's views can be seen from the fact that he prefaces his remarks with the words "by this method of reasoning" and he begins his conclusion with "upon your suppositions," indicating that this first step follows from *Cleanthes'* position. But why does Philo present this argument; that is, what has Cleanthes said that leads Philo to put this argument forth as representing Cleanthes' position? The answer is to be found in Cleanthes' version of the Argument from Design in Part II. Cleanthes had argued: "Since therefore the effects resemble each other, we are led to infer, by all the rules of analogy, that the causes also resemble; and that the Author of nature is somewhat similar to the mind of man; though possessed of much larger faculties, *proportioned to the grandeur of the work, which he has executed.*"[11] It is, therefore, Cleanthes who, early in the debate, proposed 'proportioning the cause to the effect' in those cases where only the effect can be observed.

But it might be argued that I have not yet established conclusively that Philo is not committed to the view of a finite deity on the basis of a finite effect (the design of the world). It could be argued that when Philo asserts that 'the

[9] D. 166.
[10] D. 166.
[11] D. 143, my italics.

cause ought only to be proportioned to the effect' he is to be interpreted as accepting this principle, and employing it to establish a finite deity for the design of the world. Philo, on this account, is not himself bothered by this consequence but, as his *reductio* will reveal, this consequence will adversely affect Cleanthes' position. In other words, Philo regards the proportioning of cause to effects as legitimate, and then turns this against Cleanthes, who, in Philo's opinion, must be able to establish that God is infinite to prevent having the *reductio* applied against the position he holds.

That this is an incorrect reading can be learned by noting that toward the end of Part V, Philo expresses what he regards as following from Cleanthes' hypothesis, and in so doing, omits any reference to God as finite or infinite:

In a word, Cleanthes, a man, who follows your hypothesis, is able, perhaps, to assert, or conjecture, that the universe, sometime, arose from something like design: But beyond that position he cannot ascertain one single circumstance, and is left afterwards to fix every point of this theology, by the utmost license of fancy and hypothesis.[12]

What this passage also reveals is that Philo holds that Cleanthes also should not hold to the hypothesis of a finite deity: even if we were to grant Cleanthes' mode of seeking a knowledge of God by comparing the design of the world to the design machines, the inference to a finite deity cannot be countenanced – and this obtains even though "the effect, so far as it falls under our cognisance, is not infinite."

Why does Philo refuse to allow the inference to the finitude of the deity? No direct answer is provided by Philo in Part V. However, there are other passages – in Section XI of the first *Enquiry* – in which Hume indicates why he will not accept arguments like the one Philo has presented in Part V regarding a finite deity. It will be seen that Philo has all along echoed Hume's reasons when arguing against Cleanthes.

In section XI of the first *Enquiry*, Hume examines the principle concerning the proportioning of causes to effects where the cause is to be known only through the effect:

When we infer any particular cause from an effect, we must proportion the one to the other, and can never be allowed to ascribe to the cause any qualities, but what are exactly sufficient to produce the effect ... If the cause, assigned for any affect, be not sufficient to produce it, we must either reject that cause, or add to it such qualities as will give it a just proportion to the effect.[13]

He then goes on to entertain a use for this principle in learning about the deity:

Allowing, therefore, the Gods to be the authors of the existence or order of the universe; it

[12]   D. 168–169.
[13]   E. 136.

follows, that they possess that precise degree of power, intelligence, and benevolence, which appears in their workmanship; but nothing farther can ever be proved, except we call in the assistance of exaggeration and flattery to supply the defects of argument and reasoning. So far as the traces of any attributes, at present, appear, so far may we conclude these attributes to exist.[14]

Throughout this discussion, the principle regarding the proportioning of causes to effects is treated quantitatively: it is proposed that by examining the effect, we can calculate how much of a particular attribute must be present in its cause – there may, of course, be a greater degree of the attribute in the cause, but this cannot be known by examining the effect.

However, this interpretation of the principle is rejected by Hume, and he denies that a cause can be known only through its effect, that is, where the effect cannot be classified as a member of a species whose cause is known:

... I much doubt whether it be possible for a cause to be known only by its effect (as you have all along supposed) ... It is only when two *species* of objects are found to be constantly conjoined, that we infer the one from the other; and were an effect presented, which was entirely singular, and could not be comprehended under any known *species*, I do not see, that we could form any conjecture or inference at all concerning its cause. If experience and observation and analogy be, indeed, the only guides which we can reasonably follow in inferences of this nature; both the effect and cause must bear a similarity and resemblance to other effects and causes, which we know, and which we have found, in many instances, to be conjoined with each other.[15]

For Hume, therefore, the proper application of the principle regarding proportioning causes to effects is based on observing effects and their causes constantly conjoined: to proportion a cause to an effect means assigning as the cause of an effect what we have found to be the cause of an effect of that sort. To offer a quantitative analysis of this principle without the requisite constant conjunction is to corrupt the principle.

Now, Philo refuses to infer a finite deity even though the effect presents itself as finite. He has, throughout the discussion, given full support to the Humean claims that causal knowledge requires observing cause and effect constantly conjoined, and that the design of the world does not enable us to classify the world under any known species. Philo could accept a finite deity on the basis of an effect which appears finite where the advantage of observing cause and effect constantly conjoined is not present if an only if he accepts a purely quantitative analysis of the principle enjoining the proportioning of causes to effects. Since he refuses the former, he must be denying the latter as well. Therefore, Philo's refusal to infer a finite deity establishes his refusal to treat the proportioning principle in a purely quantitative manner. According to Philo, Cleanthes' position lacks the

---

[14] E. 137. See also E. 144–145.
[15] E. 148.

required constant conjunction for causal knowledge of God, and misuses the principle that causes ought to be proportioned to their effects.

Nelson Pike writes that even if Philo has shown that Cleanthes is committed to a finite deity, this should not disturb Cleanthes, for at no time did he seek to deny this:

> The question of interest is whether Cleanthes should be disturbed by Philo's contention ... I think we can agree that Cleanthes would not be distressed in the least ... Cleanthes holds that God's attributes far exceed their counterparts in men, but he explicitly denies that they are infinite. At this point we should expect Cleanthes to be quite content with the claim that the argument from design will establish the existence of an extremely intelligent (and extremely powerful) creator although it does nothing to show that the intelligence (and power) involved in this cause is infinite.[16]

Pike makes two errors in his interpretation. First, Philo denies that the inference to a *finite* deity is countenanced, inasmuch as the requisite constant conjunction is absent in the case of God and the world. And, secondly, Pike fails to realize – what Philo correctly points out to Cleanthes – that the *reductio* in Part V is possible only if the finitude of the deity is granted:

> From the moment the attributes of the Deity are supposed finite, all these [absurdities] have place. And I cannot, for my part, think, that so wild and unsettled a system of theology is, in any respect, preferable to none at all.[17]

Philo's *reductio* can now be seen in a clear light. Allowing 'A' to stand for "The deity is a mind like the human mind," 'F' to stand for "The deity is finite," and 'R_1, R_2, R_3, R_4, R_5,' to stand for the absurdities which Philo will draw from Cleanthes' position, Philo's argument against Cleanthes can be represented as follows:

$$(A \supset F) \cdot [(A \cdot F) \supset (R_1 \cdot R_2 \cdot R_3 \cdot R_4 \cdot R_5 \cdot)] \ (C)$$

In the first conjunct above, 'A' must be represented as implying 'F' since the finitude of the deity is, for Cleanthes (D. 166 third paragraph), 'a consequence of' his anthropomorphism. That is to say, when Cleanthes argues for the intelligence of the designer of the world through the principle 'like effects prove like causes,' he is maintaining that this principle can be employed only if the principle of proportioning causes to effects is also employed. Cleanthes' anthropomorphic conception of God is a result of the former principle; the claim that the deity is finite results from the latter principle. Accordingly, we can regard his anthropomorphism as implying the finitude claim.[18]

[16]   Pike 166–167.
[17]   D. 169.
[18]   In the first *Enquiry*, Hume (prior to his critique of this method of reasoning) writes:

In the second conjunct, the antecedent must be represented as 'A·F' and not simply as 'F', inasmuch as otherwise Philo would be represented as holding that the absurdities follow simply from the claim of the finitude of the deity, and this is not the position for which he is arguing. Philo is not claiming that all representations of the deity which include the finitude claim lead to absurdities. He urges that Cleanthes' anthropomorphism implies the finitude claim, and that these two doctrines taken together lead to absurd conclusions regarding the deity. Hence, the representation of the argument which I have offered above.

Philo's primary aim in Part V is to discredit anthropomorphism. Part V opens with Philo indicating that he will show Cleanthes 'more inconveniences in his anthropomorphism'. How Philo accomplishes this is easily seen by determining what follows from (C).

1. $(A \supset F) \cdot [(A \cdot F) \supset (R_1 \cdot R_2 \cdot R_3 \cdot R_4 \cdot R_5)]$ P   (C)
2. $(A \cdot F) \supset (R_1 \cdot R_2 \cdot R_3 \cdot R_4 \cdot R_5)$ 1,   Simplification
3. $A \supset F$ 1,   Simplification
4. $A \supset (A \cdot F)$ 3,   Absorption
5. $A \supset (R_1 \cdot R_2 \cdot R_3 \cdot R_4 \cdot R_5)$ 4,2,   Hypothetical Syllogism

Given premise 1 (C) above, it follows that the absurdities which Philo draws are implied by the claim that 'the deity is a mind like the human mind,' and Cleanthes' anthropomorphism is seen to be unacceptable.

None of the following propositions, however, can be inferred from (C):

(1) 'The deity is not finite': $(\sim F)$
(2) 'The deity is finite':   (F)
(3) 'The deity is a mind like the human
     mind and the deity is not finite: $(A \cdot \sim F)$
(4) 'The deity is not a mind like the
     human mind and the deity is finite: $(\sim A \cdot F)$

In other words, within this argument nothing has been settled regarding whether the deity is or is not finite, and nothing has been established about the acceptability or unacceptability of anthropomorphism *simpliciter*. Philo has established only that Cleanthes' anthropomorphism leads to certain absurd results, once the deity is held to be finite. (Cleanthes cannot, of course, conjoin his anthropomorphism with the claim of an infinite deity even though

---

"When we infer any particular cause from an effect we must proportion the one to the other." The principle of proportioning causes to effects is, therefore, regarded as a *sine qua non* for employing the principle 'like effects prove like causes.'

this would avoid the *reductio*, since he has no evidence for the hypothesis of an infinite deity. Furthermore, in one passage (in Part XI) he indicates his resistance to the ascription of the term 'infinite' to the deity: "I scruple not to allow, said Cleanthes, that I have been apt to suspect the frequent repetition of the word, *infinite*, which we meet with in all theological writers, to savour more of panegyric than of philosophy, and that any purposes of reasoning, and even of religion, would be better served, were we to rest contented with more accurate and more moderate expressions."[19])

What are the absurdities which follow from Cleanthes' position? Philo lists five. First, once the deity is supposed finite, we cannot ascribe perfection to him, since the product, from which our knowledge of the deity is to be inferred, contains 'many inexplicable difficulties.'[20] Second, even if the world is a perfect production, we cannot determine whether the perfections of the work can be ascribed to the workman. Very often, the one who brings a designed product about is "a stupid mechanic, who imitated others, and copied an art, which through a long succession of ages, after multiplied trials, mistakes, corrections, deliberations, and controversies, had been gradually improving."[21] Third, on Cleanthes' hypothesis, we cannot establish that there is only one deity: several deities may have co-operated in framing this world. Fourth, men are mortal and renew their species by generation: why should this feature, which 'is common to all living creatures,' be excluded from the deities? Finally, why not become a perfect anthropomorphite, and assert that the deities are corporeal, a position which accords with the fact that we have never seen reason except in a human figure.

Pike interprets these five points as constituting a "fanciful hypothesis", and he holds that Philo's intention in putting it forth is to suggest that this fanciful hypothesis is as good as, or better than, the hypothesis of design in accounting for the design of the world.[22] We have already seen that this is a misreading of Philo, since his concern is to demonstrate, through these five claims, what Cleanthes' hypothesis of design yields, once the deity is supposed to be finite. Therefore, these five points do not constitute an alternative to Cleanthes' position: they follow from it. To maintain the hypothesis of design such that it will be compatible with his theism, Cleanthes must give up the claim of the finitude of the deity.

---

[19]   D. 203.

[20]   D. 166.

[21]   D. 167.

[22]   "Given the empirical facts for which we are trying to account, isn't this fanciful hypothesis as good as the hypothesis of design. It may even be better. Of course, if this alternative is *as good as* Cleanthes' hypothesis, then there would be no empirical warrant for preferring one over the other. The hypothesis of design could then be dismissed as arbitrary. On the other hand, if this alternative is actually *better*, the conclusion would be that the hypothesis of design is probably false." (Pike 165)

Philo's *reductio*, therefore, does not constitute a criticism of Cleanthes' Argument from Design, and in particular, it does not attack the position that the design of the world stems from intelligence. However, toward the end of Part V, the penultimate paragraph, Philo does not confine his remarks to the inconsistency between the hypothesis of design and Cleanthes' theism. Rather he focuses on the intelligence thesis of the Design Argument, as well as offering a general assessment of this Argument:

In a word, Cleanthes, a man, who follows your hypothesis, is able, perhaps, to assert, or conjecture, that the universe, sometime, arose from something like design: But beyond that position he cannot ascertain one single circumstance.[23]

From what was argued above, it can be seen that this passage does not follow from Philo's *reductio*. And, in fact, Philo's manner of introducing this passage establishes his awareness of this. He says that a person 'who follows your [Cleanthes'] hypothesis' is the one who can say no more than this about the deity. What needs to be understood is the hypothesis to which Philo is here referring. And I submit that the relevant hypothesis is the same one which he mentioned in the second paragraph of Part V, namely, Cleanthes' 'hypothesis of experimental theism,' which, according to Philo, cannot utilize new discoveries in science: all such discoveries "become so many objections, by removing the effect still farther from all resemblance to the effects of human art and contrivance." But, as I showed earlier, nothing said by Philo in the opening paragraphs of Part V proves that Cleanthes' employment of the principle 'like effects prove like causes' through the features means to ends relations and a coherence of parts is defective. Therefore, nothing said by Philo in the opening paragraphs of Part V establishes the unknowability of the deity as set out in the passage quoted above from the penultimate paragraph. And since the *reductio* in Part V also does not establish the deity's unknowability, it follows that nothing said by Philo in Part V supports the passage spoken by Philo at D.168–169.

The central effort in the Argument from Design, namely, the attempt to establish that the cause of the design of the world resembles human intelligence, because both the world and machines of human contrivance exhibit means to ends relations and a coherence of parts, has yet to be attacked decisively by Philo. Cleanthes' closing remarks in Part V indicate that he understands this as well.

---

[23]   D. 168–169.

CHAPTER 7

Hume's *Dialogues*: Parts VI–VIII

COMPETING COSMOGONIES

Within Part V, Philo has demonstrated the absurdities which follow from Cleanthes' anthropomorphism, once the deity is regarded as finite. In the final paragraph of Part V, Cleanthes responds to Philo's *reductio*:

These suppositions I absolutely disown, cried Cleanthes: They strike me, however, with no horror; especially when proposed in that rambling way in which they drop from you. On the contrary, they give me pleasure, when I see, that by the utmost indulgence of your imagination, you never get rid of the hypothesis of design in the universe; but are obliged, at every turn, to have recourse to it. To this concession I adhere steadily; and this I regard as a sufficient foundation for religion.[1]

This passage is important, primarily because it discloses that Philo's *reductio* has moved Cleanthes to yield on certain points to which he formerly held, and it shows that Cleanthes realizes those elements within his position which Philo has not yet attacked successfully. It is clear that Cleanthes realizes that Philo has not yet succeeded in attacking his characterization of design in the world and the manner in which he regards this characterization to support his claim of an intelligent designer, namely, that the mere presence of means to ends relations and a coherence of parts in machines and the world countenances reasoning analogically to an intelligent designer for the world. Along with this, of course, goes Cleanthes' belief that Philo has not shown that natural theology cannot be founded on the principle 'Like effects prove like causes'. What Cleanthes must be willing to give up in the light of Philo's *reductio* is that the Design Argument establishes that the designer of the world is finite.[2] For, without the finitude claim, Philo's *reductio* is eliminated. The final paragraph in Part V reveals no adamancy on Cleanthes' part to retain the finitude claim. (Further evidence of Cleanthes' willingness to give up the claim of the finitude of the deity can be obtained by examining Parts X and XI. In Part X, Philo undertakes an examination as to whether the design of the

---

[1] D. 169
[2] That Cleanthes does want to hold to a finite deity was shown in the previous chapter of this book.

world can be explained if we assume that God possesses benevolence and infinite power. While the examination is proceeding, Cleanthes appears willing to accept the hypothesis of an infinite deity. It is only when Philo shows that the hypothesis of an infinite deity possessing moral attributes similar to ours fails to account for the design of the world as we find it, that Cleanthes (at the beginning of Part XI) reintroduces the hypothesis of a finite deity to determine whether a deity who is finite and benevolent can account for the good and evil in the world. Quite obviously, therefore, Cleanthes in Part X, did not bring with him his earlier belief in a finite deity. When Cleanthes makes reference to a finite deity in Part XI, he does so in the context of putting forth an hypothesis to account for the presence of good and evil in the world, rather than as a conclusion of the Argument from Design.)

The crucial challenge has now been presented to Philo: to establish the principle error in Cleanthes' position, insofar as the argument he advanced maintains that means to ends relations and a coherence of parts are always evidence of intelligent contrivance.

Philo begins his attack on this claim by introducing the principle "that where several known circumstances are observed to be similar the unknown will also be found similar".[3] Philo urges that this principle is similar to Cleanthes' principle 'Like effects prove like causes' in that it is "no less certain, and derived from the same source of experience". Cleanthes' principle is concerned with making causal inferences, given specific resemblances in the effects observed. Philo's principle, on the other hand, is not a principle enabling us to make causal inferences. Just what Philo intends by his principle can be learned from the particular examples he offers of the employment of the principle:

Thus, if we see the limbs of a human body, we conclude, that it is also attended with a human head, though hid from us. Thus, if we see, through a chink in a wall, a small part of the sun, we conclude, that were the wall removed, we should see the whole body.[4]

In both examples, there is a concern with inferring something to be co-present with what is being observed, based on our past experience of such items being co-present. Philo maintains that the principle of co-existence is at least as certain as Cleanthes' principle 'Like effects prove like causes', since both principles derive their level of certainty from the same source – the observation of constant conjunction. The principle of co-existence requires that the observations obtained bear a specific resemblence to portions of objects (Philo's examples are confined to natural objects) previously observed. What the principle countenances is an inference to those portions

[3] D. 170
[4] D. 170

of that type of object which cannot be observed. If the principle countenances such inferences, then it must also countenance inferring that the observations obtained are those of an object of a certain sort. The usefulness of the Principle of Co-existence can therefore be stated in two ways: given the appropriate constant conjunction, the Principle of Co-Existence enables us to infer the presence of an object of a certain sort, or the presence of the unobserved portion of that sort of object.

I now proceed to Philo's employment of this principle against Cleanthes' position. Philo argues:

Now if we survey the universe, so far as it falls under our knowledge, it bears a great resemblance to an animal or organized body, and seems actuated with a like principle of life and motion. A continual circulation of matter in it produces no disorder: A continual waste in every part is incessantly repaired: The closest sympathy is perceived throughout the entire system: And each part or member, in performing its proper offices, operates both to its own preservation and to that of the whole. The world, therefore, I infer is an animal, and the Deity is the soul of the world, actuating it, and actuated by it.[5]

Allowing A, B, C, and D to stand for the four characteristics which the world has in common with an animal or organized body, Philo's argument can be stated as follows:

I   A, B, C, and D have been found by experience to be characteristics of animals. The world possesses A, B, C, and D. Therefore, from the Principle of Co-Existence it follows that the world is an animal.

II   A, B, C, and D have been found by experience to be joined to mind. The world has A, B, C, and D. Therefore, from the Principle of Co-Existence it follows that the world is joined to a mind.

Cleanthes uses the Principle of Co-Existence to take issue with Philo's argument:

... [I]t seems to me that, though the world does, in many circumstances, resemble an animal body; yet is the analogy also defective in many circumstances, the most material: No organs of sense; no seat of thought or reason; no one precise origin of motion and action. In short, it seems to bear a stronger resemblance to a vegetable than to an animal; and your inference would be so far inconclusive in favour of the soul of the world.[6]

Commentators are in general agreement that the concession by Cleanthes, that the world bears a greater resemblance to an organism than to a machine, effectively destroys his case regarding an intelligent cause of design for the

[5]   D. 170–171
[6]   D. 172

world. However, in the light of our previous discussion on the Vegetable Library analogy, it is clear that his position cannot yet be taken as refuted, inasmuch as he concedes that organisms have, as their immediate cause, internal unintelligent designing principles, but insists that the original cause of organisms is intelligence. Hence, he believes his anthropomorphism to be secure, regardless of whether the design of the world resembles the design of machines or the design of organisms.

At the beginning of Part VII, Philo inquires into the cause of the design of the world in the light of his examination in Part VI which sought to establish that the world is an organism. He prefaces his inquiry by indicating that his argument will destroy almost entirely Cleanthes' position:

But here, continued Philo, in examining the ancient system of the soul of the world, there strikes me, all on a sudden, a new idea, which, if just, must go near to subvert all your reasoning, and destroy even your first inferences, on which you repose such confidence.[8]

He goes on to argue:

If the universe bears a greater likeness to animal bodies and to vegetables, than to the works of human art; it is more probable that its cause resembles the cause of the former than that of the latter, and its origin ought rather to be ascribed to generation or vegetation than to reason or design. Your conclusion, even according to your own principles, is therefore lame and defective.[9]

This passage, and the preceding one, raise certain problems: (1) In the preceding passage, Philo indicates that his argument will 'go near' to subvert all Cleanthes' reasoning, but he does not specify just what part of Cleanthes' position this argument does not reach. (2) In the last passage quoted, Philo concludes that Cleanthes' conclusion is 'lame and defective' and this obtains 'even according to Cleanthes' own principles'. Nevertheless, Philo does not tell us which of Cleanthes' principles are involved. (3) Philo's argument begins with the claim that the universe bears 'a greater likeness' to animals and vegetables than to machines, and this raises two further questions: (a) what evidence does Philo offer for this claim? and (b) does Philo intend that the greater likeness in the case of the world and organisms gives his conclusion, that the cause of the design of the world resembles generation or vegetation, more plausibility than Cleanthes' conclusion that the cause of the design of the world resembles human intelligence?

We can begin by addressing the questions raised in (3) above. That the universe bears a greater resemblance to animals and vegetables than to machines is asserted by Philo in three different passages – p. 176, five lines

[7]   See, for example, Nathan in the Chappell volume, p. 412.
[8]   D. 176
[9]   D. 176

from the top; p. 176, fifth line from the bottom of the page; p. 171, the first new paragraph on the page. Hence, it is a claim which must be taken seriously. The evidence for this claim is difficult to determine. That the world resembles an organism is based on the Principle of Co-Existence. But this, by itself, does not establish that the resemblance is greater with respect to organisms than it is with respect to machines. To substantiate his position, Philo must show either that the very evidence employed by Cleanthes in his argument to establish that the world resembles a machine is in fact more supportive of Philo's claim that the world resembles an organism, or he must show that the data he has offered in support of his position are (in some sense) superior to the data employed by Cleanthes to support the intelligence claim.

Cleanthes' sole basis for arguing an intelligent cause of design for the world is the presence of means to ends relations and a coherence of parts. Now, each of the characteristics cited by Philo as evidence that the world resembles an organism is reducible to these very features: the first, third, and fourth characteristics[10] are clear cases of means to ends relations and a coherence of parts, while the second – a continual waste in every part is incessantly repaired – is nothing but a display of means to ends relations. Philo makes the point that the four features cited in support of the world-as-an-organism hypothesis are gained by surveying the universe "so far as it falls under our knowledge" (D.170), thereby indicating that these are characteristics which are confirmed by scientific investigation.

Cleanthes insisted that they proceed scientifically. Philo insists that investigating the world scientifically reveals some resemblances between the world and organisms – resemblances which have their basis in the means to ends relations and coherence of parts which are discovered. This gives us the insight we require to determine why Philo believes that the resemblance between the design of the world and organisms is greater than that between the world and machines: whereas scientific investigation reveals *specific* similarities between the world and organisms in terms of the means to ends relations and coherence of parts which are found, no comparable specific similarities based on these features are found by science between the world and machines. That science cannot establish that the world resembles a machine was the very point Philo had urged in the first four paragraphs of Part V. In Parts VI and VII, he elaborates on this through the Principle of Co-Existence, that is, the particular means to ends relations and coherence of parts in the design of the world appear to allow for the classification of the world as an organism, whereas no comparable classification of the world as

---

[10] "a continual circulation of matter in it produces no disorder"; "the closest sympathy is perceived throughout the entire system"; "each part or member, in performing its proper offices, operates both to its own preservation and to that of the whole".

a machine is countenanced through this Principle (or for that matter through any other principle of inference). It should also be recalled that at the end of Part V, Cleanthes challenged Philo by urging that nothing which Philo has argued refutes 'the hypothesis of design' in the universe, and that this – which amounts to the presence of means to ends relations and a coherence of parts – he regards 'as a sufficient foundation for religion'. It is entirely reasonable for Philo to address this challenge by showing that the very features of design cited by Cleanthes are, in fact, more supportive of the view of the world as an organism than they are of Cleanthes' view of the world as a machine.

I now turn to the second part of question 3, namely, should Philo be regarded as believing that the claim that the design of the world arose from generation or vegetation is more acceptable (in terms of the evidence provided) than Cleanthes' hypothesis of design? Philo does appear to be maintaining that his argument is stronger than Cleanthes' Design Argument:

...[T]here are other parts of the universe (besides the machines of human invention) which bear still a greater resemblance to the fabric of the world, and which therefore afford a better conjecture concerning the universal origin of this system. These parts are animals and vegetables. The world plainly resembles more an animal or a vegetable, than it does a watch or a knitting-loom. Its cause, therefore, it is more probable, resembles the cause of the former. The cause of the former is generation or vegetation. The cause, therefore, of the world, we may infer to be something similar or analogous to generation or vegetation".[11]

In another passage, however, he explains precisely how the superiority of his position over Cleanthes' is to be understood. His account is offered while replying to a question raised by Demea: the latter asks "Is the slight imaginary resemblance of the world to a vegetable or an animal sufficient to establish the same inference with regard to both objects, which are in general so widely different; ought they to be a standard for each other?"[12] And Philo replies:

Right ... This is the topic on which I have all along insisted. I have still asserted, that we have no *data* to establish any system of cosmogony. Our experience, so imperfect in itself, and so limited both in extent and duration, can afford us no probable conjecture concerning the whole of things. But if we must needs fix on some hypothesis; by what rule, pray, ought we to determine our choice? Is there any other rule than the greater similarity of the objects compared? And does not a plant or an animal, which springs from vegetation or generation, bear a stronger resemblance to the world, than does any artificial machine, which arises from reason and design?.[13]

Philo is asserting (a) that, strictly speaking, evidence for classifying the world in order to enable us to infer its cause of design is not available; and (b) but if, in the face of this absence of adequate evidence to classify the world, we

[11] D. 176–177
[12] D. 177
[13] D. 177

persist in forming hypotheses about it, then we should opt for that hypothesis which is based on the strongest resemblance between the world and certain items found in the world. Hence, since the world bears a stronger resemblance to an organism than it does to a machine, the machine hypothesis must be rejected. Philo holds that neither position is actually tenable; but if we are forced to choose, our selection should be guided by what it is that the world most closely resembles.

By examining the world we find that it bears some resemblances to an animal or vegetable, but not enough to justify classifying it as one or the other. Philo does not enumerate what other characteristics the world would have to possess to justify classifying it as an organism. However, from other things which he says, we can understand why such a list is not included. In Part II, Philo expressed misgivings about Cleanthes' position, partly because he saw no justification for concluding that thought is the productive principle of the whole world, simply because it is a productive principle in parts of the world: there are other productive principles as well, and Philo was at a loss to know how they are to be ruled out. In Parts VI and VII the discussion centers around means to ends relations and a coherence of parts which are found in organisms, and which originate from generation and vegetation. Hence, the mere presence of these characteristics does not guarantee that the productive principle involved is thought. Other principles may also be responsible for design which manifests these characteristics:

In this little corner of the world alone, there are four principles, *reason, instinct, generation, vegetation*, which are similar to each other, and are the causes of similar effects ... Any one of these four principles above mentioned (and a hundred others which lie open to our conjecture) may afford us a theory, by which to judge of the origin of the world; and it is a palpable and egregious partiality, to confine our view entirely to that principle, by which our own minds operate".[14]

We also know how Philo (and Hume) hold that the productive principle can be inferred and others ruled out: we must find a close correspondence (or specific resemblance) between the features exhibited by the object in question, and other objects whose cause is known; it is this which provides for the proper employment of the principle 'Like effects prove like causes'. In short, for Philo, the concern in causal reasoning is with classification at the level of species.[15] And no classification of the world with respect to species is possible, because of the absence of the relevant (specific) resemblance between the design of the world and known species of objects. If this classification

---

[14]   D. 178
[15]   "when two species of objects have always been observed to be conjoined together, I can infer, by custom, the existence of one whenever I see the existence of the other". (D. 149)

according to species is not forthcoming, then a classification according to genus is not permissible. This, then, explains why Philo does not provide a list of features which, if exhibited by the world, would enable us to classify it as an organism: the only lists of features which are relevant are those pertaining to species of objects, and there is no species within the world to which the world bears so close a resemblance that it can be regarded as another member of that species.

It might be objected here that Philo could, or should, nevertheless, have provided a list of features which would enable a generic classification of the world, e.g. as an organism, since for objects to be considered a species of a given genus, certain common features must be posited in the generic classification. On this account, even if we could not determine the kind of organism the world is, or most closely resembles, and even if it is the only instance of a particular species of organism, it may yet have enough in common with all other organisms to allow for a generic classification as an organism. Hence, a list of features still seems appropriate.

The issue to be raised is how Philo believes the question of the generic classification of the world is to be settled, if it cannot be approached through its connection with a known species. In such cases, the generic classification can be settled only through a familiarity with the cause of design. Given that the world exhibits all the features singled out by Philo in Part VI, and granting that its cause of design is generation or vegetation, than it can be classified as an organism. However, the cause of design of the world is precisely the issue which Philo and Cleanthes are attempting to settle. Therefore, if the world cannot be classified under a known species, it cannot be given a generic classification either.

Philo's employment of the Principle of Co-existence, therefore, is defective, since he violates his own teaching that a generic classification, when it cannot be based on a familiarity with the cause of design, must proceed through a classification according to species. In the case of the world, this cannot be done. Our discussion above makes it clear that Philo is aware that his argument in Parts VI and VII is, strictly speaking, unacceptable. We will shortly examine why, despite this awareness on his part, he persists in his argument.

The second question I raised earlier concerned the fact that in arguing to generation or vegetation as the cause of the design world, Philo concludes that Cleanthes' conclusion is lame and defective, "even according to your own principles". Philo is, therefore, maintaining that he has argued here against Cleanthes by employing the principles used by Cleanthes. Which principles does he have in mind? Now, the term 'principle' is variously employed within the *Dialogues*. This much however, is clear: whenever either Philo or Cleanthes uses this term, the referent is held to possess a guiding function.

Accordingly, human reason (p. 139), thought, heat, and cold (p. 147) atheism and scepticism (p. 139) are all spoken of as principles. Since the concern in Philo's argument in Parts VI and VII is with establishing a more probable conjecture regarding the cause of the design of the world than is attainable from Cleanthes' argument, the 'principles' he has in mind must be those utilized by Cleanthes in the Argument from Design, i.e. the meaning of 'principles' here must be 'inference-guiding'. Philo's argument to establish generation or vegetation as the cause of the design of the world in Part VII is based on the principle 'Like effects prove like causes'. In the second paragraph of Part VI, Philo refers to 'Like effects prove like causes' as the principle which Cleanthes supposes to be the foundation of all religion. Since Cleanthes' Design Argument is also based on this principle, it must be one of those to which Philo is referring.

In Part VII Philo urges that causal knowledge regarding animals and vegetables is as certain as that pertaining to machines: "... when I see an animal, I infer, that it sprang from generation; and that with as great certainty as you conclude a house to have been reared by design".[16] But we also know that he holds that all causal knowledge must be based on the observation of constant conjunction. I submit, therefore, that given the sense of principle as a rule by which to draw inferences, the rule to judge what causes what through the observation of constant conjuction must also be one of the principles being referred to by Philo in the passage under consideration. Philo insists that when we argue to the cause of the design of the world, we find that thought has no advantage either through the Principle 'Like effects prove like causes' (since the world looks more like an organism than a machine) or through the principle enjoining experience or the observation of objects constantly conjoined as the means of determining what causes what.

Granting that Philo's concern in Part VII with 'principles' is a concern with rules for drawing inferences, it can be shown that the two 'principles' which I have discussed are the only ones with which Philo is dealing. In Part II, Philo singles out these two as the only rules of inference relevant to Cleanthes' argument: "That all inferences, Cleanthes, concerning fact, are founded on experience, and that all experimental reasonings are founded on the supposition, that similar causes prove similar effects, and similar effects similar causes: I shall not, at present, much dispute with you" (D. 147). Also, in the second version of the Argument from Design (p. 145–146) where the inference-guiding rules are made explicit, only the two I have discussed are mentioned.

In Part VI, Philo employs the Principle of Co-existence to argue that the world is an organism, and, as we have seen, he understands that his procedure

---

[16]   D. 178

violates the very lesson which he is attempting to get Cleanthes to grasp. Nevertheless, we can now understand why he argues as he does, even though his reasoning is defective: through his employment of the Principle of Co-existence, he is illustrating the *correct approach* to providing the Argument from Design with premises. And this requires that the classification of the world under a known species *precede* the use of the principle 'Like effects prove like causes'. It is important to realize, therefore, that Philo is not simply providing a counter argument to Cleanthes' Argument. Philo is illustrating how Cleanthes ought to have begun his inquiry, namely, through attempting to classify the world, rather than by beginning with the (unwarranted) assumption that machines of human contrivance provide the paradigm for all causal inferences where the effect displays means to ends relations and a coherence of parts.

Philo's argument against Cleanthes which has been examined above goes near to subverting all Cleanthes' reasoning. I now turn to the first question raised earlier: determining that part of Cleanthes' position which Philo's argument does not reach.

It is clear that in Parts VI and VII Philo has effectively destroyed Cleanthes' efforts within the Argument from Design itself to establish the legitimacy of a causal inference to an intelligent designer merely through the presence of means to ends relations and a coherence of parts. The issue of classification shows Cleanthes' procedure in the argument to be defective. From our treatment of the Articulate Voice, it can now be established that this illustrative analogy is without force in strengthening Cleanthes' position. The means to ends relations and coherence of parts apprehended in what is heard from the clouds are precisely what justify an inference to the belief that what is heard is a voice. With this classification and our knowledge of the cause of voices, we are justified in concluding that the cause of what is heard from the clouds in intelligence. However, since a similar classification of the world as a machine on the basis of the means to ends relations and coherence of parts which we find is not possible, it follows that the Voice Analogy is not helpful in illustrating Cleanthes' position. The Voice analogy does, in fact, illustrate Philo's claim that, unless the features of design exhibited allow a proper classification of what is being observed under a known species, an inference to the cause of design is not justified.

Philo has succeeded in showing that a classification of the world which would allow the use of the principle 'Like effects prove like causes' cannot be accomplished. And in this respect Cleanthes' efforts have failed. But what Philo has conceded is that if we still persist in our efforts at classification, then "Is there any other rule than the greater similarity of the objects compared?", and on this method of proceeding, we find that the world bears a stronger resemblance to a plant or animal than it does to a machine (D. 177). What

Philo must now show is that even if this is the most convincing claim we can make about the nature of the world, it will not assist Cleanthes in seeking to establish that the cause of the design of the world is an intelligent being. We know that Cleanthes is not bothered by a classification of the world as an organism: in the Vegetable Library analogy, he argued that when reasoning by analogy about the cause of the design of the Vegetable Library, we must acknowledge that only intelligence, posited as the *original* cause of the Vegetable Library, can adequately explain the activities and design of the vegetable volumes. Both the activities of the volumes and their particular design exhibit means to ends relations and a coherence of parts, and to the extent that any organism displays these features, the same orignal cause must be posited. It is at this point, therefore, that Philo must address the second of Cleanthes' illustrative analogies. This, then, is (at least part of) what Philo's argument has thus far not challenged.

That Philo is about to address the Vegetable Library analogy can be learned from the fact that the central claim of that analogy is reintroduced in Part VII as a challenge to Philo:

But methinks, said Demea, if the world had a vegetative quality, and could sow the seeds of new worlds into the infinite chaos, the power would be still an additional argument for design in its Author. For where could arise so wonderful a faculty but from design? Or how can order spring from any thing, which perceives not that order which it bestows?[17]

Philo's answer is given in two parts, and his answer addresses two inconsistent positions adopted earlier by Cleanthes.

At times, Cleanthes insists that the immediate cause which experience discloses for a particular phenomenon should be regarded as a satisfactory causal account for that phenomenon, even though we are unable to trace that cause further back to its cause, and so on. This is particularly evident in Part IV, when Cleanthes is confronted with the cause of the ideas in God's mind.

Even in common life, if I assign a cause for any event; is it any objection, Philo, that I cannot assign the cause of that cause, and answer every new question, which may incessantly be started? And what philosophers could possibly submit to so rigid a rule? philosophers, who confess ultimate causes to be totally unknown, and are sensible, that the most refined principles, into which they trace the phenomena, are still to them as inexplicable as these phenomena themselves are to the vulgar. The order and arrangement of nature, the curious adjustment of final causes, the plain use and intention of every part and organ; all these bespeak in the clearest language an intelligent cause or Author. The heavens and the earth join in the same testimony: The whole chorus of nature raises one hymn to the praises of its Creator: You alone, or almost alone, disturb this general harmony. You start abstruse doubts, cavils, and objections: You ask me, what is the cause of this cause? I know not; I care not; that concerns not me. I have found a Deity; and here I stop my enquiry. Let those go farther, who are wiser or more enterprising.[18]

---

[17] D. 178–179
[18] D. 163

Now, to the extent that this is Cleanthes' position, Philo urges that vegetation and generation must be accepted as the causes of organisms, and therefore, as the causes of the organic library, since these are the designing principles which are found constantly conjoined with the resultant organisms. Experience discloses that design (means to ends relations and a coherence of parts) can orginate from non-intelligent sources:

A tree bestows order and organization on that tree which springs from it, without knowing the order: an animal, in the same manner, on its offspring: a bird, on its nest: And instances of this kind are even more frequent in the world, than those of order, which arise from reason and contrivance.[19]

Philo correctly points out that if, in the case of organisms, the immediate cause is not regarded as providing an adequate causal account – a position Cleanthes maintained when putting forth the Vegetable Library analogy – and an intelligent original cause is posited, then we have begged the question. Philo explains this in the following way:

To say that all this order in animals and vegetables proceeds ultimately from design is begging the question; nor can that great point be ascertained otherwise than by proving *a priori*, both that order is, from its nature, inseparably attached to thought, and that it can never, of itself, or from original unknown principles, belong to matter.[20]

Cleanthes has insisted throughout that support for hypotheses be sought within experience. In his discussion of the organic library, he also insisted that the ultimate cause of the organic volumes be sought. It is Philo's answer to this line of inquiry which constitutes the second part of his answer to the Vegetable Library analogy.

Philo argues that once the question of ultimate causes is raised, Cleanthes will find that his reasoning has no empirical support:

Judging by our limited and imperfect experience, generation has some privileges above reason: For we see every day the latter arise from the former, never the former from the latter.[21]

Again, in the next paragraph Philo points out that "reason, in innumerable instances, is observed to arise from the principle of generation, and never to arise from any other principle".

If Cleanthes insists on seeking an ultimate cause, the problems which arise are clear: if we begin with the view of the world as an organism, there is no support in experience for an intelligent original cause, and if we begin with the world as a machine, there is some support for the claim that it ultimately arose from generation. Therefore, on this mode of proceeding, Cleanthes

[19] D. 179
[20] D. 179
[21] D. 180

either can have no support for his intelligence claim, or an ultimate cause (generation/vegetation) which cannot serve his purpose.

Ultimately, therefore, Philo confronts Cleanthes with a dilemma from which he believes Cleanthes cannot escape – a dilemma which is based on Cleanthes' two assertions, namely, that a satisfactory causal account can be obtained from the immediate cause, and that a satisfactory causal account can be obtained only by tracing the phenomenon back to an ultimate or original cause.

At this stage, therefore, – the end of Part VII – Philo has effectively destroyed any plausibility in Cleanthes' position, insofar as the latter holds that we can reason analogically to an intelligent cause for the design of the world. Philo's success covers the Argument from Design as well as Cleanthes' two illustartive analogies. Cleanthes finds that he has no answer to any of the objections raisd by Philo. At the end of Part VII, Cleanthes says:

I must confess, Philo, replied Cleanthes, that of all men living, the task which you have undertaken, of raising doubts and objections, suits you best, and seems, in a manner, natural and unavoidable to you. So great is your fertility of invention, that I am not ashamed to acknowledge myself unable, in a sudden, to solve regularly such out-of-the way difficulties as you incessantly start upon me: Though I clearly see, in general, their fallacy and error. And I question not, but you are yourself, at present, in the same case, and have not the solution so ready as the objection; while you must be sensible, that common sense and reason is entirely against you, and that such whimsies as you have delivered, may puzzle, but never can convince us".[22]

It seems appropriate, therefore, that Philo's critique should cease with Part VII. In Part VIII, however, we find him continuing his attack on Cleanthes' position: Philo prefaces his remarks in this section by addressing Cleanthes' claim that the doubts and objections which Philo has raised are 'natural and unavoidable' given his 'fertility of invention':

What you ascribe to the fertility of my invention, replied Philo, is entirely owing to the nature of the subject. In subjects adapted to the narrow compass of human reason, there is commonly but one determination, which carries probability or conviction with it; and to a man of sound judgment, all other suppositions, but that one, appear entirely absurd and chimerical. But in such questions as the present, a hundred contradictory views may preserve a kind of imperfect analogy: and invention has here full scope to exert itself.[23]

What Philo has yet to show is the extent to which we can be sceptical in trying to understand the nature of God.

If we proceed as Philo has done in Parts VI and VII, then we must allow that, since a proper classification of the world according to species is not possible, the design of the world could have resulted from generation, vegetation, instinct, or reason, inasmuch as each is capable of bringing about

[22]   D. 181
[23]   D. 182

design exhibiting means to ends relations and a coherence of parts. Hence, the impression might have been given by Philo at the end of Part VII that, although the analysis is inadequate for the reasons Philo set out, the list of principles from which the design of the world originated has but four (serious) candidates. Therefore, it might seem that the list of candidates is of determinate length, and that we can conclude – to the extent that any knowledge of God is possible – that the cause of the design of the world resembles one (or more) of these principles. Part VIII reveals that Philo is intent on proving that our scepticism can be extended well beyond what was argued up to Part VII, with the result that the list of candidates shown to be capable of designing the world is open-ended. In this way, he shows that there is no justification for confining the list to a determinate number of candidates.

The second way in which Philo will seek to prove that our scepticism can be extended beyond the discussion in Part VII concerns the matter of an ultimate cause. Thus far we have seen that to the extent that experience offers any data in regard to ultimate causes, we learn that intelligence arises from generation, while generation is never observed to arise from intelligence. (Philo could have added that instinct is also observed to arise from generation.) Therefore, when inquiring into an ultimate cause for the design of the world, the list of candidates is even smaller than the list of candidates dealing with the immediate cause of the design of the world: reason and instinct are both found to arise from generation, while generation and vegetation arise from other instances of reason and vegetation. In Part VIII Philo will argue that, when reasoning by analogy, we cannot confine our list of ultimate principles to generation and vegetation. The list of ultimate principles will also be seen to be open-ended. Also, in some instances, experience will disclose no support for explanation through an ultimate cause.

I now turn to Part VIII to examine Philo's manner of extending scepticism beyond any determinate list of designing principles.

He begins with the 'old Epicurean hypothesis':

This is commonly, and I believe, justly, esteemed the most absurd system, that has yet been proposed; yet I know not, whether, with a few alterations, it might not be brought to bear some faint appearance of probability. Instead of supposing matter infinite, as Epicurus did; let us suppose it finite. A finite number of particles is only susceptible of finite transpositions: And it must happen, in an eternal duration, that every possible order or position must be tried an infinite number of times. The world, therefore, with all its events, even the most minute, has before been produced and destroyed, and will again be produced and destroyed, without any bounds and limitations. No one, who has a conception of the powers of the infinite, in comparison of finite, will ever scruple this determination.[24]

---

[24]   D. 182

Demea immediately inquires whether we are justified in accepting an account of matter in motion which yields means to ends reations and a coherence of parts, but which omits all reference to a 'voluntary agent or first mover'. Philo assures Demea that experience itself discloses that matter can acquire motion without a known voluntary agent or first mover:

And where is the difficulty, replied Philo, of that supposition .. Motion, in many instances, from gravity, from elasticity, begins in matter, without any known voluntary agent; and to suppose always, in these cases, an unknown voluntary agent, is mere hypothesis; and hypothesis attended with no advantages. The beginning of motion in matter is as conceivable *a priori* as its communication from mind and intelligence.[25]

The fact that motion in matter can be brought about through non-intelligent causes does not prove that such causes have the capacity to generate the design which we find the world. It might seem, therefore, that when Hume proposes 'other systems of cosmogony' in Part VIII, he is relying on his position, developed from his analysis of causality, that *a priori* anything may cause anything. And this might appear appropriate since 'worlds have never been formed under our eyes'. Leon Pearl reads Philo's efforts in Part VIII in this manner, and urges that this procedure cannot be held to be an effective argument against Cleanthes:

Unlike the position that the world is a living organism, the above is in broad outline an explanatory hypothesis for the fact that the world is an orderly system. But why should this hypothesis be considered as good or better than that of design? Hume introduces it as possibly true. But 'possibly' in what sense? *A priori*? But in that case Hume's point would have no bearing on the argument from design; since the argument did not consist in a logical deduction of a world designer from the fact that the world exhibits order. The possibility, if it is to undermine the design argument, must be grounded like the design argument, on experience. The issue turns on the question: Is the Epicurean hypothesis empirically at least as well grounded as that of design? And the answer Hume should have given is that it is not. Unlike design, Hume simply did not have a known sample of objects exhibiting order which originated in accordance with the Epicurean hypothesis.[26]

I now propose to show that this reading of Part VIII is incorrrect. To do this, I will focus on Pearl's claim that the Epicurean hypothesis is offered as an *a priori* possibility, and show that this is not Philo's basis for the hypothesis: Philo holds that the Epicurean hypothesis can be stated in such a manner that it is at least as well grounded as the Design Hypothesis. Therefore, there is – to use Leon Pearl's words – ' a known sample of objects exhibiting order which orignated in accordance with the Epicurean hypothesis'.

That Philo believes he is proceeding empirically in a manner analogous to the Design Argument is learned from the opening paragraph in Part VIII

[25]   D. 182–183
[26]   Leon Pearl, "Hume's Criticism of the Design Argument", The *Monist* 54, 1970. p. 283.

wherein he claims the 'in such questions as the present, a hundred contradictory views may preserve a kind of imperfect analogy' and that he could 'propose other systems of cosmogony, which would have *some faint appearance of truth*' (italics added). However, this does not, of course, establish that he does offer hypotheses which rival the Design Argument. A close study of the text reveals that Philo does exactly what he claims to be able to do.

Philo begins by calling upon our experience of the world to establish that matter always appears to us to be in motion:

And whatever the causes are, the fact is certain, that matter is, and always has been in continual agitation, as far as human experience or tradition reaches. There is not probably, at present, in the whole universe, one particle of matter at absolute rest.[27]

The opening words of this passage indicate that our experience is too limited to enable us to provide an exhaustive enumeration of the sources of motion in matter. Philo had earlier selected gravity, elasticity, and electricity, but he does not hold that there is evidence to support the claim that these are the only sources of motion in matter. The number of sources of motion in matter – actual or possible – Philo refuses to specify, given our limited experience of the world. And this – the absence of a definitive list of the sources of motion in matter – works to the advantage of scepticism. As we will see, Philo will argue that any source of motion in matter could have contributed to bringing about the present order. Further, since we lack a knowledge of all such sources of motion, Philo will argue his position through the presence of motion itself, without any reference to, or knowledge of, the actual causes of motion. In short, Philo will account for the order of the world through the mere presence of motion in matter – a feature of matter which appears to have no exceptions – without taking into account how matter acquired motion, and he will argue that his account possesses at least as much empirical support as the Argument from Design possesses.

Since he has already shown in Parts VI and VII that the means to ends relations and coherence of parts which we find do not allow us to classify the world (in any strict sense) according to a known species or genus, his concern in Part VIII need not, and, in fact, will not be to show additional known species to which the world bears some (imperfect) analogy. Part VIII is silent on the matter of such classifications, and, therefore, we can conclude that Philo believes that he has offered enough on this. As such, it becomes evident that Part VIII will not concern itself with *Cleanthes'* version of the Argument from Design – the first version presented in the *Dialogues*, p. 143 – wherein certain features that the world exhibits in its design are compared to the same

---

[27]   D. 183

features in machines of human contrivance. It will be recalled that Part II contained two versions of the Argument from Design: the second version (p. 145–146) is the one which avoids the concern with classification, and emphasizes that matter appears to be unable to arrange itself so as to form an object displaying means to ends relations and a coherence of parts, whereas we find that the human mind can arrange its own ideas so as to form the plan of objects possessing design. Part VIII, therefore, is largely concerned with this second version of the Argument from Design, and will show that experience supports the claim that design can arise in matter without an intelligent source of order.

The passage in the original argument where the issue of intelligence and matter as sources of design is brought up reads:

For aught we can know *a priori*, matter may contain the source or spring of order originally, within itself, as well as mind does; and there is no more difficulty in conceiving, that several elements, from an *internal unknown cause*, may fall into the most exquisite arrangement, than to conceive that their ideas, in the great universal mind, from a like *internal unknown cause*, fall into that arrangement. The equal possibility of both these suppositions is allowed.[28]

From the italicized portion of this passage we learn that no allowance is made for inquiring into the cause of the order exhibited in mind or matter: the extent of the inquiry is simply whether order can be observed to originate in each. The original argument claims that order can be observed to originate only in mind, not in matter (premise 5):

By experience we find (according to Cleanthes), that there is a difference between them. Throw several pieces of steel together, without shape or form; they will never arrange themselves so as to compose a watch: Stone, and mortar, and wood, without an architect, never erect a house. But the ideas in a human mind, we see, by an unknown, inexplicable oeconomy, arrange themselves so as to form the plan of a watch or house. Experience, therefore, proves, that there is an original principle of order in mind, not in matter.[29]

Therefore, if Philo can establish that order can be observed to originate in matter, he will have provided an alternative account to that in the original argument, which possesses at least as much empirical support as that argument possesses.

In arguing his case, Philo begins by asking: "Is there a system, an order, an oeconomy of things, by which matter can preserve that perpetual agitation, which seems essential to it, and yet mainatin a constancy in the forms, which it produces?" (D. 183). And he answers:

There certainly is such an oeconomy: For this is actually the case with the present world. The

---

[28] D. 146, my italics
[29] D. 146

continual motion of matter, therefore, in less than infinite transposistions must produce this oeconomy or order; and by its very nature, that order, when once established, supports itself, for many ages, if not to eternity.[30]

The preservation of the design brought about is explained through the presence of means to ends relations and a coherence of parts – the essential features of the design:

But wherever matter is so poised, arranged and adjusted as to continue in perpetual motion, and yet preserve a constancy in the forms, its situation must, of necessity, have all the same appearance of art and contrivance which we oberve at present. All the parts of each form must have a relation to each other, and to the whole: And the whole itself must have a relation to the other parts of the universe; to the element, in which the form subsists; to the materials, with which it repairs its waste and decay; and to every other form, which is hostile or friendly. A defect in any of these particulars destroys the form; and the matter, of which it is composed, is again set loose, and is set into irregular motions and fermentations, till it unite itself to some other regular form. If no such form be prepared to receive it, and if there be a great quantity of this corrupted matter in the universe, the universe itself is entirely disordered ... a chaos ensues, till finite, though innumerable revolutions produce at last some forms, whose parts and organs are so adjusted as to support the forms amidst a continual succession of matter.[31]

If Philo had offered no more than this in defense of his competing hypothesis in Part VIII, then Leon Pearl's claim would be correct, for Philo would be offering this position *a priori*: since worlds have not been formed under his eyes, he has no waying of knowing, through experience, that this account is accurate, namely, that order can originate in matter.

But this is not all that Philo offers. Philo does find empirical evidence that order can originate through matter in motion without an intelligent designer.

It is in vain, therefore, to insist upon the uses of the parts in animals or vegetables, and their curious adjustment to each other. I would fain know how an animal could subsist, unless its parts were so adjusted? Do we not find, that it immediately perishes whenever this adjustment ceases, and that its matter corrupting tries some new form? It happens, indeed, that the parts of the world are so well adjusted, that some regular form immediately lays claim to this corrupted matter: And if it were not so, could the world subsist? Must it not dissolve as well as the animal, and pass through new positions and situations; till in a great, but finite succession, it falls at last into the present or some such order?[32]

The relevant experience (or analogy) has been found in the matter of organisms which both exhibits design, and which, upon the destruction of the particular form, 'tries some new form'. According to Philo, the behaviour of matter from which organisms are formed is typical of what is observed to be the case with matter generally. Wherever matter is so arranged that an

[30] D. 183
[31] D. 183–184
[32] D. 185

adjustment of means to ends results, the arrangement has a tendency to self-preservation (an expression used one page earlier, D. 184); wherever the adjustment of means to ends is disturbed, the arrangement has a tendency to self-destruction; and wherever the destruction of such an arrangement occurs, the 'corrupted matter' continues on until it becomes part of another adjustment of means to ends relations. In short, experience discloses that design can originate in matter in motion in addition to (what was never disputed by Philo) intelligence.

Besides offering a counter claim to the fifth premise in the second version of the Argument from Design, the last passage quoted establishes that there are no general characteristics by which we can determine whether order originated in mind or in matter: the very features which Cleanthes regards as evidence of design originating from mind – means to ends relations and a coherence of parts – are seen to be a feature of all design, regardless of origin, inasmuch as without these features no design can exist. Without the presence of means to ends relations and a coherence of parts, no design can come into existence or continue to exist, whereas with these features the design has a tendency to self-preservation. Accordingly, both mind and matter are bound by the same conditions in yielding design.

From Philo's argument in Part VIII, we learn that any source of motion in matter could have originated the present order, and, therefore, it is in vain to attempt to provide a determinate list of principles through which the world could have achieved its design. But Philo is saying much more than that a determinate list of designing *principles* is not obtainable. Given that matter is always in motion, and that stability in arrangement depends only on matter achieving an adaptation of means to ends and coherence of parts, what appears to be the result of some designing principle may, in fact, originate in a 'blind unguided force'. A designing principle for Hume is a force – albeit one whose essence is unknown by us – which, when exerted, is disposed to produce effects of a certain type. A blind unguided force, on the other hand, would be one which also causes motion in matter, but it would not, each time it is exerted, be disposed to produce effects of a certain type. Philo's point is that even if matter were set in motion by a blind unguided force, a stability in arrangement would be reached once the parts of matter achieved means to ends relations and a coherence of parts. Hence, the design of the world could appear to be the result of a designing principle, either in mind or matter, and actually stem from a force which has no disposition or tendency to design at all. Therefore, what Philo is challenging in Part VIII is not only the view that means to ends relations and a coherence of parts are evidence of mind as the principle of design; he is also challenging a datum accepted by Cleanthes, namely, that design is evidence of a *principle* of design. Philo urges that given the manner in which matter is found to behave in terms of design coming into existence, passing out of existence, and abiding, the design of the world can be accounted for (at least as well as the Design Argument is able to do so) without reference to a principle of design. Hence, the plausibility of the Epicurean account as Philo restates it.[33] Accordingly, we cannot even decide whether the present order originates from a designing principle or a blind unguided force in matter: the present order is compatible with both alternatives and appears to support both equally. (The mysteriousness of the causes of order in mind and in matter has already been discussed by Philo in Part IV of the *Dialogues*, p. 162–163).

In the account of matter in which there is no employment of designing principles in explaining the present order, it must also be the case that the regularities which are observed within the world, from which the account of the design of the whole world is fashioned, are to be explained without reference to principles of design. All generation, stability, and decay of forms may be the result of an arrangement which all matter has assumed, which permits the present order to continue, but which has not been achieved through any designing principles. This explains why, in delivering his version of the Epicurean hypothesis, no reference whatever is made to designing principles –either with regard to the whole world or within the world. The distinction between principles of order and forces generating motion in matter is, therefore, understood not to be one which can be made simply through an examination of the effects – even when generation and decay are observed to occur in a regular manner. This, of course, stems from our complete ignorance of principles and forces, and is not a position adopted by common sense. Common sense will always treat regularities in nature as resulting from certain principles of order. The sceptic, however, can exploit our ignorance of principles of design in nature, and provide an account of design which omits all reference to these principles.

Given that the sceptic is able to attack one of the data of the Design Argument, namely, that design is evidence of a principle of design, Philo is able to complete his sceptical attack on this argument, inasmuch as he is able to challenge the principle 'Like effects prove like causes' (premise 11) and the principle enjoining the observation of constant conjunction as the guide to causal knowledge (premise 1). The principle regarding constant conjunction assumes that observed regularities are evidence of a power in one object to bring about the observed effect in the second; and the principle 'Like effects prove like causes' assumes that where effects are similar, we are entitled to infer similar principles of order or guides for matter as their cause. However, on the Epicurean account which Philo offers in Part VIII, both are challenged: observed regularities in nature are not regarded as evidence of a

[33] See D. 184–85

power in one object to bring about the effects observed in the one regularly conjoined with it, and similar effects are not taken as evidence of similar principles of order in objects which bring them about. The regularities and similarities observed are all accounted for through the adaptation of means to ends and coherence of parts which matter has achieved in accordance with the tendency we observe in matter to hold forms achieving such adaptations, and the tendency of matter to arrange itself so as to accomodate all matter when a particular form is upset. Hence, on the Epicurean hypothesis, no object is accurately called a 'cause' of another, and similar effects are not actually the products of similar *principles* of order. Once the use which Cleanthes makes of these principles is challenged by the Epicurean hypothesis, we are made to see that Philo's objections to the Design Argument go beyond the particular principle of order for which Cleanthes' has argued, and include any principle of order which we might select. The order of the world may have resulted from a designing principle or it may not have so resulted, and Philo's point is that we cannot, on the basis of data available, decide between these.[34]

I mentioned earlier that part of Philo's effort in Part VIII will be to deal with the question of an ultimate cause for the design of the world. We can now deal with this topic.

Because the Epicurean hypothesis accounts for design without reference to 'principles' of design and 'powers' in objects to bring about observed effects in other objects, it is evident that this hypothesis is incompatible with the claim that there is an ultimate *cause* or *principle* of design for the world.

But what of the motion which is observed to be present in matter? If it is caused, then, perhaps, we can still maintain an original cause of the design which has come about. Such a cause would not be directly responsible for the design of the world – no principles of design are countenanced – but it could be considered an original cause in the sense that without it, matter would not be in motion, and therefore, without this cause, no design in matter could come about. At times, Philo holds that we are simply ignorant of the causes of motion in matter: "*And whatever the causes are*, the fact is certain, that matter is, and always has been in continual agitation, as far as human experience or tradition reaches".[35] In other passages, he suggests that motion

---

[34] That Philo's sceptical attack would extend to the principle 'Like effects prove like causes' and to claims regarding *principles* of order based on observing objects constantly conjoined was actually anticipated (by Philo) in a passage in Part II shortly after the second version of the Argument from Design was presented. Philo says at that point: "That all inferences, Cleanthes, concerning fact, are founded on experience, and that all experimental reasonings are founded on supposition, that similar causes prove similar effects, and similar effects similar causes; I shall not, *at present*, much dispute with you" (D. 147, italics added). There is, then, a clear warning that even these matters will be attacked by the sceptic.

[35] D. 183 *(italics added)*.

in matter may be internal; and if this is the case, there would not be an ultimate or original cause of motion in matter: "Besides, why may not motion have been propogated by impulse through all eternity, and the same stock of it, or nearly the same, be still upheld in the universe? As much as is lost by the composition of motion, as much is gained by its resolution".[36]

Now, it appears that Philo opts for one of these alternatives, at least insofar as he is concerned to develop the Epicurean hypothesis. On two occasions in Part VIII, he mentions that motion in matter is eternal.[37] This might seem inconsistent with Philo's scepticism; but it can be accounted for. Recall that Philo is putting forth hypotheses which, as he puts it, 'preserve a kind of imperfect analogy' or 'have some faint appearance of truth'.[38] When dealing with the topic of ultimate causes in Part VII, we came across an example of such an imperfect analogy – his words in Part VII in this connection are 'some faint shadow of experience' (D. 180) – wherein he argued that if we postulate reason to be the immediate cause of the design of the world, then the ultimate cause should be taken to be generation.[39] In Part VIII, Philo appears to favour eternal motion in matter. The reason for this must be that this hypothesis does possess a 'faint appearance of truth'. Since matter is found to be in 'continual agitation',[40] the hypothesis of matter which is eternally in motion bears an 'imperfect analogy' to our experience of matter. Therefore, if we decide to take a position on the motion observed in matter, we should hold that this motion had no beginning. Further, if motion in matter had no beginning, then matter too must be without beginning; hence, there is no need to pursue further whether matter was caused to exist.

Finally, then, on the issue of ultimate causes, since the Epicurean hypothesis holds matter to be eternal, and, therefore, without an ultimate cause which can account for the features that matter exhibits, including those pertaining to its design, it follows that no account in terms of ultimate causes can explain why all design in matter depends upon the presence of means to ends relations and a coherence of parts.

We can see, therefore, that the Epicurean hypothesis is incompatible with any attempt to posit an original cause for the design of the world. And since this hypothesis is grounded in the same features of design as the Argument

---

[36] D. 183
[37] D. 182, middle of the second paragraph (line 8–10); and D. 184, three lines from the bottom of the page.
[38] D. 182
[39] "Reason, in innumerable instances, is observed to arise from the principle of generation, and never to arise from any other principle". (D. 180)
[40] "... matter is, and always has been in continual agitation, as far as human experience or tradtion reaches. There is not probably, at present, in the whole universe, one particle of matter at absolute rest". (D. 183)

from Design, namely, means to ends relations and a coherence of parts, it follows that the design of the world is as compatible with the denial of an ultimate cause as it is compatible with the affirmation of such a cause. In short, the evidence does not enable us to decide whether there is an original or ultimate cause for the design of the world.

Toward the end of Part VIII, Cleanthes raises a number of criticisms to the Epicurean hypothesis – criticisms which Philo acknowledges to be relevant. After pointing out additional difficulties in the Design Argument, Philo cautions that because of the subject matter, those with opposing views should not condemn each other:

... these instances, I say, may teach, all of us, sobriety in condemning each other and let us see, that as no system of this kind ought ever to be received from a slight analogy, so neither ought any to be rejected on account of a small incongruity. For that is an inconvenience from which we can justly pronounce no one to be exempted.

All religious systems, it is confessed, are subject to great and inseparable difficulties. Each disputant triumphs in his turn; while he carries on an offensive war, and exposes the absurdities, barbarities, and pernicious tenets of his antagonist.[42]

Since no system of cosmogony can be defended satisfactorily, in the end the victory belongs to the sceptic, and a suspense of judgment is the only reasonable position:

... all of them, (i.e. those proposing 'religious systems'). on the whole, prepare a complete triumph for sceptic; who tells them, that no system ought ever to be embraced with regard to such subjects: For this plain reason, that no absurdity ought ever to be assented to with regard to any subject. A total suspense of judgment is here our only reasonable resource. And if every attack, as is commonly observed, and no defence, among theologians, is successful; how complete must be *his* victory, who remains always, with all mankind, on the offensive, and has himself no fixed station or abiding city, which he is ever on any occasion, obliged to defend.[43]

Part VIII closes with this passage. Cleanthes has now been shown that the argument he advances and attempts to support is no stronger than a variety of others which account for the design of the world in many different ways. In a number of passages, Cleanthes confesses, in line with Hume's account of the dogmatist who 'sees objects only on one side, and has no idea of any counterposing argument', that these competing religious systems (cosmogonies) have never occurred to him,[44] nor does he have any response

---

[41]   D. 185, last paragraph. We need not cite Cleanthes' criticisms here.
[42]   D. 186
[43]   D. 186–187
[44]   D. 172, after Philo has argued that the world is an organism and not a machine, Cleanthes responds: "This theory, I own, replied Cleanthes, has never before occurred to me, though a pretty natural one; and I cannot readily, upon so short an examination and reflection, deliver any opinion with regard to it.

to them.[45] By the end of Part VIII, he is made to see that reasoning by analogy will not yield knowledge of the nature of God. On the interpretation offered here, Cleanthes has been loosened from his dogmatism, and now realizes that he should suspend judgment on the topic of God's nature.

Although Cleanthes' suspense of judgment has been brought about by Philo's sceptical objections to the Design Argument, there is a clear indication in the last passage quoted above, that with the argument in Part VIII now complete, Philo will no longer participate in the discussion *as a pyrrhonian*. When commenting on the sceptic's victory in this passage, Philo signals a shift from excessive scepticism by referring to the victory of the sceptic as 'his' victory (the word 'his' in the text is italicized for emphasis). Thus, we find that, prior to Part XII where the concern with the claim of the intelligence of the deity is once again brought up for discussion, Philo alerts us to an impending alteration in his position. On our reading, the shift will be to mitigated scepticism – the position which Hume explained in the first *Enquiry* as resulting from Pyrrhonism, or excessive scepticism, "when its undistinguished doubts are, in some measure, corrected by common sense and reflection".[46] The confirmation of this reading must await an examination of Part XII.

---

[45] D. 181, the end of Part VII, Cleanthes tells Philo: "I must confess Philo, replied Cleanthes, that of all men living, the task which you have undertaken, of raising doubts and objections, suits you best, and seems, in a manner, natural and unavoidable to you. So great is your fertility of invention, that I am not ashamed to acknowledge myself unable, in a sudden, to solve regularly such out-of-the-way difficulties as you incessantly start upon me."

[46] E. 161

CHAPTER 8

Hume's *Dialogues*: Part XII

MITIGATED SCEPTICISM AND NATURAL THEOLOGY

The victory claimed for the Pyrrhonian at the end of Part VIII paves the way for the confusion and controversy among commentators regarding a correct reading of Part XII, the last section of the *Dialogues*, in which Philo appears to reverse himself and make certain positive assertions about God. In this chapter, I will show that Part XII connects to the first eight sections of the *Dialogues* in the manner outlined at the start of this book.

THE GENERAL THESIS RESTATED

It has been my contention that when the *Dialogues* opens, Cleanthes is represented as a dogmatist, and therefore, as one who is likely to err in his reasoning because he lacks the necessary preparative to the study of philosophy – the inculcation of sceptical considerations on the uncertainty and narrow limits of human reason. Since the sole argument which Cleanthes offers is the Argument from Design, it is in connection with this argument that we are likely to discover certain errors. Cleanthes admits no role for scepticism in inquiry, exhibits no doubt, caution, or modesty in defining his position, and lacks an impartiality in putting forth his argument – this latter being exhibited through his claim that the Argument from Design tends to the confirmation of the 'true religion'. In short, Cleanthes fits the pattern Hume finds in all dogmatists: "... while they see objects only on one side, and have no idea of any counterpoising argument, they throw themselves precipitately into the principles, to which they are inclined; nor have they any indulgence for those who entertain opposite sentiments."[1]

Hume's suggested cure is that the dogmatist be exposed to the argument of the Pyrrhonian; this we witnessed through Philo in Parts II through VIII. Philo urged that he was arguing with Cleanthes 'in his own way', and showed the latter that the Argument from Design, insofar as it seeks to establish

---

[1] E.161

analogically the intelligence of God and his externality to what He has designed, is indefensible. The Argument from Design was shown to involve an infinite regress (Part IV), to be susceptible of reduction to absurdity (Part V), and to utilize data which are equally supportive (and therefore not supportive at all) of an open-ended list of alternative hypotheses to a Designer of the world who is intelligent and external (Part VI–VIII). Cleanthes has no answer to Philo's pyrrhonian objections; at the end of this sceptical attack, Philo proclaims a complete victory for the Pyrrhonian: the only reasonable response, he urges at the end of Part VIII, is a total suspense of judgment.

In accordance with Hume's analysis in the first *Enquiry*, I indicated that the problem with a pyrrhonian attack is that it generates 'undistinguished doubts', that is, it does not differentiate between what is acceptable in an account or argument and what is unacceptable, and consequently, in its efforts at counterbalancing the dogmatist's position, it overshoots the mark. Hence, the doubts which the Pyrrhonian introduces must, as Hume urges, be 'corrected by common sense and reflection'. (E.161) At this stage, the position adopted is that of the 'mitigated sceptic or academical Philosophy'[2] – a position which results initially through the influence of nature itself. It is nature, operating through common sense, which forces the Pyrrhonian doubts to loosen their full hold on us.[3] In one sense, then, the Pyrrhonian doubts are 'undistinguished' in that they pay no heed to the influence of nature or instinct in generating and countenancing certain of the beliefs which we hold.

What, then, does Hume mean by 'reflection' correcting the 'undistinguished doubts' raised by the Pyrrhonian? Pyrrhonism will attempt to prove that the empirical data selected cannot support the hypothesis under discussion. Nevertheless, when Pyrrhonism is constructive in nature, it does acknowledge the relevance of empirical evidence to questions of fact. For a constructive Pyrrhonian, conclusions which are supported by the available empirical data will be accepted. But, now, if a Pyrrhonian has attacked a position which, we subsequently learn, has its origin in nature rather than in supportive empirical data, in other words, if a Pyrrhonian has attacked a natural belief, what role can 'reflection' serve in correcting the 'undistinguished doubts' generated by the sceptic? In fact, in such cases, it may seem that there is no useful role for 'reflection', for with natural beliefs there never is adequate empirical evidence for the belief in question.

Although it is true that if a belief is a natural belief then it cannot be justified through evidence, Hume did believe that 'reflection' still has a useful role to play in correcting the 'undistinguished doubts' of the Pyrrhonian. This

---

[2]   E.161
[3]   See E.162, E.158–159, the first chapter of this book.

can best be determined by looking at his own 'reflective' treatment of all the accepted cases of natural belief. His approach is this: granting that we hold a belief in causality, external objects, and the self, which the empirical data cannot justify, it is still open to us to inquire what claims the available empirical data do support with respect to each of these. For example, our natural inclination in the case of objects which are constantly conjoined is to believe that such objects are causally related and, therefore, necessarily connected – a position which the sceptic can attack as indefensible, given the empirical data available. But Hume argues that this sceptical attack does overshoot the mark somewhat, since some meaning can be attached to causality in the light of certain relations which can be established between what we consider to be the cause and what we hold to be the effect of that cause: this results in the two definitions of cause as a natural and a philosophical relation.[4] Therefore, although the available data do not support the belief in a necessary connection between causes and effects, they do support a certain empirical conception of what a cause is. This 'reflective' effort is the work of the mitigated sceptic, the one for whom 'philosophical decisions are nothing but the reflections of common life, methodized and corrected'.[5]

Similar 'reflective' efforts in the light of sceptical doubts are seen in the case of the other natural beliefs as well. Regarding personal identity, we find that after Hume raises sceptical objections to claims that "we are every moment intimately conscious of what we call our SELF; that we feel its existence and its continuance in existence; and are certain, beyond the evidence of a demonstration, both of its perfect identity and simplicity",[6] he points out what selfhood amounts to in the light of the empirical data:

For my part, when I enter most intimately into what I call *myself*, I always stumble on some particular perception or other, of heat or cold, light or shade, love or hatred, pain or pleasure. I never can catch myself at any time without a perception, and never can observe any thing but the perception. ... The mind is a kind of theatre, where several perceptions successsively make their appearance; pass , re-pass, glide away, and mingle in an infinite variety of postures and situations. There is properly no simplicity in it at one time, nor identity in different; whatever natural propension we may have to imagine that simplicity and identity.[7]

In the case of external objects, we experience a succession of resembling perceptions, but we are not informed through experience of the continued and independent existence of what we perceive, nor for that matter, of the identity of the succession of perceptions.

---

[4] T.170
[5] E.162
[6] T.251
[7] T.252–253

When the sceptic attacks our belief in causality, personal identity, and external objects, the basis for his criticisms is found in Hume's theory of perceptions, namely, the belief never has an impression through which it can be *justified*.[8] In all cases, other than those of natural beliefs, the criticism of a belief through the impressional test would not be the sign of an excessive sceptic:

When we entertain, therefore, any suspicion that a philosophical term is employed without any meaning or idea (as is but too frequent), we need but inquire, *from what impression is that supposed idea derived*? And if it be impossible to assign any, this will serve to confirm our suspicion. By bringing ideas into so clear a light we may reasonably hope to remove all dispute, which may arise, concerning their nature and reality.[9]

However, in the case of a natural belief, an analysis which confines itself to the impressional test is a sign of an excessive sceptic, for the resultant critique ignores both the 'natural' and 'reflective' aspects of these beliefs which we have discussed.

PHILO'S MITIGATED SCEPTICISM

As Part XII opens, we are given unambiguous signs by Philo that his treatment of the topic of God will follow Hume's treatment of our natural beliefs. He begins Part XII by admitting that he is "less cautious on the subject of natural religion than on any other", thereby revealing that the arguments he has put forth are themselves in need of evaluation.[10] Philo continues by asserting that his former lack of caution in arguing against Cleanthes had a two-fold basis:

I must confess, replied Philo, that I am less cautious on the subject of natural religion than on any other; both because I know that I can never, on that head, corrupt the principles of any man of common sense, and because no one, I am confident, in whose eyes I appear a man of common sense, will ever mistake my intentions.

Each of these deserves some comment. First, Philo defends his lack of caution in argument by urging that his procedure can never corrupt common sense principles. Now, Cleanthes' common sense principles in regard to causal reasoning are two in number: that experience, or observing objects constantly

---

[8]   On Hume's account of impressions and ideas, see my Reason and Conduct in Hume and his Predecessors, Chapter 2.

[9]   E.22

[10]   This emphasis on 'caution' in our philosophic reasonings is also made by the mitigated sceptic in section XII of the first *Enquiry* following Hume's discussion of how the Pyrrhonian can attack the position of the dogmatist. See E.161–162.

conjoined, is the only proper guide as to what causes what; and that causal inferences are to be guided by the principle 'Like effects prove like causes'. And in regard to *natural* arguments, Cleanthes holds that because the observation of means to ends relations and a coherence of parts leads, with such forcefulness, to the belief in an intelligent designer, regardless of where these features of design are observed, we ought to assent to this belief in these cases. This is an instantiation of the principle "to assent, wherever any reasons strike him with so full a force, that he cannot, without the greatest violence, prevent it".[11] We can take it, therefore, that in Part XII Philo is admitting that no sceptical argument can so effect us that we will abandon our common sense principles – even though we may do so momentarily. This is a view of Philo's with which we are already familiar. In Part I he acknowledged:

To whatever length any one pushes his speculative principles of scepticism, he must act, I own, and live, and converse like other men; and for this conduct he is not obliged to give any other reason that the absolute necessity he lies under of so doing.[12]

The second point made by Philo in the passage under discussion is that he is less cautious on the subject of natural religion than any other, because no one who sees him as a man of common sense will ever mistake his intentions. My analysis of Philo's arguments in Part II and Parts IV through VIII reveals that Philo's intention was to show that Cleanthes' principles – particularly those dealing with causal *reasoning* – cannot be applied, as Cleanthes had attempted to apply them, to natural religion. In Part I, Philo had already warned against this effort of Cleanthes', while at the same time urging him to confine his speculations to the empirical:

So long as we confine our speculations to trade, or morals, or politics, or criticism, we make appeals, every moment to common sense and experience, which strengthen our philosophical conclusions, and remove (at least, in part) the suspicion, which we so justly entertain with regard to every reasoning that is very subtle and refined. But in theological reasonings, we have not this advantage; while at the same time we are employed upon objects, which we must be sensible, are too large for our grasp, and of all others, require most to be familiarised to our apprehension. We are like foreigners in a strange country, to whom everything must seem suspicious, and who are in danger every moment of transgressing the laws and customs of the people with whom they live and converse. We know not how far we ought to trust our vulgar methods of reasoning in such a subject; since even in common life and in that province which is peculiarly appropriated to them, we cannot account for them, and are entirely guided by a kind of instinct or necessity in employing them.[13]

[11] D.154
[12] D.134. We should recall here that in Part VIII even our principles regarding causal knowledge were brought into doubt by the sceptic.
[13] D.135

We have yet to ask what Philo means when he says that he is 'less cautious' in natural religion than in other areas of inquiry. Our study of Philo's criticisms provides the required insight. In arguing against Cleanthes' position on God, Philo himself employs principles and utilizes data, without directly questioning whether his procedure is justified. Hence, in this respect, he violates his own position in Part I, in which he argued against such inquiries. Nevertheless, Philo's purpose in doing so was to show Cleanthes the difficulties involved in, and the alternatives to, the Design Argument. Since Philo's aim was not to inquire into God's nature, but to show why our ordinary procedures are inadequate to such an investigation, and, therefore, ultimately to show that no system of cosmogony is defensible, Philo holds that his procedure in the earlier chapters is justified. Part I had already anticipated this result:

All sceptics pretend, that, if reason be considered in an abstract view, it furnishes invincible arguments against itself, and that we could never retain any conviction or assurance, on any subject, were not the sceptics reasonings so refined and subtile, that they are not able to counterpoise the more solid and natural arguments, derived from the senses and experience. But it is evident, whenever our arguments lose this advantage, and run wide of common life, that the most refined scepticism comes to be upon a footing with them, and is able to oppose and counterbalance them. The one has no more weight than the other. The mind must remain in suspense between them; and it is that very suspense or balance, which is the triumph of scepticism.[14]

Nevertheless, the Pyrrhonian attack generates what Hume calls 'undistinguished doubts', and it is because of this, that Philo acknowledges that he has been less cautious than he would otherwise be. His arguments sought to discredit *all* that Cleanthes had defended; no attempt was made to distinguish within Cleanthes' position elements which are acceptable. In any case, by admitting that his scepticism possessed a certain lack of caution in argumentation, Philo is allowing for a reappriasal of Cleanthes' – as well as his own – position. Part XII provides this re-appraisal.

That the stand which Philo is about to defend is his own can be learned from the fact that after expressing himself he confesses: "These, Cleanthes, are my unfeigned sentiments on this subject; and these sentiments, you know, I have ever cherished and maintained".[15] Before defending his position, he makes explicit that his approach has both a natural (common sense) and a reflective aspect – putting it exactly in line with Hume's mitigated scepticism. Philo asserts: "You are sensible, that, notwithstanding the freedom of my conversation, and my love of singular arguments, no one has a deeper sense of religion impressed on his mind, or pays more profound adoration to the

[14] D.135–136
[15] D.219

divine Being, as he discovers himself to reason, in the inexplicable contrivance and artifice of nature".[16]

CORRECTING THE 'UNDISTINGUISHED' PYRRHONIAN DOUBTS THROUGH 'COMMON SENSE'

Philo begins by elaborating on the 'sense of religion impressed on his mind':

A purpose, an intention, or design strikes everywhere the most careless, the most stupid thinker; and no man can be so hardened in absurd systems, as at all times to reject it.[17]

We have already discussed this passage in dealing with Nathan's account of rationality (Part IV). What will now be presented will provide a further elaboration on the natural belief aspect of the *Dialogues*, with the bulk of our attention being paid to Philo's words in Part XII.

The first point which Philo makes in this passage is that no one who gives any attention to the world can avoid believing that its organization is purposive or intentional. By including 'the most stupid thinker, Philo is pointing out that the attention paid to the design of the world can be crude and unsophisticated; by including 'the most careless' thinker he is including the Pyrrhonian whose scepticism is broken by 'carelessness and inattention'. A further point is also being made with the reference to 'the most careless thinker': when the Pyrrhonian is careless and inattentive, his state of mind is very much like that of the common person, particularly in regard to what he is naturally inclined to believe.[18] Therefore, Philo intends that the ordinary consciousness is also struck by the purposive or intentional character of the design of the world.

By asserting that 'no man can be so hardened in absurd systems, as at all times to reject it' Philo is admitting that we can hold certain hypotheses about the design of the world which oppose the natural belief view of purposiveness, although he does not believe that the design hypothesis can always be rejected by such people.

Which rival views does Philo have in mind in his reference to 'absurd systems'? Of all the systems of cosmogony developed by Philo in Parts VI through VIII, it is only the ones discussed in Part VIII to which the label 'absurd' is ascribed. When Philo introduces the 'old Epicurean hypothesis' in the second paragraph of Part VIII (D.182) he says that 'this is commonly, and I believe, justly, esteemed, the most absurd system that has yet been

---

[16] D.214
[17] D.214
[18] See D.133 last paragraph to D.134.

proposed', and when he begins his own version of this hypothesis three paragraphs later, he claims 'that it is not absolutely absurd or improbable'. The sense of these two references appears to be that certain hypotheses can be more or less absurd, although it is not clear what determines whether they are to be so regarded.

What characterizes the hypotheses in Part VIII as opposed to those in Parts VI and VII is that in the latter the design of the world is always attributed to a principle of design (for example, generation and vegetation), whereas the hypotheses in Part VIII all seek to account for design through matter in motion, without any employment of principles of order. It is because these latter hypotheses are the furthest removed from common sense which holds that design requires some principle of design, that Philo holds that they can be called 'absurd'. The Epicurean hypothesis makes no reference to principles of order, and it accounts for a given arrangement of particles by holding that in an eternal duration 'every possible order or position must be tried an infinite number of times'. Philo's hypothesis also makes no use of principles of order, but, as we saw, it does attempt to account for design through analogy with the behaviour of the matter of organisms.

Where the theory employs a principle of order, it may be false, but is not held to be absurd. Where the theory employs no principle of order, it is called 'absurd'. Why does Philo not say that the hypothesis which he propounds in Part VIII is as absurd as the 'old Epicurean hypothesis'? The degree of absurdity is determined by the extent to which an account of design is sought through analogy with design as it is found to originate in (parts of) the world. Therefore, because the 'old Epicurean hypothesis' makes no use of analogy, it is held to be the 'most absurd system'. Because Philo's version utilizes the design found in organisms, it is held to be less absurd that the old Epicurean hypothesis. In any case, when Philo speaks of 'absurd' systems in Part XII, he is referring to theories which explain design without reference to a principle or principles of design.

Of the systems of cosmogony which can be proposed, Philo holds that, in the end, it is 'absurd systems' which offer the strongest opposition to the hypothesis of design, and yet this opposition cannot be sustained indefinitely. Two questions arise: a) why is it that only those accounts which do not employ principles of order can offer the strongest alternative to the design hypothesis? and b) why does Philo claim that no one can be so hardened in absurd systems as to reject always the design hypothesis?

The first question is easily answered. As we have seen, systems of cosmogony fall into two categories, those employing principles of order and those which do not. Now, the procedure for confirming a system of cosmogony which postulates an ordering principle is clear: either worlds would have to be formed under our eyes, or the design of the world must bear sufficient resemblance to some species within the world to utilize the principle 'like effects prove like causes'. And, in regard to this Philo has been adamant, namely, the first disjunct can obviously not be satisfied in the case of God and the world, and neither can the second disjunct, since the world does not bear sufficient resemblance to any know species of objects to be classified as a member of that species. Therefore, no principle of order, the effects of which are familiar to us, can be used to explain the design of the world. And if we have recourse to principles other then these, we cease to employ analogical reasoning.

The 'absurd systems', on the other hand, lack this classification requirement. Hence, Philo correctly holds that they are unaffected by the fact that the world is without specific resemblance to things in the world. But yet he holds that even 'the absurd systems' must give way at some point to the hypothesis of design. We must now ask why this is so.

The answer to our question can be discerned by examining two different passages, the first being Philo's comments on science in Part XII which immediately follow the passage presently under discussion; the second is the debate on absurd systems between Philo and Cleanthes which begins with the third last paragraph of Part VIII and continues through to the end of the next paragraph.

In the third last paragraph of Part VIII, Cleanthes raises certain objections to the 'absurd system' proposed by Philo:

> It is well, replied Cleanthes, you told us, that this hypothesis was suggested on a sudden, in the course of the argument. Had you had leisure to examine it, you would soon have perceived the insuperable objections, to which it is exposed. No form, you say, can subsist, unless it possess those powers and organs, requisite for its subsistence: Some new order or oeconomy must be tried, and so on, without intermission; till at last some order, which can support and maintain itself, is fallen upon. But according to this hypothesis, whence arise the many conveniences and advantages which men and all animals possess? Two eyes, two ears, are not absolutely necessary for the subsistence of the species. Human race might have been propogated and preserved, without horses, dogs, cows, sheep, and those innumerable fruits and products which serve to our satisfaction and enjoyment. If no camels had been created for the use of man in the sandy deserts of African and Arabia, would the world have been dissolved? If no loadstone had been framed to give that wonderful and useful direction to the needle, would human society and the human kind have been immediately distinguished? Though the maxims of nature be in general very frugal, yet instances of this kind are far from being rare; and any one of them is a sufficient proof of design, and of a benevolent design, which gave rise to the order and arrangement of the universe.[19]

Cleanthes' criticism centers around the fact that if the system of cosmogony developed by Philo offered the correct account, then all there is should be explicable simply in terms of the survival hypothesis. In other words, the only

[19]   S.185

maxim which would be required in studying what there is would be that at any level of inquiry the adaptation of means to ends and coherence of parts which we find are to be understood exclusively in terms of the maintenance of the order within which theses features are found. And, he urges, much that we find cannot be accounted for through this maxim; hence, the maxim itself must be rejected, and along with it, the system of cosmogony in which it is rooted. When Philo, in the next paragraph, sets out to respond to Cleanthes' criticism, he admits that all systems of cosmogony have difficulties – therefore, the one he developed is not peculiar in being defective – and he proceeds to point out some of the difficulties in Cleanthes' position:

But can we ever reasonably expect greater success in any attempts of this nature? Or can we ever hope to erect a system of cosmogony, that will be liable to no exceptions, and will contain no circumstance repugnant to our limited and imperfect experience of the analogy of nature? Your theory itself cannot surely pretend to any such advantage; even though you have run into anthropomorphism, the better to preserve a conformity to common experience. Let us once more put it to trial. In all instances which we have ever seen, ideas are copied from real objects, and are ectypal, not archetypal, to express myself in learned terms: You reverse this order, and give thought the precedence. In all instances which we have ever seen, thought has no influence upon matter, except where that matter is so conjoined with it, as to have an equal reciprocal influence upon it. No animal can move immediately any thing but the members of its own body; and indeed, the equality of action and re-action seems to be an universal law of nature: But your theory implied a contradiction to this experience.[20]

What is particularly interesting in Philo's response is the fact that he does not attempt to meet Cleanthes' criticism by showing that the Design Hypothesis also cannot provide an entirely satisfactory basis for maxims through which to study the world. Instead of arguing for this, he brings up disanalogies between the divine intelligence hypothesis of the Design Argument and human intelligence. The second and third paragraphs in Part XII show clearly why this omission was allowed, namely, Philo believes that the maxims of science which stem from the Design Hypothesis are, in fact, the ones which science employs, and, he appears to be saying, ought to employ, in its inquiries:

A purpose, an intention, or design, strikes everywhere the most careless, the most stupid thinker; and no man can be so hardened in absurd systems, as at all times to reject it. *That nature does nothing in vain*, is a maxim established in all the schools, merely from the contemplation of the works of nature, without any religious purpose; and, from a firm conviction of its truth, an anatomist, who has observed a new organ or canal, would never be satisfied till he had discovered its use and intention. One great foundation of the Copernican system is the maxim, *that nature acts by the simplest methods, and chooses the most proper means to any end*; and astronomers often, without thinking of it, lay this strong foundation of piety and religion. The same thing is observable in other parts of philosophy: And thus all the sciences almost lead us insensibly to

[20]   D.186

acknowledge a first intelligent Author; and their authority is often so much the greater, as they do not directly profess that intention.

It is with pleasure I hear Galen reason concerning the structure of the human body. The anatomy of a man, says he, discovers above 600 different muscles; and whoever duly considers these, will find, that in each of them nature must have adjusted at least ten different circumstances, in order to attain the end which she proposed; proper figure, just magnitude, right disposition of the several ends, upper and lower position of the whole, the due insertion of the several nerves, veins, and arteries: So that, in the muscles alone, above 6000 several views and intentions must have been formed and executed. The bones he calculates to tbe 284: The distinct purposes, aimed at in the structure of each, above forty. What a prodigious display of artifice, even in these simple and homogeneous parts? But if we consider the skin, ligaments, vessels, glandules, humours, the several limbs and members of the body; how must our astonishment rise upon us, in proportion to the number and intricacy of the parts so artificially adjusted. The farther we advance in these researches, we discover new scenes of art and wisdom: But descry still, at a distance, farther scenes beyond our reach; in the fine internal structure of the parts, in the oeconomy of the brain, in the fabric of the seminal vessels. All these artifices are repeated in every different species of animal, with wonderful variety, and with exact propriety, suited to the different intentions of nature, in framing each species. And if the infidelity of Galen, even when these natural sciences were still imperfect, could not withstand such striking appearances; to what pitch of pertinacious obstinacy must a philosopher in this age have attained, who can now doubt of a supreme intelligence?[21]

Purposive design, Philo urges, strikes anyone who contemplates nature. We have already seen, and Philo repeats here, this belief in purposiveness is not identical to the observation of means to ends relations and a coherence of parts. When Philo maintains that any one who contemplates nature is struck by purposiveness, he does not mean that the act of contemplation invariably discloses specific purposes. His point is rather that by observing the adaptation of means to ends and coherence of parts throughout nature we are struck with a belief in purposiveness. Hence, this belief in purpose is actually prior to the investigation of nature. Philo's point is that there is a causal connection between the observation of means to ends relations and a coherence of parts and a belief in purposive design: the belief in purposive design does not await an understanding of a given case of purposiveness. This explains why, in the first paragraph quoted (quotation 21 above), Philo asserts that the maxims of science, which involve a purposive view of the design of the world, can be obtained from 'the contemplation of the works of nature'. It is also important to realize that in these two paragraphs Philo is not concerned with reasoning analogically to purposiveness in design. What he is saying here does not in any way rely upon noting resemblances between the world and machines. We are, he points out, 'struck' by the machine-like or purposive nature of the world, and not reasoning to it. His point, therefore, is that science does not require a system of cosmogony which is arrived at through reason before it can obtain maxims needed for the study

[21]   D.214–215

of nature. The observation of nature, he is saying, impresses us with the needed beliefs required to provide those maxims for science which will prove to be its most dependable guide.

This concession by Philo in the second and third paragraphs of Part XII helps to bring him in line with Cleanthes' position in Part III, in which the latter, through the two illustrative analogies, maintained that there was an immediate or natural inference from the observation of means to ends relations and a coherence of parts present in the Articulate Voice and Living Vegetable Library to an intelligent cause of design. The use by Cleanthes of these particular illustrative analogies can now be understood. The Articulate Voice example corresponds to the Physical Sciences, while the Vegetable Library example corresponds to the Organic Sciences. In Part XII, when Philo develops his view of the purposive nature of the world he selects astronomy and anatomy – each representative of the physical and organic sciences respectively. The Articulate Voice analogy, therefore, can be understood to represent all natural phenomena studied by the physical sciences, while the Vegetable Library Analogy is representative of the natural phenomena studied by the organic sciences. The point, therefore, which Cleanthes, and as we now see, Philo, want to make is that no science can be regarded as representing an area of inquiry which would not lend itself to a purposive type of inquiry. Since all of nature exhibits means to ends relations and a coherence of parts, our observations of nature will naturally lead us to a purposive view of what we find, and this will result in a study of nature in terms of ends or purposes.

In the first chapter, I set out the criteria for natural beliefs based on what Hume says regarding established or non-controversial cases of such beliefs. When dealing with Cleanthes' illustrative analogies in Part III, I indicated respects in which Cleanthes' views on 'natural' arguments differ, or at least do not appear to accord with, Hume's views on natural beliefs. I now propose to examine fully the extent to which the position taken in the early paragraphs of Part XII by Philo, and agreed to by Cleanthes, accord with Hume's account of natural belief. The position I will defend is that the belief in an intelligent designer of the world satisfies all the criteria of a natural belief and, therefore, must be regarded as being such a belief.

1) A Belief Classified as a Natural Belief Cannot Be One Which Can Be Fully Analyzed in Terms of Hume's Account of Perceptions, or Impressions and Ideas

As in the case of other natural beliefs, the position taken in the *Dialogues* is that there is no adequate or proper impression of God. Early in Part II, Philo argues:

In reality, Cleanthes, continued he, there is no need of having recourse to that affected scepticism, so displeasing to you, in order to come at this determination. Our ideas reach no further than our experience: We have no experience of divine attributes and operations: I need not conclude my syllogism: You can draw the inference yourself. And it is a pleasure to me (and I hope to you too) that just reasoning and sound piety here concur in the same conclusion, and both of them establish the adorably mysterious and incomprehensible nature of the sumpreme Being.[22]

Again, as with the other natural beliefs, there are certain perceptions which are involved in our belief in God:

... as all perfection is entirely relative, we ought never to imagine, that we comprehend the attributes of this divine Being, or to suppose, that his perfections have any analogy or likeness to the perfections of a human creature. Wisdom, thought, design, knowledge; these we justly ascribe to him; because these words are honourable among men, and we have no other language or other conceptions, by which we can express our adoration of him. But let us beware, lest we think, that our ideas any wise correspond to his perfections, or that his attributes have any resemblance to these qualities among men. He is infintely superior to our limited view and comprehension ...[23]

Because a Natural Belief Goes Beyond the Data of Experience, the Awareness Accompanying a Natural Belief is Always a Substitute for the Putative Object of that Belief

Through observation, we find means to ends relations and a coherence of parts. We have already seen that when we attempt to reason about the machine-like character or purposive nature of the world on the basis of these features, reason will be confronted by opposing and equally strong accounts which it can generate. Hence, at least in the earlier Parts of the book, Philo maintained that reason is unable to establish that what there is is purposively designed. In Part XII, Philo holds firm on this point: in the second paragraph he speaks of his profound adoration for the divine being 'as he discovers himself to reason, in the inexplicable contrivance and artifice of nature'. Nevertheless, Philo holds that the observation of means to ends relations and a coherence of parts causes a belief in an intelligent designer and, therefore,

[22] D.143
[23] D.142

in purposive design. How we are struck – to use Philo's term – by the observation of means to ends relations and a coherence of parts is analogous to Hume's account of our belief in causality. Whereas in causality the awareness we require is power or necessary connection, in natural theology the required awareness is purposive design. Neither awareness is obtainable through observation or reasoning; hence, there is no proper awareness either of power or of purposiveness. In causality, the determination of the mind which follows our observation of objects constantly conjoined is 'spread'. on external objects, and this, for Hume, is the perception which is substituted for the awareness of power. With natural theology, the following account emerges. Our observations of the world do not disclose any perception through which the purpose of its particular order can be discerned, nor that it was designed by an intelligent being. However, through the observation of means to ends relations and coherence of parts we come to believe that the whole world is like a machine. Contemplating the world results in a belief that all there is is purposively designed; and yet there is no perception of this purpose, and Philo holds that this is not an area we either can or ought to pursue. This can be rendered intelligible by noting that what Philo does believe comes before the mind when we contemplate the world is the anthropomorphic conceptions of 'wisdom, thought, design, and knowledge'.[24] Philo's point, therefore, must be that the observation of means to ends relations and a coherence of parts throughout nature is followed by an anthropomorphic conception of God as the cause of design, and it is this anthropomorphic conception of God which explains why the world is believed to be purposively designed. Once we hold the belief that the cause of the design of the world is an intelligent being, we will believe that its design is purposive, even though the purpose of the design is not known, and it is not known whether it was purposively designed. In causality, a habit of mind is the basis of a belief in power; in natural theology, an anthropomorphic conception of God is the basis of a belief in purposive design. In both cases, we, in a sense, misrepresent the data of experience, and go beyond it – the misrepresentation in natural theology arising through the fact that we have no evidence that the world was intelligently designed, and yet the anthropomorphic conception of God supports a belief in intelligent contrivance.

[24]   D.142

In the Case of a Natural Belief, We Are Unable to Explicate the Putative Referent of the Belief

This, of course, follows from 1) and 2). Since the source of our belief in purposiveness is not found in a perception (impression or idea) which reveals purpose or intention, we no more know the purpose of the design of the world than we know causal connections between objects. Moreover, just as we have no proper awareness of power even when we make causal inferences, so we cannot establish that the world was purposively designed, even when we achieve success with teleological explanations within the world. Causal inferences are made without knowing whether and how objects are causally related; inferences about purpose are made without knowing whether natural objects were purposively designed, and without knowing the cause or source of design.

What We Believe Naturally May Not Be At All

We come to believe naturally in causal connections, external objects, and a continuing self, and yet there may not be causal connections between objects, or external objects, or a proper identity to the self. Philo indicates that when science proceeds as though the world was intellligntly designed, it enjoys great success, insofar as it offers teleological explanations for the means to ends relations and coherence of parts which it uncovers. The maxims of science discussed by Philo – that nature does nothing in vain, and that nature acts by the simplest methods, and chooses the most proper means to any end – require that there is (an) intelligence using the idea of ends to guide and organize the interrelationships of the means. He has insisted throughout that if we are to prove this, we must either observe the cause producing the effect, or find sufficient resemblances between the world and machines to classify the world as a machine. Since neither disjunct can be satisfied, it follows that we can never prove that the world was purposively designed. Therefore, just as there may not be causal connections, or external objects, or a proper identity to the self, so what there is in nature may not be intelligently contrived and, therefore, may not be purposively designed.

But a natural belief is compatible with however matters really are. For example, our belief in causal connections is compatible with whatever the true account of how effects are brought about. Philo holds a similar position in regard to the Design Hypothesis: we are unable to provide through reason an adequate system of cosmogony, and, therefore, we cannot determine how the world achieved its design. Nevertheless, science has had great success in its quest for teleological explanations. Here, again, therefore, the approach is compatible with whatever the true system of cosmogony.

A Natural Belief is Unavoidable and Universal

In our preliminary discussion on natural belief, I showed that the unavoidability of such beliefs requires that given certain perceptions with certain specifiable characteristics, the imagination will be led to generate the awareness or belief in question. With causality, for example, the perceptual feature must be constant conjunction, and with external objects these features are constancy and coherence. With our belief in an intelligent designer of the world, Philo is equally clear: when we observe means to ends relations and a coherence of parts, we are struck by the belief in intelligent contrivance.

If the belief in an intelligent designer for the world is unavoidable as explicated above, and, therefore, universal, it should follow that no exceptions can be found. However, in Hume's writings on religion, there is an acknowledgment that the belief in an intelligent designer is not universal.[25] Within the *Dialogues* itself, we find Cleanthes denying the strict universality of this belief:

It sometimes happens, I own, that the religious arguments have not their due influence on the ignorant savage and barbarian; not because they are obscure and difficult, but because he never asks himself any question in regard to them. Whence arises the curious structure of an animal? From the copulation of its parents. And these whence? From *their* parents. A few removes set the objects at such a distance, that to him they are lost in darkness and confusion; nor is he actuated by any curiosity to trace them farther. But this is neither dogmatism, nor scepticism, but stupidity; a state of mind very different from your sifting, inquisitive disposition, my ingenious friend.[26]

Why the 'ignorant savage and barbarian' fail to come to the belief in an intelligent designer can be understood by examining a passage spoken by Cleanthes two paragraphs earlier in Part III, in which he speaks of those who do hold the belief in an intelligent designer:

Consider, anatomize the eye: Survey its structure and contrivance; and tell me, from your own feeling, if the idea of a contriver does not immediately flow in upon you with a force like that of sensation. The most obvious conclusion surely is in favour of design; and it requires time, reflection and study, to summon up those frivolous, though abstruse, objections, which can support infidelity. Who can behold the male and female of each species, the correspondence of their parts and instincts, their passions and whole course of life before and after generation, but must be sensible, that the propagation of the species is intended by nature. Millions and millions of such instances present themselves through every part of the universe; and no language can

[25] See the *Natural History of Religion*, p. 31
[26] D.155

convey a more intelligible, irresistible, meaning, than the curious adjustment of final causes. To what degree, therefore, of blind dogmatism must one have attained, to reject such natural and such convincing arguments?

Throughout this passage, Cleanthes seeks to make one point: those who believe in an intelligent contriver are precisely the ones who have attended to the adjustments or adaptations of means to ends throughout nature. In his comments on the ignorant savage and barbarian, he is pointing out that their view is, at best, confined to the immediate cause, and in the case of natural phenomena, this immediate cause will not be an intelligent being. Cleanthes is, therefore, calling attention to the fact that not every observation of a causal situation leads to a belief in an intelligent cause; the belief in an intelligent cause of design requires a more comprehensive view than one or two observed instances of causality. It requires an awareness that the causal relations which are observed – whether within a given natural item, or within the chain of causes and effects by which these items come into existence – have been adjusted to each other: once this adjustment is apprehended, we will normally be struck with the belief in an intelligent cause of design.

It should be pointed out that this view as to why the ignorant savage and barbarian do not believe in an intelligent designer for the world is made by Hume in a number of different passages in the *Natural History of Religion*. The first passage is no more than an elaboration of Cleanthes' point regarding these non-believers:

But a barbarous, necessitous animal (such as man is on the first origin of society), pressed by such numerous wants and passions, has no leisure to admire the regular face of nature, or make inquiries concerning the cause of those objects, to which from his infancy he has been gradually accustomed. On the contrary, the more regular and uniform, that is, the more perfect nature appears, the more is he familiarized to it, and the less inclined to scrutizine and examine it ... an animal, compleat in all its limbs and organs, is to him an ordinary spectacle, and produces no religious opinion or affection. Ask him, whence that animal arose; he will tell you, from the copulation of its parents. And these, whence? From the copulation of theirs. A few removes satisfy his curiosity, and set the objects at such a distance, that he entirely loses sight of them. Imagine not, that he will so much as start the question, whence the first animal; much less, whence the whole system, or united fabric of the universe arose.[27]

In the second passage from the *Natural History of Religion*, Hume contrasts the barbarian with the astronomer and anatomist – these latter being precisely the ones to whom Philo called attention in the second and third paragraphs of Part XII when speaking of being struck by a purpose or intention in nature:

Ignorant of astronomy and the anatomy of plants and animals, and too little curious to observe the admirable adjustment of final causes; they remain still unacquainted with a first and supreme

---

[27] N.H.R. 35

creator, and with that infintely perfect spirit, who alone, by his almighty will, bestowed order on the whole frame of nature.[28]

In the opening sentence to the General Corrollary of the *Natural History of Religion*, Hume writes:

Though the stupidity of men, barbarous and uninstructed, be so great, that they may not see a sovereign author in the more obvious works of nature, to which they are so much familiarized; yet it scarcely seems possible, that any one of good understanding should reject that idea, when once it is suggested to him.[29]

This, of course, is a position to which both Philo and Cleanthes must assent, since each holds that we will be struck by the belief in intelligent contrivance, once the adjustment of means to ends is apprehended.

In the light of the above remarks, the issue of the universality of the belief in an intelligent designer for the world tends to dissolve. A natural belief is regarded by Hume as unavoidable and universal, because in each case the imagination will generate the belief, provided we apprehend certain perceptions with certain specifiable characteristics. Now, in the case of the belief in an intelligent designer of the world, Hume, Philo, and Cleanthes all agree that where the belief is not present in ignorant savages and barbarians, this is due to the fact that the relevant perceptions have not been apprehended: each is committed to the view that once the adaptation of means to ends has been observed, the belief will occur. Once it is understood that a natural belief for Hume is universal in the sense that there must be an experience of a certain kind for the belief to be generated, the universality of the belief in an intelligent designer is established. This conditional analysis of the unavoidability and universality of another natural belief, causality, is clearly illustrated by Hume in a passage in the first *Enquiry* where he writes:

It seems evident that, if all the scenes of nature were continually shifted in such a manner that no two events bore any resemblance to each other, but every object was entirely new, without any similitude to whatever had been seen before, we should never, in that case, have attained the least idea of necessity, or of a connection among these objects. We might say, upon such a supposition, that one object or event has followed another, and not that one was produced by the other. The relation of cause and effect must be utterly unknown to mankind. ... Our idea, therefore, of necessity and causation arises entirely from the uniformity observable in the operations of nature, where similar objects are constantly conjoined together, and the mind is determined by custom to infer the one from the appearance of the other.[30]

The conditional analysis of natural beliefs in Hume will remove the case of ignorant barbarians and savages as an obstacle to the claim that the belief in

---

[28]   N.H.R. 42
[29]   N.H.R. 46
[30]   E.82

an intelligent designer of the world is a natural belief. However, an additional difficulty to the natural belief claim can be found in some of the learned, that is, in those who hold to systems of cosmogony which conflict with the Design Hypothesis. The difficulty here, of course, is, that unlike the barbarian and the savage, these people have apprehended the adaptations of means to ends in nature, and nevertheless, hold to a rival view. In Part II, Philo mentions that "though sometimes the ancient philosophers reason from final causes, as if they thought the world the workmanship of God; yet it appears rather their favourite notion to consider it as his body, whose organization renders it subservient to him".[31] And in Part XII, he allows that alternative accounts can be held, although he indicates that no one who holds to an alternative account can at all times reject the Design Hypothesis: "... no man can be so hardened in absurd systems, as at all times to reject it".[32]

To what extent, then, do systems of cosmogony among the learned challenge the natural belief character of the Design Hypothesis? According to the last passage quoted above, Philo holds that although alternative accounts may be offered, the Design Hypothesis must eventually strike even these people. Hence, just as the sceptic is able to put forth a variety of systems of cosmogony, so may others as well, and just as the sceptic is eventually struck by the purposive nature of design, so will those others who propose alternative accounts. If the belief in an intelligent designer for the world is a natural belief, then no system of cosmogony can be rationally defended, and, consequently, any such theory will give way to the natural belief: in the end, the purposiveness of nature will strike us and command our attention.

Within the discussion of the *Dialogues*, this is all that Philo offers in defense of the universality of the belief in an intelligent designer among the learned. Nevertheless, it might be said that this is not adequate to establish the universality of the belief in an intelligent designer. It can be shown that different accounts which have been offered, for example in the case of theories of evolution, have a much stronger hold on their proponents than Philo appears willing to allow, and that this hold lasts beyond what one might expect having read the *Dialogues* on the matter. I want now to show that even in the light of such considerations, the universality of the belief in an intelligent designer can be defended. To show this, we must examine the other Humean natural beliefs.

I begin with the natural belief in causality. In the Treatise, Bk. I, Pt. III, Sect. XIV, Hume shows an awareness of many different views among the learned which attempt to explain 'the secret force and energy of causes':

---

[31] D.171
[32] D.214

In this research we meet with very little encouragement from that prodigious diversity, which is found in the opinions of those philosophers, who have pretended to explain the secret force and energy of causes. There are some, who maintain, that bodies operate by their substantial form; others, by their accidents or qualities; several, by their matter and form; some, by their form, and accidents; others by certain virtues and faculties distinct from all this. All these sentiments again are mix'd and vary'd in a thousand different ways.[33]

In some instances, the power to produce effects is concluded to be in the deity, and not in matter:

The small success, which has been met with in all the attempts to fix this power, has at last obliged philosophers to conclude, that the ultimate force and efficacy of nature is perfectly unknown to us, and that 'tis in vain we search for it in the known qualities of matter. In this opinion they are almost unanimous; and 'tis only in the inference they draw from it, they discover any difference in their sentiments. For some of them, as the *Cartesians* in particular, having establish'd it as a principle, that we are perfectly acquainted with the essence of matter, have very naturally inferr'd, that it is endow'd with no efficacy ... Matter, say they, is in itself entirely inactive, and depriv'd of any power, by which it may produce, or continue, or communicate motion: But since these effects are evident to our senses, and since the power, that produces them must be somewhere, it must lie in the Deity, or that divine being, who contains in his nature all excellency and perfection.[34]

In these passages taken from the *Treatise*, we find an acknowledgement of alternative accounts of causality among the learned: all agree that effects come into existence, but disagreement arises among the learned as to how to account for effects. Similarly, all agree that the world displays design or order, but there is disagreement among the learned as to how this order is best explained. Hume's response in both cases is the same: since the means by which effects come into existence has been totally shut off from us, no reasoned account can be shown to be satisfctory, and, in fact, all can be criticized (see T.157–160); since the means by which the world achieved its design has been totally shut off from us, no reasoned account can be shown to be satisfactory, and all can be criticized (including the Argument from Design). When dealing with our belief in the external world in "Of Scepticism with Regard to the Senses", Hume discusses the Lockean view – he calls it the philosophical system – and concedes that it "is found by experience to take hold of many minds".[35] Whether in connection with the belief in causality, external objects, or the self, the fact that the learned have put forth alternate views on these matters does not disturb their natural belief character. For, as Hume repeatedly points out, once they leave their study, the learned, to quote from "Of Scepticism with Regard to the Senses" return to our vulgar

---

[33] T.158
[34] T.159
[35] T.213

and natural notions".[36] The point made by Hume in the *Natural History of Religion* (p. 31, p. 42, p. 96), by Cleanthes, particularly throughout Part III, and Philo at the end of Part X and in the second and third paragraphs of Part XII – all of these passages show agreement that our natural notion is to believe the design of the world is the product of intelligent contrivance. This is the view, or better, the only view which strikes us when we contemplate nature. In one passage, Philo points out that the Design Hypothesis often strikes us when studying nature, even when we approch nature as infidels. The relevant passage here is the one where Philo discusses Galen:

All these artifices are repeated in every different species of animal, with wonderful variety, and with exact propriety, suited to the different intentions of nature in framing each species. And if the infidelity of Galen, even when these natural sciences were still imperfect, could not withstand such striking appearances; to what pitch of pertinacious obstinacy must a philosopher in this age have attained, who can now doubt of a supreme intelligence?"[37]

To complete our discussion of the unavoidability and universality of the belief in an intelligent designer of the world, we must take the sceptic into account. When, at the end of Part VIII Philo speaks of the victory of the sceptic, he makes it clear that the sceptic 'has himself no fixed station or abiding city, which he is ever, on any occasion, obliged to defend', meaning by this that the sceptic has no system of cosmogony, no reasoned solution to the question of the cause of the design of the world. The sceptic "tells them, that no system ought ever to be embraced with regard to such subjects".[38] Although the sceptic has no system of cosmogony, "he must", as we saw in Part I, "act, and live, and converse like other men; and for this conduct he is not obliged to give any other reason than the absolute necessity he lies under if so doing".[39] He urges against carrying his speculation beyond the empirical. In a number of passages, Philo holds that even the sceptic will be struck by the purposive nature of the design of the world:

... when we argued concerning the natural attributes of intelligence and design, I needed all my sceptical and metaphysical subtlety to elude your grasp. In many views of the universe, and of its parts, particularly the latter, the beauty and fitness of final causes strike us with such irresistible force, that all objections appear (what I believe they really are) mere cavils and sophisms; nor can we then imagine how it was ever possible for us to repose any weight on them".[40]

The sceptic warns against holding a system of cosmogony, but he too, like the vulgar and the learned, is struck by the purposive character of the design of

[36] T.216
[37] D.215
[38] D.186
[39] D.134
[40] D.201–202

the world. And if he is not struck by the purposiveness in design *qua* sceptic, he will be so struck, according to Philo, once he returns to his more usual state of mind.

In the light of the above discussion, I conclude that the claim that the belief in an intelligent designer of the world is unavoidable and universal entirely accords with Hume's views of these features in the context of other natural beliefs.

A Natural Belief is Always One Which is 'An Affair of Too Great Importance to be Trusted to our Uncertain Reasonings and Speculations'.

In our earlier discussion of natural belief, I showed that the great importance of natural beliefs is two-fold: such beliefs provide the basis for certain types of empirical knowledge, and they provide us with essential ways of approaching our experiences in order to get on in the world. I shall take each of these in turn in discussing the Design Hypothesis.

Is there a sense in which the belief in an intelligent designer of the world is necessary to acquiring empirical knowledge? The answer offered in the *Dialogues* is unambiguously affirmative. Once the adaptation of means to ends is apprehended, we are struck by the purposiveness of the design and the intelligence of the cause of design. These beliefs, in turn, render our search for causes in nature systematic. The systematization of our search for causes is founded on the maxims – mentioned in the second paragraph of Part XII – which naturally suggest themselves once the belief in purposive or intelligent contrivance has struck us. Without the belief in an intelligent designer of the world, our search for causes in nature would be a search for physical sequences and nothing else. Through the belief in an intelligent designer, an understanding of the presence of particular causes can be obtained in terms of the purpose which these causes assist in realizing. In the second paragraph in Part XII, Philo comments on the activities of an anatomist who has been struck by purposiveness in design: *"That nature does nothing in vain*, is a maxim established in all the schools, merely from the contemplation of the words of nature, without any religious purpose; and from a firm conviction of its truth, an anatomist, who has observed a new organ or canal, would never be satisfied till he had also discovered its use and intention".[41] The belief in an intelligent designer, therefore, guides our study of nature, and establishes the manner in which nature is to be studied.

Since the belief in intelligent contrivance is not arrived at through reason, alternative accounts which reason can generate can provide different maxims

---

[41]   D.214

for the study of nature. But Philo is clear on the following. First, no system of cosmogony, including the Design Argument, can be satisfactorily defended (Parts VI–VIII); hence, no system can be held because it has been proved by reason. Second, in general, once you begin studying nature in terms of the presence of means to ends relations and a coherence of parts, you are struck by the purposive nature of the design. Third, science, which has proceeded in accordance with this view of nature, has had great success in attempting to understand the world. Fourth, Philo is confident that additional scientific investigations based on this teleological view of nature will encounter similar successes. Philo is confident that the belief in intelligent contrivance stands in no danger of being refuted, or rendered questionable, by what we find in nature: everywhere in nature we find means to ends relations and a coherence of parts, and whenever such is the case, a teleological account will strike us as appropriate – a propriety which additional scientific research will confirm. Philo affirms that all of nature is of a piece in this regard:

Could I meet with one of this species (who, I thank God, are very rare) I would ask him: Supposing there were a God, who did not discover himself immediately to our senses; were it possible for him to give stronger proofs of his existence, than what appear on the whole face of nature? What indeed could such a divine Being do, but copy the present oeconomy of things; render many of his artifices so plain that no stupidity could mistake them; afford glimpses of still greater artifices, which demonstrate his prodigious superiority above our narrow apprehensions; and conceal altogether a great many from such imperfect creatures? Now, according to all rules of just reasoning, every fact must pass for undisputed, when it is supported by all the arguments which its nature admits of, even though these arguments be not, in themselves, very numerous or forcible: How much more, in the present case, where no human imagination can compute their number, and no understanding estimate their cogency?[42]

This paragraph – the fourth one in Part XII – is tied to the preceding one in which Philo asserts that Galen, and other non-believers "could not withstand such striking appearances" of art and wisdom. Hence, the fourth paragraph which was quoted is still concerned with the fact that we are struck by intelligent contrivance, and not by our ability to reason to an intelligent designer. The reference to 'all rules of just reasoning' in this passage does not, therefore, refer to the rules for analogical reasoning; in other words, he is not here defending the *Argument* from Design; he is defending the reasonableness of following the propensity we have to believe in purposiveness in nature whenever we observe the adaptation of means to ends. The success of science in seeking to understand nature teleologically makes it reasonable to expect that science will continue to be successful in pursuing nature as the product of intelligent contrivance, and this reasonableness stems from the fact that the whole of nature is of a piece in exhibiting means to ends relations and a

[42]   D.215–216

coherence of parts. Hence, in the end, Philo is confident that a teleological account of nature will continue to prove satisfactory, and that, therefore, nothing in nature will be encountered which will call for a different type of explanation. Philo is saying that because Nature endorses the purposive account of the study of nature, there is no reason to believe that any other approach to the study of nature will prove to be more successful.[43] When we try to argue to an intelligent designer for the world on the basis of means to ends relations and a coherence of parts, it can be shown a) that the argument does not accord with the rules of analogical reasoning (Part II), b) that it leads to an infinite regress (Part IV), c) that it can be reduced to absurdity (Part V), and d) that it is no better than, and in some cases weaker than, competing systems of cosmogony (Part VI–VIII). On the other hand, when we proceed to understand the world as the product of intelligent contrivance, we encounter great success. It is important to realize that the success encountered in studying the world teleologically does not in any way establish that we have gained any insight into the cause of the design of the world. For, it is characteristic of natural beliefs that, through them, nothing is learned as to how matters really are. For Hume, the successful employment of a natural belief for obtaining empirical knowledge is never relevant to understanding the true nature of what is believed. Our ability to make causal judgments is in no way relevant to explaining the true nature of a cause; similarly, statements about body and the self are not relevant to explaining the nature of body or the self. In fact, our abilities here do not even reveal whether there are causes, bodies, and selves. The *Dialogues* holds that the belief in intelligent contrivance follows this pattern: the belief in intelligent contrivance is useful in obtaining empirical knowledge, but no such knowledge is relevant to actually understanding the true nature of the design of the world, and its cause of design. To know what a cause is requires apprehending the necessary connection between causes and effects. To know that the world is the product of intelligent contrivance requires an awareness, either directly (through observation) or indirectly (through analogy), of the cause of the design of the world. As we have already seen, means to ends relations and a coherence of parts are neither identical to, nor do they ensure, that what there is is purposively designed. In arguing about body, Hume shows that constancy and coherence do not ensure that there is body. Nevertheless, these features cause a belief in body. Constant conjunction is, strictly speaking, neither identical to, nor in any strict philosophical manner does it ensure, a causal connection. One should not make the mistake of thinking that the success of

---

[43] A parallel here with the other natural beliefs is in order. For example, given that Nature endorses a view of causality based on constant conjunction and a resultant impression of reflection which arises in the mind, there is no reason to believe that any other approach to the study of causes and effects will show itself to be more successful.

science is different in this regard, and reveals the nature of the design of what there is and the nature of its source of order.

Our natural beliefs provide us with essential ways of approaching our experience in order to get on in the world. And the preceding discussion has disclosed that the belief in an intelligent designer has relevance to our search for causes. First, the purposive view of nature guides us in our efforts at connecting the various causes which we find in nature, and, in fact, often suggests to us that such a unity exists where this unity is far from obvious. Second, the maxims of parsimony, which the belief in intelligent contrivance includes, guide our efforts at reducing the number of causes which we encounter. Experience or the observation of objects constantly conjoined provides the basis for our awareness of what causes what. Part XII reveals how the belief in an intelligent designer assists us in dealing with the causes which we find in nature. This is particularly useful in the context of scientific investigations of nature.

Philo's position is that all the sciences are advanced when all there is is regarded as having been intelligently designed. In the second paragraph of Part XII, he twice points out that the purposive foundation of the sciences is often revealed through the maxims of science rather than through explicit references to an intelligent designer:

One great foundation of the Copernican system is the maxim, that nature acts by the simplest methods, and chooses the most proper means to any end; and astronomers often, *without thinking of it*, lay this strong foundation of piety and religion. The same thing is observable in other parts of philosophy: And thus all the sciences *almost lead us insensibly* to acknowledge a first intelligent Author; and their authority is often so much greater, as they do directly profess that intention.[44]

Science is not theology. And the business of science is not to gain theological insights. Hence, the scientist is not seeking to make contributions to theology. On the other hand, Philo maintains that scientific investigations are advanced when what there is is regarded as the product of intelligence. Since the focus of science is nature and not the source of the design of nature, it is sufficient for the advancement of science if its maxims and procedures regard what there is as purposive or intentional. Explicit references to an intelligent designer are not required.

With this I have completed my treatment of the belief in an intelligent designer as a Humean natural belief. And I have shown that this belief satisfies all the features of natural belief so that it can be included in this class. This, then, constitutes the 'common sense' aspect of the correction of Philo's 'undistinguished' Pyrrhonian doubts. On my account, there remains the

---

[44]   D.214–215. Italics in text omitted.

additional effort, namely, to correct the 'undistinguished' Pyrrhonian doubts through 'reflection'.

CORRECTING THE 'UNDISTINGUISHED' PYRRHONIAN DOUBTS
THROUGH 'REFLECTION'

The sceptical objections which Philo has advanced in the earlier chapters stem from Cleanthes' insistence that the principle 'like effects prove like causes' can be used to establish an anthropomorphic conception of God, given the presence of means to ends relations and a coherence of parts in the design of the world and the design of machines. As we have seen, it is this position which leads to the consideration of an infinite regress in Part IV, *a reductio ad absurdum* of anthropomorphism in Part V, and an open-ended list of competing cosmogonies in Parts VI–VIII. The cumulative effect of these sceptical objections is to show that an anthropomorphic conception of the deity, and along with it a purposive view of design, cannot be supported; that no account based on the features of design cited by Cleanthes can, strictly speaking, be shown to be an acceptable system of cosmogony; and that a suspense of judgment on the topic of the nature of God is the only reasonable position to adopt.

But Philo's sceptical arguments also challenged certain 'common sense' beliefs which we hold about causality. (It will be recalled that, early in Part XII, Philo emphasized that common sense principles cannot be corrupted by the sceptic's arguments, and that he himself is a man of common sense.) His arguments (in Part IV) generated doubts as to whether causal claims can be put forth which do not lead to an infinite regress; Philo's version of the Epicurean hypothesis (in Part VIII), which accounts for all design without reference to powers in objects and principles of order or design, raised doubts about the propriety of employing constant conjunction as a guide to what causes what, and about employing the principle 'like effects prove like causes' when reasoning about what causes what.

We will see that in correcting the 'undistinguished' pyrrhonian doubts through 'reflection', Philo reintroduces our common sense beliefs regarding causality: the concern with an infinite regress disappears, principles of order and powers in objects to produce change are accepted (although never explained), and constant conjunction and the principle 'like effects prove like causes' are regarded as our only means of gaining knowledge of causes. It is only in the context of Philo's pyrrhonian attack on the Argument from Design with his admitted 'lack of caution' when advancing the sceptic's arguments that our common sense beliefs in regard to causality come to be challenged.

Throughout his attack on the Argument from Design, Philo has insisted that the features of design in the world cited by Cleanthes cannot prove that anthropomorphism is true. Nevertheless, at no point in the first eight Parts of the *Dialogues* does Philo establish what conclusion about the cause of the design of the world is supported by the means to ends relations and coherence of parts which we find in the world and in machines. Or, what comes to the same thing, he has not yet shown the significance of the differences between the design of the world and machines when we attempt to learn about the cause of the design of the world. As a result, Philo has again exhibited a lack of caution in his arguments. It remains for Part XII to disclose the causal inferences which can be made about God from the similarities and differences present in the design of the world and machines.

In the opening chapter of this book, we saw that for the mitigated sceptic 'philosophic decisions are nothing but the relfections of common life, methodized and corrected'. And I pointed out that Hume's account of perceptions (impressions and ideas) and his Experimental Method (which is largely concerned with ensuring accuracy in causal reasoning) are the main doctrines which are utilized by the mitigated sceptic in reaching philosophical decisions. It will be shown that both doctrines are involved in correcting by 'reflection' the 'undistinguished' doubts generated by Phio's sceptical attack on the Argument from Design.

In the fifth paragraph of Part XII, Cleanthes expresses his agreement with what has been said (by Philo) in the preceding paragraphs of this Part:

> I shall farther add, said Cleanthes, to what you have so well urged, that one great advantage of the principle of theism is, that it is the only system of cosmogony which can be rendered intelligible and complete, and yet can throughout preserve a strong analogy to what we everyday see and experience in the world. The comparison of the universe to a machine of human contrivance is so obvious and natural, and is justified by so many instances of order and design in nature, that it must immediately strike all unprejudiced apprehensions, and procure universal approbation. Whoever attempts to weaken this theory, cannot pretend to succeed by establishing in its place any other that is precise and determinate: It is sufficient for him, if he starts doubts and difficulties; and by remote and abstract views of things, reach that suspense of judgment, which is here the utmost boundary of his wishes. But besides that this state of mind is in itself unsatisfactory, it can never be steadily maintained against such striking appearances as continually engage us into the religious hypothesis. A false, absurd system, human nature, from the force of prejudice, is capable of adhering to with obstinacy and perseverence: But no system at all, in opposition to a theory, supported by strong and obvious reason, by natural propensity, and by early education, I think it absolutely impossible to maintain or defend.[45]

Cleanthes holds two positions on the question of the cause of the design of the world: he believes that there is a 'natural argument' for an intelligent designer, wherein the requirement of constant conjunction is waived in seeking causal understanding, and an analogical argument (in Part II) in which it is maintained that the resemblances between the world and machines

---

[45] D.216

of human contrivance are sufficient to establish that the cause of the design of the world resembles human intelligence. As explicated by Cleanthes, both require the same evidential data – means to ends relations and a coherence of parts. Since Philo in Part XII acknowledges the force of the natural argument, discussed here as natural belief, it is understandable that he is described in Part III as "a little embarrassed and confounded", once Cleanthes has put forth his two illustrative analogies. Philo, we now realize, never intended to take issues with the natural argument, nor do any of his criticisms challenge this position. What Philo throughout has objected to is the *Argument* from Design: in the fifth paragraph of Part XII Cleanthes has yet to understand that Philo has no intention of accepting this argument *as Cleanthes has stated it*. When Philo, at the end of Part X, supports the intelligence claim and dismisses his own sceptical objections, it must be understood that the intelligence claim is not the one obtained from the analogical argument, but rather from the natural argument:

Formerly, when we argued concerning the natural attributes of intelligence and design, I needed all my sceptical and metaphysical subtlity to elude your grasp. In many views of the universe, and of its parts, particularly the latter, the beauty and fitness of final causes strike us with such irresistible force, that all objections appear (what I believe they really are) mere cavils and sophisms; nor can we then imagine how it was ever possible for us to repose any weight on them.[46]

Sceptical objections cannot maintain their force against natural instinct.[47]

However, sceptical objections cannot be disregarded when arguments are presented which attempt to prove what we naturally believe. Against such arguments, sceptical objections do exhibit their force, and generate a suspense of judgment. Philo's admission that he exhibited a lack of caution when presenting his sceptical objections to the Design Argument provides him with the opportunity to assess these objections. It is in the sixth paragraph of Part XII that Philo begins the 'reflective' assessment of his sceptical objections:

So little, replied Philo, do I esteem this suspense of judgment in the present case to be possible, that I am apt to suspect, there enters somewhat of a dispute of words into this controversy, more than is usually imagined. That the works of nature bear a great analogy to the productions of art is evident; and according to all the rules of good reasoning, we ought to infer, if we argue at all concerning them, that their causes have a proportional analogy. But as there are also considerable differences, we have reason to suppose a proportional difference in their causes; and in particular ought to attribute a much higher degree of power and energy to the supreme cause than any we have observed in mankind. Here then the existence of a Deity is plainly ascertained by reason; and if we make it a question, whether, on account of these analogies, we can properly call him a *mind* or *intelligence*, notwithstanding the vast difference, which may reasonably by supposed between him and human minds; what is this but a mere verbal controversy? No man can deny the analogies between the effects: To restrain ourselves from enquiring concerning the

---

[46] D.201–202
[47] E.160–161

causes is scarcely possible: From this inquiry, the legitimate conclusion is, that the causes have also ana analogy: And, if we are not contented with calling the first and supreme cause a God or Deity, but desire to vary the expression; what can we call him but Mind or Thought, to which he is justly supposed to bear a considerable resemblance?[48]

This passage makes clar that Philo is again concerned with the principle 'Like effects prove like causes' and, therefore, with the extent to which we can reason analogically to an intelligent designer of the world. He is also explicit on what the 'dispute of words' mentioned in the first sentence is about: the verbal dispute concerns whether the resemblances between the world and the productions of art warrant calling the cause of the design of the world a mind or intelligence, in the light of the differences which exist between the effects being compared. What cannot be disputed, Philo asserts, is that there are resemblances between the world and the productions of art, and this justifies concluding that 'the causes have also an analogy'. Now, this concession might be taken as evidence that, the differences between the world and the productions of art notwithstanding, Philo is prepared to alter the position he has all along maintained, namely, that "we ought never to imgine, that we comprehend the attributes of this divine Being, or to suppose, that his perfections have any analogy or likeness to the perfections of a human creature".[49] It will now be shown that Philo has not altered his position, and that, in fact, he goes to great lengths to emphasize that there is no change in his position.

A sign that the position espoused in the sixth paragraph of Part XII accords with his earlier position is presented in the last sentence of this paragraph in which he says that 'if we are not contented with calling the first and supreme cause a God or Deity, but desire to vary the expression; what can we call him but Mind or Thought, to which he is justly supposed to bear a considerable resemblance?' It will be recalled that in Part II, Philo spoke of 'justly' ascribing wisdom, thought, design, and knowledge to God, and the reason given for this is that "those words are honourable among men, and we have no other language or other conceptions, by which we can express our adoration of him".[50] He then goes on to warn us: "But let us beware, lest we think that our ideas any wise correspond to his perfections, or that his attributes have any resemblance to these qualities among men".[51] The final sentence in Paragraph VI of Part XII is reminiscent of Philo's earlier view, and should alert us to the fact that no change in position is being advocated.

It might be said, however, that we cannot use the final sentence in the sixth

---

[48] D.216–217
[49] D.142
[50] D.142
[51] D.142

paragraph as a sign that no change in position has occurred, because this presupposes that the word 'justly' is being used univocally in the two passages, and of course, this can only be established by proving that no change in position does take place. I will now show that Philo's elaboration of paragraph six (in the seventh paragraph) clearly discloses that he remains firm on the unknowability of the divine nature through reason.

He begins the seventh paragraph by elaborating on the nature of a 'verbal dispute' – the type of dispute he claims is involved in trying to decide whether "on account of these analogies, we can properly call him [i.e. God] a *mind* or *intelligence*, notwithstanding the vast difference, which may reasonably be supposed between him and human minds". He explains that the only remedy for a verbal dispute arises "from clear definitions, from the precision of those ideas which enter into any argument, and from the strict and uniform use of those terms which are employed". A verbal dispute, therefore, requires that both the language and ideas employed not allow for accuracy in judgment: "But there is a species of controversy, which, from the very nature of language and of human ideas, is involved in perpetual ambiguity, and can never, by any precaution or any definitions, be able to reach a reasonable certainty or precision".[52] Philo locates verbal disputes in "the controversies concerning the degrees of any quality or circumstance". He offers three examples of such disputes:

Men may argue to all eternity, whether Hannibal be a great, or a very great, or a superlatively great man, what degree of beauty Cleopatra possessed, what epithet of praise Livy or Thucydides is entitled to, without bringing the controversy to any determination".

And he locates the difficulty in each in the fact that we have no precise measure for quantifying these qualities:

The disputants may here agree in their sense and differ in their terms, or *vice versa*; yet never be able to define their terms, so as to enter into each other's meaning: Because the degrees of these qualities are not, like quantity or number, susceptible of any exact mensuration, which may be the standard in the controversy".[53]

In other words, in regard to certain qualities, an accurate calculation of the degrees of that quality present in an object cannot be achieved.

Philo insists that "the dispute concerning theism is of this nature, and consequently is merely verbal, or perhaps, if possible, still more incurably ambiguous".[54] He shows this by addressing himself both to the theist and the atheist. His initial comments are addressed to the theist:

[52] D.217
[53] D.218
[54] D.218

I ask the theist, if he does not allow, that there is a great and immeasurable, because incomprehensible, difference between the *human* and the *divine* mind: The more pious he is, the more readily will he assent to the affirmative, and the more will he be disposed to magnify the difference: He will even assert, that the difference is of a nature which cannot be too much magnified".[55]

Although there is a reference in this passage to 'the human and divine mind', the differences between them are characterized as 'great and unmeasurable, because incomprehensible'. Not only can the differences not be measured, they cannot be understood! Since this is the position which Philo has urged from the outset, it might seem that his discussion of the theist's position in Part XII makes no attempt to correct the sceptical objections advanced earlier. This, however, is a misreading of the theist's position as set out in Part XII.

It will be recalled that in the opening paragraphs of Part V of the *Dialogues*, Philo spoke of 'the true system of theism' which maintains that scientific discoveries reveal the immense grandeur and magnificence of the works of nature, and thereby show that 'the farther we push our researches of this kind, we are still led to infer the universal cause of All to be vastly different from mankind, or from any object of human experience and observations'. In the opening paragraph of Part V, Philo explains the relevance of differences in design to the application of the principle 'like effects prove like causes': "Now it is certain, that the liker the effects are, which are seen, and the liker the causes, which are inferred, the stronger is the argument. Every departure on either side diminishes the probability, and renders the experiment less conclusive". In Rule 6 of the 'Rules by which to judge of causes and effects' in Section XI of the *Treatise of Human Nature*, Hume expresses the same point in the following manner: "The difference in the effects of two resembling objects must proceed from that particular, in which they differ. For as like causes always produce like effects, when in any instance we find our expectation to be disappointed, we must conclude that this irregularity proceeds from some difference in the causes".[56] When discussing the opening paragraphs of Part V of the *Dialogues*, I showed that Philo's claim that differences between the design of the world and machines weaken the attempt to reason analogically about God would be acceptable provided that Cleanthes had included the machine-like character of the world as a premise in his Argument, or Philo had been able to establish that the features of design which Cleanthes argued are evidence of an intelligent principle of design can arise from non-intelligent sources of order. Since Cleanthes does not include the machine-like character of the world as a premise in his Argument, and

[55] D.218
[56] T.174

since it is in Parts VI through VIII of the *Dialogues* that Philo shows that means to ends relations and a coherence of parts can arise from non-intelignt sources of order, it is clear that Philo's critique in the early paragraphs of Part V, of Cleanthes' use of the Principle 'like effects prove like causes', is not yet complete. Consequently, his position that scientific discoveries show God to be vastly different from us has not yet been established. Even in the opening paragraphs of Part V, therefore, Philo exhibits a lack of caution in presenting his argument. In Part XII, Philo again makes reference to the position of the theist that the differences between the design of the world and machines do seriously weaken Cleanthes' use of the principle 'like effects prove like causes'; the theist's position is now acceptable, given that the sceptic has by this time established that design can arise from non-intelligent sources of order.

What, then, of the data which Cleanthes offers in the Argument from Design to support the claim of resemblance between us and God? Philo's views on the proper use of the data are expressed in his comments addressed to the atheist.

I next turn to the atheist, who, I assert, is only nominally so, and can never possibly be in earnest; and I ask him, whether, from the coherence and apparent sympathy in all the parts of this world, there be not a certain degree of analogy among all the operations of nature, in every situation and in every age; whether the rotting of a turnip, the generation of an animal, and the structure of human thought be not energies that probably bear some remote analogy to each other. It is impossible he can deny it: He will readily acknowledge it. Having obtained this concession, I push him still farther in his retreat; and I ask him, if it be not probable, that the principle which first arranged, and still maintains, order in this universe, bears not also some remote inconceivable analogy to the other operations of nature, and among the rest to the oeconomy of human mind and thought. However reluctant, he must give his assent.[57]

In this passage, Philo is calling attention to the coherence of parts which Cleanthes' Argument from Design has employed. When Philo advanced competing cosmogonies in the earlier Parts of the *Dialogues*, he attempted to account for the design of the whole world through a comparison with the design found in parts of the world, especially organisms. Since no system of cosmogony can be shown to be properly grounded, the sceptic urges a suspense of judgment as the only reasonable position to adopt. One of the matters which Philo's presentation of competing cosmogonies does reveal is that all sources of design are bound by the same features of design, namely, means to ends relations and a coherence of parts. Now, whereas a suspense of judgment is held by Philo to be reasonable when systems of cosmogony are compared and contrasted, Philo has not yet established what position is reasonable in natural theology, once we grant that no system of cosmogony

[57]   D.218

can be accepted, and that all sources of design are bound by identical features of design. An alteration in the sceptic's position may, therefore, be in order.

Philo's argument proceeds in two stages, each engaging the principle 'like effects prove like causes'. In the first stage of his argument, he claims that the coherence of parts evident in all parts of the world countenances the conclusion that 'there is a certain degree of analogy among all the operations of nature'. In Rule 5 of the 'Rules by which to judge of causes and effects' in the *Treatise of Human Nature*, Hume writes: "... where several different objects produce the same effect, it must be by means of some quality, which we discover to be common amongst them. For as like effects imply like causes, we must always ascribe the causation to the circumstance, wherein we discover the resemblance".[58] Philo's point is that the resemblance found among all the effects in the world is so general, that in applying a rule of this sort, no specificity can be achieved when we attempt to determine the particular resemblance among the operations of nature. This explains why, in comparing the rotting of a turnip, the generation of an animal, and the structure of human thought, he concludes that these are energies 'that probably bear some remote analogy to each other'.

In the second stage of the argument, Philo calls upon the atheist once again to apply the principle 'Like effects prove like causes', but in this case, the order observed throughout the world is compared to the order observed to result from the other operations of nature. The basis of comparison is coherence in design (as it was in the first stage), and once again this feature reveals no 'specific resemblance' between the design of the world and the designs resulting from the operations of nature within the world. The comparison of the design of the whole world with specific effects in nature in terms of coherence of design yields a conclusion which seems epistemologically much weaker than the conclusion obtained in the first stage: in the first stage of the argument 'some remote analogy' is conceded among all the operations of nature, whereas in the second stage 'some remote *inconceivable* analogy'[59] is conceded between the principle of design of the whole world and the other operations of nature.

That the second stage is not espitemologically weaker than the first can be learned by reading several lines further when Philo reconciles the position of the theist and atheist. For, at that point, the atheist agrees that 'the original principle of order bears some remote analogy' to the operations of nature, with the term 'inconceivable' omitted. Relying on Hume's doctrine of impressions and ideas. Philo has insisted throughout the book that the operations of nature are unknown to us: "But reason, in its internal fabric

---

[58] T.174
[59] italics added

and structure, is really as little known to us as instinct or vegetation; ... The effects of these principles are all known to us from experience: But the principles themselves, and their manner of operation, are totally unknown''.[60] As such, even when natural objects are compared in terms of coherence of design, the remote analogy between their causes should be regarded as 'inconceivable'. If the principles cannot be known or understood at all, any claim of analogy between them must be inconceivable. Therefore, regardless of whether Philo includes the term 'inconceivable' or not, any claim of analogy between principles of order must be regarded as being 'inconceivable'. What Philo has shown is that this problem of 'inconceivability' is not peculiar to natural theology: in light of the fact that all principles of design and their manner of operation are totally unknown, no claim of analogy between principles of order can be thought.

What the atheist assents to is that it is probable that the principle which first arranged, and still maintains, order in this universe, bears "some remote inconceivable analogy to the other operations of nature, and among the rest to the oeconomy of human mind and thought". Accordingly, thought has no primacy when a comparison is attempted between God and the operations of nature. The 'remote inconceivable analogy' which the atheist allows between the principle of design of the world and the structure of human thought is also allowed between the principle of design of the world and the other operations of nature. What directs the atheist to single out thought is nothing more than Philo's effort to contrast the atheist's position with the theist's position which focuses on intelligence: it is not that the resemblance between God and thought can be shown to be greater than that between God and the other operations of nature. In no case can more be established between God and any operation of nature than 'some remote inconceivable analogy', and, as we have seen, no knowledge or understanding of God is contained therein.

The theist holds that the differences between God and us are 'great and immeasurable, because incomprehensible'. The atheist will allow 'some remote inconceivable analogy' between the principle of order of the world and thought. I submit, therefore, that in the end the unknowability of the divine nature is upheld.

The verbal dispute between theist and atheist can now be clearly grasped: since neither holds a position for which there are ideas which are determinate in nature, the degree of resemblance or difference between God and human intelligence cannot be ascertained:

The theist allows, that the original intelligence is very different from human reason: The atheist allows, that the original principle of order bears some remote analogy to it. Will you quarrel,

[60]   D.178

Gentlemen, about the degrees, and enter into a controversy, which admits not of any precise meaning, nor consequently of any determination? If you should be so obstinate, I should not be surprised to find you sensibly change sides; while the theist on the one hand exaggerates the dissimilarity between the supreme Being, and frail, imperfect, variable, fleeting, and mortal creatures; and the atheist on the other magnifies the analogy among all the operations of nature, in every period, every situation, and every position. Consider then, where the real point of controversy lies, and if you cannot lay aside your disputes, endeavour, at least, to cure yourself of your animosity.[61]

The 'undistinguished' doubts of the Pyrrhonian have now been corrected by 'reflection'. In regard to the claim that there is 'some remote inconceivable analogy' between God and human intellignce, it is obvious that no additional sceptical attack is either anticipated or offered.

Relying on the position attributed to the atheist, Philo offers the final pronouncement on the topic under discussion:

If the whole of natural theology, as some people seem to maintain, resolves itself into one simple, though somewhat ambiguous, at least undefined proposition, *that the cause or causes of order in the universe probably bear some remote analogy to human intelligence*: If this proposition be not capable of extension, variation, or more particular explication: if it afford no inference that affects human life, or can be the source of any action of forbearance: And if the analogy, imperfect as it is, can be carried no farther than to the human intelligence, and cannot be transferred, with any appearance of probability, to the other qualities of the mind: If this really be the case, what can the most inquisitive, contemplative, and religious man do more than give a plain, philosophical assent to the proposition, as often as it occurs; and believe that the arguments, on which it is established, exceed the objections which lie against it? Some astonishment indeed will naturally arise from the greatness of the object: Some melancholy from its obscurity: Some contempt of human reason, that it can give no solution more satisfatory with regard to so extraordinary and magnificent a question.[62]

It is particularly noteworthy that the work of the sciences and the fact that "all the sciences almost lead us insensibly to acknowledge a first intelligent Author" is not included in this final pronouncement, in which is contained all that human reason can, with justification, express about God. This confirms the point made earlier that the concern in the early paragraphs of Part XII is not with *reasoning* about God. That the success of science can be totally ignored in offering all that human reason can say about God does make sense if the belief in an intelligent designer which is spoken of in those early paragraphs is a natural, rather than a reasonable, belief. In reasoning about God, the scientist can be no more successful than the atheist, and, therefore, if reasoning were the only guide to the cause of the design of the world, he would not be justified in holding that all there is in nature is the product of intelligence.

[61]   D.218–219
[62]   D.227

The position which I have adopted in regard to Pamphilus is that we can accept what he says, except where there are indications in the text that this should not be done. It is given to Pamphius to offer, in the last paragraph of the *Dialogues*, an assessment of all three speakers. He says:

Cleanthes and Philo pursued not this conversation much farther; and as nothing ever made greater impression on me than all the reasonings of that day; so I confess, that, upon a serious review of the whole, I cannot but think, that Philo's principles are more probable than Demea's; but that those of Cleanthes approach still nearer to the truth.

According to this passage, Cleanthes has the best case. However, at the end of the penultimate paragraph of Part XII, a clear warning is offered to the effect that Pamphilus is not in a position to assess what has been said. Philo closes this paragraph by saying:

To be a philosophical sceptic is, in a man of letters, the first and most essential step toward being a sound, believing Christian; a proposition which I would willingly recommend to the attention of Pamphilus: And I hope Cleanthes will forgive me for interposing so far in the education and instruction of his pupil.[63]

We have seen that Cleanthes had no grasp of the role of scepticism in argumentation. Pamphilus is Cleanthes' student. That Philo singles him out to emphasize the need for scepticism indicates that Philo recognizes a less than adequate appreciation in Pamphilus of scepticism. Pamphilus' assessment, therfore, is not to be trusted.

---

[63]   D.228

Bibliography

Aiken, H.D., *Hume's Dialogues Concerning Natural Religion*, New York, 1948.

Anderson, J., "Design", *American Journal of Philosophy* 13, (1935), 241–256 (reprinted in 1962 in Anderson, *Studies in Empirical Philosophy*, Sydney).

Andic, M., "Experimental Theism and the Verbal Dispute in Hume's 'Dialogues' ", *Arch. Gesch. Phil.* 56 (1974), 239–246.

Anscombe, G.E.M., "Whatever has an Existence Must Have a Cause: Hume's Argument Exposed", *Analysis 34* (1973), 145–151.

Attfield, R., *God and the Secular* (esp. chp. 5–6), Cardiff, 1978.

Ayer, A.J., *Hume*, Oxford University Press, Oxford, 1980 (Design, argument from: p. 23, 93–95; Natural beliefs: p. 19, 36, 38, 71; Religion: p. 10, 21, 92).

Baroncelli, F., "Di una possible lettura dei Dialoghi ... di Hume", *Proteus* 3, 35–49.

Basu, D.K., "Who is the Real Hume in the *Dialogues*?", *Indianapolis Phil. Quarterly* 6, (1978), 21–28.

Beanblossom, R.E., "A New Foundation for Humean Scepticism", *Phil. Studies* 29 (1976), 207–210.

Beauchamp, T.L., "An Analysis of Hume's Essay 'On Suicide' ", *Review of Metaphysics* 31 (1976), 73–95.

Boys Smith, J.S., "Hume's Dialogues Concerning Natural Religion", *Journal of Theological Studies* 37 (1936), 337–349.

Brentano, F. *Vom Dasein Gottes*, Ch. 21–24, Hamburg, 1929.

Bricke, J. "On the Interpretation of Hume's *Dialogues*", *Religious Studies* 11 (1975), 1–18.

Britton, K., *Philosophy and the Meaning of Life*, Ch. 5, Cambridge, 1969.

Brockway, G.M., *Leibniz, Hume, Kant and the Contemporaries on the Problem of Evil*, University of Wisconsin (Diss.), 1973, Chp.2.

Burch, R., "Bayesianism and Analogy in Hume's *Diaglogues*", *Hume Studies 5* (1980), 94–109.

Burns, H.R. *Hume's Attitude Towards Religion*, St. Louis University (Diss.), 1974.

Butler, R.J., "Natural Belief and the Enigma of Hume", *Archiv für Gesch. d. Phil.* 42 (1960), 73–100 [(1974), 281–294].

Campbell, Alexander, *David Hume und die fundamental-theologische Frage*, Manuscript, University of Vienna.

Capaldi, Nicholas, *David Hume: The Newtonian Philosopher*, Twayne Publishers, Boston, 1975, p. 24, 27, 55–56, 79, 105, 176, 188–197.

Carabelli, Giancarlo, "Enlightment Philosophy and the Eighteenth Century Booktrade" [on the *Dialogues*], *Enlightenment Essays* 1, (1970), 169–178.

Carabelli, Giancarlo, "Hume e la retorica dell' ideologia (Uno studio dei 'Dialoghi sulla religione naturale' " *La Nuova Italia Editrice*, Florence, 1972, Ch. II, VII, IX, & X.

Carabelli, Giancarlo, "L'alibi strutturale di Hume nei *Dialogues*....'', *Strumenti critici 2* (1968), 87–110.

Chappell, V.C., *Hume*, New York, Doubleday, 1966. (i) Capitan, William H., "Part X of Hume's *Dialogues*", 387–396; (ii) Noxon, James, "Hume's Agnosticism", 360–383; (iii) Nathan, George J., "Hume's Immanent God", 396–423.

Clarke, B.L., "The Argument from Design: A Piece of Abductive Reasoning". *International Journal of Philosophy of Religion* 5 (1974), 65–78.

Clive, G., "Hume's Dialogues Reconsidered", *Journal of Religion* 39 (1959), 110–119.

Doore, G., "The Argument from Design: Some Better Reasons for Agreeing With Hume", *Religious Studies* 16 (1980), 145–161.

Duerlinger, J., "The Verbal Dispute in Hume's 'Dialogues' ", *Arch. Gesch. Phil.* 53 (1971) 22–34.

Dunham, J.H., *The Religion of Philosophers*, Temple University Publications, Philadelphia, 1947, Ch. 7.

Elliott, P.P., *Arguments for Theism from Design in Nature with Special Reference to Hume, Paley, and Kant*, Oxford University (Diss.), 1926.

Force, J.E., "Hume in the *Dialogues*, the Dictates of Convention, and the Millennial Future State of Biblical Prophecy", *S-West Journal of Philosophy* (1977), 131–141.

Francken, Wijnaendts, *David Hume*, H.D. Tjeenk Willink & Zoon, Haarlem, 1907, 128–136.

Franklin, J., "More on Part IX of Hume's *Dialogues*, *Phil. Quarterly* 30, (1980), 69–71.

Gaskin, John C.A., "The Design Argument: Hume's Critique of Poor Reason", *Religious Studies* 12, (1976), 331–345.

Gaskin, J.C.A., "God, Hume, and Natural Belief", *Philosophy* 49 (1974), 281–294.

Gaskin, J.C.A., "Hume's Criticism of the Argument from Design", *Revue*

Internationale de Philosophie 30 (1976), 64–78.

Gaskin, J.C.A., Hume's Critique of Religion", *Journal of the History of Philosophy* 14 (1976), 301–311.

Gaskin, J.C.A., *Hume's Philosophy of Religion*, Macmillan Press, London, 1978

Gawlick, G., *David Hume, Dialoge über natürliche Religion*, Hamburg, neu bearbeitet, 1968 (Paulsen translation revised with introduction).

Gawlick, G., "Hume and the Deists: a Reconsideration", in Morice, *David Hume, Bicentenary Papers*, 128–138.

Grieg, J.Y.T., *David Hume*, London, 1931.

Harward, D.W., "Hume's *Dialogues* Revisited", *International Journal of Philosophy of Religion* 6 (1975), 33–42.

Haskin, D., "English Bards and a Scottish Previewer", *New Blackfriars* 55 (1974), 33–42.

Hearn, T.K., "Norman Kemp Smith on 'Natural Belief' ", *Southern Journal of Philosophy* 7 (1969), 3–7.

Heath, P.L., "The Incredulous Hume", *American Philosophical Quarterly* 13 (1976), 159–163.

Henry, W.L., *A Study of David Hume versus His Eighteenth-Century English Contemporaries on the Question of Natural Theology*, Vanderbilt University (Diss.), 1974.

Henze, D.F., "On Some Alleged Humean Insights and Oversights", *Religious Studies* 6 (1970), 369–377. (A discussion of *Dialogues*, parts X–XI).

Hendel, C.W., *Studies in the Philosophy of David Hume*, New York, 1963, 302–309, and Ch. 11.

Hodges, M., and Lachs, J., "Hume on Belief", *Review of Metaphysics* 30 (1976), 3–18.

Hochfeldowa, A.D., *Hume: Dialogii o religii naaturalnej; Naturalna historia religii*, Warsaw, 1962.

Hoerster, N., "David Hume: Existenz und Eigenschaften Gottes" in J. Speck, *Grundprobleme der grossen Philosophen; Philosophie der Neuzeit*, I, Gottingen, 1979, 240–275.

Howells, E.G., *Hume and teleology: A Background Study of Hume's Interest in the Argument from Design*, Stanford University (Diss.), 1975.

Hurlbutt, R.H., "David Hume and Scientific Theism", *Journal of the History of Ideas* 17 (1956), 486–497.

Hurlbutt, R.H., *Hume, Newton, and the Design Argument*, Lincoln, 1965.

Jacobson, N.P., "The Uses of Reason in Religion: A Note on David Hume", *Journal of Religion* 39 (1959), 103–109.

James, E.D., "Scepticism and Religious Belief: Pascal, Bayle, Hume", in R.R. Bolgar, *Classical Influences on Western Thought A.D. 1650–1870*, Cambridge, 1979, p. 93–104.

Jeffner, A., "Butler & Hume on Religion: A Comparative Analysis", *Phil. Review* 77 (1966), 369–372.

Johnson, A.L., "Hume's Response to the Pressure to Conform in Religious Beliefs", *S.W. Phil. Studies* 2 (1977), 95–101.

Jones, P., "Hume's Two Concepts of God", *Philosophy* 47 (1972), 322–333.

Keen, C.N., "Reason in Hume's *Dialogues*", *Phil. Papers* 5 (1976), 121–134.

Kemp Smith, N., *Hume's Dialogues Concerning Natural Religion*, Oxford Press, Landow, 1935 (2nd Ed., 1947). (*Journal of Philosophy* 32, 665–666; *Mind* 45, 334–349; *Philosophy* 12, 173–190; *Philosophy* 13, 84–86).

Klinefelter, D.S., "Scepticism and Deism in Hume's Philosophy of Religion", *Journal of American Acad. Religion* 45 (1977), 222.

Kuntz, P.G., "Hume's Metaphysics: A New Theory of Order", *Religious Studies* 12 (1976), 401–428.

Laing, B.M., "Hume's Dialogues Concerning Natural Religion", *Philosophy* 12 (1937), 175–190.

Laird, J., *Hume's Philosophy of Human Nature*, E.P. Dutten & Co., New York, 1932, Ch. X, p. 285–306.

Leroy, A., *La Critique et La Religion Chez David Hume*, Libraire Felix Alcan, Paris, 1930, Deuxieme Partie, p. 246–293.

Löwisch, D.J., *Immanuel Kant und David Hume's 'Dialogues Concerning Natural Religion': ein Versuch zur Aufhellung der Bedeutung von Humes Spätschrift für die Philosophie Immanuel Kants, im besonderen für die 'Kritik der reinen Vernunft'*, Bonn, 1964.

Löwische, D.J., "Kants Kritik der reinen Vernunft und Humes Dialogues..." *Kant Studien* 56 (1966), 170–207.

Lucas, F.L., *The Art of Living, Four 18th Century Minds*, London, 1959, 1–78.

Luers, A., *David Hume religonphilosophische Anschauugen*, Berlin (Diss.), 1959.

Maclagan, W.G., "Hume's Attitude to Religion", *Proceedings of Royal Phil. Society of Glasgow* 74 (1949), 83.

Mathews, G., "Theology and Natural Theology", *Journal of Philosophy* 61 (1964), 99–108.

McFarland, J.D., *Kant's Concept of Teleology*, Chp. 3: "The Speculative Background and Hume's Dialogues", Edinburgh, 1970.

McMahon, D.B.S., *David Hume's Philosophy of Religion*, University of Wisconsin (Diss.), 1972.

McPherson, T., "The Argument from Design", *Philosophy* 32 (1957), 219–228.   Merlan, P., "Hamann et les Dialogues de Hume", *Revue Met.* 59 (1954), 285–289.

Michael, S.J., *An Examination of the Role of Natural Belief in David Hume's Philosophy of Religion*, Harvard University (Diss.), 1968.

Morcavallo, B., "Recenti Discussione sui Dialoghi sulla Religione Naturale di David Hume", U. de Sienna (Studi Filosofie), 1978, p. 59–85.

Morcavallo, E.C., "Hume and the Deists: a Reconsideration", in Morice, *David Hume, Bicentenary Papers*, 1978, 128–138.

Morehead, R., *Dialogues on Natural and Revealed Religion*, Edinburgh & London, 1830.

Morehead, R., *Philosophical Dialogues*, London, 1845.

Morice, G., *David Hume, Bicentenary Papers*, Edinburgh & Texas University Press, 1978.

Morrisroe, M., "Characterization as Rhetorical Device in Hume's Dialogues", *Enlightenment Essays 1* (1970), 95–107.

Morrrisroe, M., "Hume's Rhetorical Strategy: A solution to the Riddle of the *Dialogues Concerning Natural Religion*", *Texas Studies in Literature & Language* 11 (1969), 963–967.

Morrisroe, M., *The Rhetoric of the Dialogues of David Hume*, University of Texas (Diss.), 1966.

Mossner, E.C., "Hume and the Legacy of the Dialogues", in Morice, *David Hume, Bicentenary Papers*, 1–22.

Mossner, E.C., "The Enigma of Hume", *Mind* 45 (1936), 334–349.

Mossner, E.C., "Hume's *Dialogues Concerning Natural Religion*: An Answer to Dr. Laing", *Philosophy* 13 (1938), 84–86.

Mossner, E.C., "The Religion of David Hume", *Journal of the History of Ideas* 39, 653–663.

Nathan, G.J., "The Existence and Nature of God in Hume's 'Theism' ", in Livingston & King, *Hume: a Re-evaluation*, New York, 1976.

Nathan, G.J., "Hume's Immanent God", in V.C. Chappell, *Hume*, New York, 1966, 396–423.

Norton, Capaldi & Robinson, *McGill Hume Studies*, Austin Hill Press, San Diego, 1979. [(a) Battersbay, Christine, "*The Dialogues* as Original Imitation: Cicero and the Nature of Hume's Skepticism", 239–253; (b) Penelhum, Terence "Hume's Skepticism and *The Dialogues*", 253–278; (c) Wadia, Pheroze, "Philo Confounded"].

Noxon, J., "Hume's Agnosticism", *Phil. Review* 73 (repr. 1966 in Chappell, *Hume*), 248–261.

Noxon, J., "Hume's Concern With Religion", in Merrill & Shahan, *David Hume: Many Sided Genius*, 1976, 59–82.

Noxon, J., *Hume's Philosophical Development: A Study of his Methods*, At the Clarendon Press, Oxford, 1973 (Argument from Design: 26, 78–79, 96–108, 167–175).

Noxon, J., "In Defence of 'Hume's Agnosticism' ", *Journal of the History of Philosophy* 14 (1976), 469–473.

Parent, W.A., "An Interpretation of Hume's *Dialogues*", *Review of Metaphysics* 30 (1976), 96–114.

Parent, W.A., "Philo's Confession", *Phil. Quarterly* 26 (1976) 63–68.

Parsons, J.E., Jr., "Hume's *Dialogues Concerning Natural Religion*: II", *Independent Journal of Philosophy* 3 (1978), 119–126.

Passmore, J.A., *Hume's Intentions*, Cambridge Press, 1952, 68–69.

Pearl, L., "Hume's Criticism of the Design Argument", *The Monist* 54 (1970), 270–284.

Pears, D.F., *David Hume: A Symposium*, Macmillan & Co. Ltd., London, 1963 (Esp. "Hume on Religion" by B.A.O. Williams, 77–89).

Penelhum, T., *Hume*, The Macmillan Press, London, 1975, Ch. 8, 180–196.

Penelhum, T., "Hume's Skepticism and the *Dialogues*", in D.F. Norton et al., *McGill Hume Studies*, 1979, 253–278.

Peters, R.S., "Hume's Argument from Design", in W.B. Todd (ed.), *Hume and the Enlightenment: Essays Presented to Ernest Campbell Mossner*, Edinburgh, 1974.

Phillips, D.Z., *Religion Without Explanation*, Basil Blackwell, Oxford, 1976, 9–25.

Pike, N., *David Hume, Dialogues Concerning Natural Religion*, Indianapolis and New York, 1970.

Plantinga, A., *God and Other Minds*, Ithaca & London, 1967, Ch. 4 (The Teleological Argument).

Popkin, R.M., *David Hume, Dialogues Concerning Natural Religion and the Posthumous Essays*, Hackett Publishing, Indianapolis, 1980.

Porter, B.F., *Deity and Morality*, London, 1968, Ch. 2.

Price, J.V., *David Hume, Dialogues Concerning Natural Religion*, Oxford, 1976 (*PB* 18 (1977), 49–54; *P* 52 (1977), 362–364; *TLS* (2 Aug. 1977), 984; *Hermathena* no. 123 (1977), 76–87).

Price, J.V., *David Hume*, Twayne Publishers, New York, 1968, 128–144.

Price, J.V., *The Dialogues of Hume and Cicero on Natural Religion*, University of Texas (Diss.), 1960.

Price, J.V., "The First Publications of David Hume's *Dialogues*", *Papers of the Biblio. Society of America* 68 (1974), 119–127.

Price, J.V., "Sceptics in Cicero and Hume", *Journal of the History of Ideas* 25 (1964), 97–106.

Priestly, J., *Letters to a Philosophical Unbeliever, Part 1*, Bath, 1780.

Pucelle, J., *Hume ou L'ambiguité*, Editions Seghers, Paris, 1969, 85–95.

Rabbitte, E., "Hume's Critique of the Argument from Design", *Phil. Studies* 5, Ireland (1955), 100–117.

Salmon, W.C., "Religion and Science: A New Look at Hume's

Dialogues", *Phil. Studies* 33 (1978), 143–176.

Santucci, A., *Sistema e ricerca in David Hume*, Editori Laterza, Bari, 1969, 240–23.

Stove, D.C., "Part IX of Hume's *Dialogues"*, *Phil. Quarterly* 28 (1978), 199–212.

Swinburne, R.G., "The Argument from Design", *Philosophy* 43 (1968), 199–212.

Taylor, A.E., Laird, J. & Jessop, T.E., "The Present Day Relevance of Hume's *Dialogues Concerning Natural Religion"*, *Proceedings of the Aristotellian Society* Suppl. Vol. 18 (1939), 179–228.

Todd, W.B., (ed.), *Hume and the Enlightenment*, The University Press, Edinburgh, 1974 (Esp. Peters, R.S., "Hume's Argument from Design", 83–99).

Tweyman, S., "L'Incidence Des Organismes Sur La Croyance Dans Une Intelligence Créatrice", *Revue de l'Université de Moncton* (dec. 1979).

Tweyman, S., "The Vegetable Library and God", *Dialogue* 18 (1979), 517–527.

Tweyman, S., "Le Sceptique Comme Pédagogue", *Revue de l'Université de Moncton* (jan. 1980), 115–123.

Tweyman, S., "Le Sceptique Comme Pédagogues-II", *Revue de l'Université de Moncton* (jan. 1981), 87–94.

Tweyman, S., "Remarks on Wadia's 'Philo Confounded' ", *Hume Studies* 6 (1980), 155–161.

Tweyman, S., "An Inconvenience of Anthropomorphism", *Hume Studies*, April 1982.

Tweyman, S. "The Sceptic as Teacher", *Spindrift*, Vol. I, Number 1, Spring 1981.

Tweyman, S., "The Articulate Voice and God", *Southern Journal of Philosophy*, July 1982.

Tweyman, S., "The Reductio in Part V of Hume's Dialogues", *Southern Journal of Philosophy*, vol. XXI, Number 3 (Fall 1983), 453–459.

Tweyman, S., "A propos d'une difficulté logique dans l'argument de Cleanthe", *Hume Studies*, Volume X, Number 1, April, 1984.

Tweyman, S., "An Enquiry concerning Hume's Dialogues" included in a *Festschrift* in honour of Professor Robert F. McRae, Caravan Press, New York, 1986.

Tweyman, S., "Reason and Conduct in Hume and His Predecessors, Martinus Nijhoff, The Hague, 1974.

Vestre, B., *Hume and Scepticism*, University of Oslo (Diss.), 1976.

Wadia, P.S., "Professor Pike on Part III of Hume's Dialogues", *Religious Studies* 14 (1978), 325–342.

Wadia, P.S., "Philo Confounded", in Norton et al., *McGill Hume*

164

Studies, Austin Hill Press, San Diego, 1979.

Wells, G.A., "Religion in Vico and Hume", *Trivium Lampeter* 11 (1976), 12–20.

Wollheim, R., *Hume on Religion* (Natural History of Religion, Dialogues, and various essays), London, 1963.

Wood, F.E., "Hume's Philosophy of Religion as Reflected in the Dialogues", *S-West Journal of Philosophy* 2 (1971), 186–193.

Yandell, K.E., "Hume on Religious Belief", in Livingston & King, *Hume: A Re-evaluation*, New York, 1976.

Yandell, K.E., "Hume's Explanation of Religious Belief", *Hume Studies* 5 (1979), 94–109.

Zimmern, H., *Schopenhauer*, London, 1932, 96–97.

Index